ENLIGHTENED

PUBLIC FINANCE

FISCAL LITERACY FOR DEMOCRATS, INDEPENDENTS, MILLENNIALS AND COLLEGIANS

GIRARD MILLER

Dedicated to the memory of the author's early mentors,
H.M. Kagi, A.K. Scotty Campbell and J.J. Bleiman.

ISBN: 978-1-54397-987-9 (print)
ISBN: 978-1-54397-988-6 (ebook)

CONTENTS

Introduction and Highlights vii

Part I: Fiscal Facts of Life – The Federal Budget, Deficits and Debt 1

Synopsis 6

TOPIC 1:   National Defense and Military Spending. 15

TOPIC 2:   Entitlement programs: Social Security, Medicare and Medicaid. 19

TOPIC 3:   Social Security. 21

TOPIC 4:   Medicare. 25

TOPIC 5:   Medicaid. 30

TOPIC 6:   Interest. 33

TOPIC 7:   Domestic discretionary spending and projected "crowding out" 40

TOPIC 8:   Implications of the Fiscal Facts 42

Part II: Federal tax policy and funding options 45

Synopsis 46

TOPIC 9:   The politics of tax reform 48

TOPIC 10: Progressive taxation: theory, history and reality 60

TOPIC 11: Tax preferences: lower rates, deductions and loopholes 69

TOPIC 12: Social Security and Medicare Taxes 77

TOPIC 13: The Estate Tax (now tarred as the "Death Tax") 87

TOPIC 14: Corporate taxes 95

TOPIC 15: Capital Gains and Dividends Taxation 105

TOPIC 16: Carried interest 113

TOPIC 17: Passthough business income tax deduction (QBID)..........118

TOPIC 18: The Alternative Minimum Tax (AMT).......................123

TOPIC 19: Financial transactions tax: The case for an FTT 143

TOPIC 20: The Value Added Tax (VAT): A viable funding source
for universal health care? 167

TOPIC 21: Tariffs 190

TOPIC 22: Wealth Tax 195

Part III: Health Care Finance 199

Synopsis...205

TOPIC 23: Medicare at Cost. 208

TOPIC 24: Medicaid expansion. 212

TOPIC 25: Universal health care coverage 216

TOPIC 26: Medical cost reductions 231

Part IV: Infrastructure 239

Synopsis 244

TOPIC 27: "Marble-cake" fiscal federalism and infrastructure
policy...250

TOPIC 28: Infrastructure economics in the digital and green era 261

TOPIC 29: Enlightened infrastructure funding: timing, incentives
and strategies 272

Appendix: "Pinocchio" Fact-Checking and Smell-Testing Scorecard 287

Glossary of Acronyms 291

Postscript:Recession Re-Sets? 293

Introduction and Highlights

This book helps readers understand the world of public finance well enough to make wiser political decisions. Political candidates, their campaign staffs and their supporters are encouraged to learn from it. Journalists, unaffiliated voters and students can become fiscally literate by using this text as a handy and informative reference guide. Unlike a college textbook, it is written for Democrats and Independents, by an Independent Democrat who once served on the Governmental Accounting Standards Board and worked for decades in the financial and investment industries as a qualified financial expert. This "Cliff Notes" section provides a synopsis of some of the most important take-aways. Each paragraph includes the associated Topic number that can be found in the table of contents where the corresponding page numbers are provided.

Part I: Fiscal Facts of Life: Budgets, Deficits and Debt

- The federal budget is running a $1 trillion annual deficit. Each year's annual shortfall is equivalent to the total value of all real estate property that has been built in New York City *over four centuries*. Annual deficits add up to become the national debt. The total national debt is now $22 trillion and will exceed $30 trillion within a decade under the most optimistic of all scenarios. That's today's equivalent of the combined value of every American's home nationwide. As this debt piles up, annual interest costs are compounding. Interest on the national debt will double (and could easily triple) from its current annual cost of $400 billion, and will become the largest single category of federal expenditure before the end of the coming decade. Without timely intervention to fix the annual budget deficits, interest expense will inevitably cannibalize federal programs for housing, education, environmental protection, transportation infrastructure and nutrition assistance. (Introduction and Topic 6)

- *This indisputable fiscal inevitability is just as insidious, imminent and "inconvenient" as global warming, climate change and rising sea levels.* (Topics 7 and 8) Here as well, deniers are liars.

> By 2030, Baby Boomers will have pushed Social Security and Medicare spending higher by $1 trillion annually. Today's tax rates cannot possibly cover these ballooning demographic costs.

- The Baby Boom generation is retiring rapidly now, just by virtue of age. 10,000 Baby Boomers retire every day, and will continue to do so for another dozen years. As they leave the workforce, taxes they now pay will shrink and automatic spending for their Social Security and Medicare escalates quickly. Their Medicare costs rise exponentially with age, as their medical procedures become more frequent and more costly with each passing year. By 2030, Baby Boomers will have pushed Social Security and Medicare spending higher by $1 trillion annually. Today's tax rates will not cover these ballooning demographic costs. (Topics 2 and 3)

- Just to put today's *annual* federal budget deficit into balance, every American household would need to contribute $8,500 in cash from its family pocketbook *every year*. If translated into what we personally consume, it would require a national tax of 7½ percent of everything we buy, from automobiles to haircuts to fast food, insurance, cellphones, college tuition, dentists, groceries, vacations, movies, electricity, rent and house payments. (Introduction)

- Naïve proposals to "monetize" the debt by printing money, borrowing even more, and inflating ourselves out of one predicament and into another will hurt countless Americans, including the elderly, everybody's savings and retirement plans including public pensions, and the entire middle class. (Synopsis and Topic 6)

> Without both tax *and* deficit reform, Millennials and collegians will suffer most.

- Millennials and today's collegians have the most to suffer if voters fail to demand that Congress and the White House address the annual budget deficit problem during the next Presidential term. The heaviest financial burdens will thereafter fall predominantly on their shoulders. Baby Boomers could face a mandatory reduction of their Social Security benefits by 2034 if Congress fails to act. The Medicare trust fund will be depleted by 2026, only one Senate term from now. The idea of "Medicare for All" becomes a cruel joke if Medicare benefits for retirees must be paid with federal IOUs in 2027 and forever thereafter. (Topic 8)

- Higher taxes are inevitable, just to preserve existing social programs, retirement benefits and national defense. (Synopsis and Topic 7) Any politician who tells Americans otherwise is either delusional or a pathological liar.

Part II: Tax Policy and Tax Reform Options

- The Liberal, Progressive and Centrist wings of the Democratic party have overlapping yet differing views of tax reform and fiscal policy. Despite widespread agreement that the Trump Tax Cuts were a give-away to big business and the wealthy, there is not yet a consensus about where tax reform should be focused, where to draw the line on progressively higher tax rates, and how to use the revenue. (Topic 9)

- Not a single politician has presented a realistic revenue plan to fund their proposed new spending *and* to reduce the federal deficit. Both Democrats and Republicans keep sweeping the federal deficit and the national debt under the rug, while political candidates try to sell us fancy new furniture on a credit card. (Topics 20 and 25)

> Democrats should enter the 2020 elections with a plan to match their new spending with equal reductions of the budget deficit, funded by the tax reforms described in this book. This will re-shape the party's image with the centrist voters who will decide the election.

- Without a major new tax source, there is not a viable combination of tax reforms and tax restorations, no matter how many, that would fund a universal health insurance program. That's true regardless of whether or not it is built on a single-payer or multiple-payer model. (Topics 20 and 25)

- Various tax reforms are necessary to simultaneously reduce the current federal budget deficit and provide revenues for new spending. That would require a comprehensive forward-looking, positive fiscal plan. Simple arithmetic shows that it will take all of the patches and reforms in the existing federal tax structure listed below, just to balance the existing federal budget deficit. Even more and higher taxes will be needed to fund new spending on universal health care and college tuition relief. To balance the budget *and* finance these additional aspirations, the U.S. will most likely require a brand-new consumption tax or an equivalent alternative that nobody has yet devised. (Topic 20)

> Part II identifies and quantifies a dozen tax reforms to help balance the budget and fund infrastructure, expanded health care coverage and tuition relief. The Appendix shows numbers for each, in one table.

- Part II is the meat-and-potatoes of fiscal literacy: It includes revenue estimates, economic and policy context, and informative explanations of each of the following tax-reform and tax-increase policy options:

    o Restoration of Obama-era personal income tax rates to make the tax code more progressive. (Topic 10)

    o Raising corporate income tax rates to higher levels that will still be competitive in the global capital markets, and taxing stock buybacks. The politics and economics of a carbon tax are also discussed in this section. An industrial emissions tax on utilities and gas-flaring polluters is the low-hanging fruit for fiscally literate environmentalists. (Topic 14)

o   Increasing taxes on investors' capital gains, dividend income, and the privileged "carried interest" of high-fee investment managers. (Topics 15 and 16)

o   Re-formulating an effective, progressive Alternative Minimum Tax; one that applies to all sources of income, without tax preferences, with a keen focus on the One Percenters and the ultra-rich. (Topic 18)

o   Broadening the estate tax and restoring cuts made in 2017, despite its limitations as a revenue source, with a primary focus on social equity. (Topic 13)

o   Raising the payroll taxes for Social Security and Medicare to make those programs actuarially sustainable. This includes low-hanging fruit on the FICA tree that can generate $35 billion annually by eliminating the wage cap on the employer side of earned income, as a first step. (Topics 10 and 12)

o   Establishing a new tax on financial transactions: a "tax on Wall Street trading" (Topic 19)

o   Reforming the new Trump tax loophole for "business pass-through" income, so that the remaining benefit is focused on small businesses and self-employed, and not the billionaire campaign financiers who have exploited the *Citizens United* court decision to manipulate election campaigns with disproportionate influence. (Topic 17)

o   In the broadest possible terms, in what we call "order of magnitude," none of any of the above tax reforms and tax increases by themselves will generate materially more than $100-150 billion of new revenues annually, without combining them with others. In comparison to today's budget deficits, each of these tax reforms alone will solve only 1/10th of our ongoing revenue shortfall. Importantly, all of them together will not pay for universal national health insurance and certainly not a single-payer plan. One strategy outlined in Topic 25 presents a formula that could provide affordable basic health care with a full-throated tax reform package– but without eliminating the ongoing annual budget deficit.

> Nothing short of a generational tax reform can accomplish the competing objectives of budgetary balance, universal health care and affordable college.

o   Even combined with all of the above tax reforms and increases, it will still require an additional new tax to provide sufficient revenues to fund universal basic health insurance and public college tuition. A consumption-based value-added tax (VAT), along with all the progressive tax reforms listed above, would reduce deficit spending *and* finance needed infrastructure, basic health care and public college education for all. This would require a generational tax reform that Millennials and collegians should study carefully as a blueprint for sharing the fiscal burdens that have been thrust upon them by inaction of preceding generations and a dysfunctional Congress. But nothing short of that will accomplish these four competing priorities. (Topic 20)

o Blockchain technology could make logistics and administration of a VAT more feasible. (Topic 20)

o The most 'outside-the-box' idea to be found in this book is its rationale for a national referendum on the generational fiscal policy revolution that a new VAT accompanied by progressive tax reforms would require. This is such a major bipartisan and multi-generational undertaking, with such major impacts on all Americans, that We the People ought to vote on it. (Topics 20 and 25) Otherwise a "package deal" dies on the vine.

> Part II enables readers to tell when a Pinocchio award is deserved by politicians making phony promises and deceptive claims about revenues.

- Unlike the exaggerated claims of tax reform revenues by several political candidates who often cite 10-year revenue projections, this book presents realistic fact-based estimates of the annual revenue of each tax reform and tax increase capsulized above. Readers of Part II can readily understand the feasibility of various spending and taxing plans now being pitched by political candidates. Although the Congressional budget process requires a 10-year forecast for reliable budget projections, ordinary citizens are deceived when candidates make specious references to multi-year "big numbers" revenue forecasts as a way to finance annual costs. Part II enables readers to tell when a Pinocchio award is deserved by politicians making phony promises and deceptive claims about revenues from specific tax reforms and tax increases. (Topics 10-19)

- *Just as one example, a financial transactions tax (Topic 19) would cover the costs of only five weeks of single-payer Medicare for All, in given year. The remaining unfunded costs would double Trump's budget deficits unless the income tax for all Americans at all income levels is also increased by a factor of 75% with a top income tax rate of 69% plus state and local taxes. That kind of health-care finance does not sound like a winning platform for 2020.*

- Other issues are addressed in Part II, including trade-war tariffs, wealth taxes, and taxation of "silver spoon" trust fund distributions through an AMT. (Topics 21, 23, and 18, respectively)

Part III: National Health Care Policy

- Americans spend $4 trillion annually on health care. No other country spends this much per capita or as a percent of GDP. Yet our high spending and high costs have failed to yield better overall health outcomes. (Introduction)

- 30 million Americans still have no health insurance. Expanding coverage to those citizens without offering subsidized benefits to other middle-class consumers is the Rubik's cube facing Democrats in their search for a solution to affordable care. (Introduction)

- 75 million Americans now receive Medicaid health benefits at federal and state expense. An astounding 39 percent of all children in the USA are presently enrolled in Medicaid. States pay 38 percent of total Medicaid costs. States spend 25 percent of their budgets for their share of Medicaid; more than what they spend on either higher education or transportation. (Topic 23)

- Republican promises to "Repeal and Replace" the Affordable Care Act (aka Obamacare) went only half-way by chiseling away at its revenue foundations, but with no "replacement." Trump promised "great health care" and has delivered nothing. Voters delivered a strong message of discontent in many Congressional districts which swung to the Blue column in the last election, at least in part because of their anxiety over national health care policy. (Introduction)

> The Medicare trust fund will be depleted in 2026. Medicare for All will be a cruel hoax if it is paid with federal IOUs.

- "Medicare for All" and the concept of a single-payer system to replace the entire private insurance industry has drawn widespread attention among many Democrats, and media coverage has elevated the issue to the level of national debate. Many advocates of Medicare for All mistakenly believe that today's Medicare is free after age 65 and is already "paid up" at retirement. Most readers are unaware of existing income-based premium surcharges already imposed to help cover costs of benefits that were supposedly paid for by payroll taxes collected during workers' lifetimes. (Introduction)

- The economics of universal health insurance are described in Part III. It is fiscally impossible to replace the multi-payer system with a nationalized health insurance model that eliminates premiums and co-pays, without raising existing taxes to painful levels or instituting major new taxes. Even with all this new revenue, a Medicare for All approach will leave the current federal budget deficits untouched. ***Without a major*** *new nationwide tax, a single-payer system will be built on a fiscal house of cards.* (Topic 25) Escalating interest owed on the national debt will ultimately undermine the health care program. (Topic 7)

- There are viable options, however, for expansion of health insurance to a large segment of the population that is now uninsured and under-insured. "Medicare at Cost" is a viable strategy, by which current Medicare benefits could be made available over time to all families at the actuarial cost. Older participants would pay more than younger enrollees, and families would pay more than singles. Because Medicare administration is non-profit, with much lower marketing and overhead costs, premiums for Medicare at Cost could be lower than equivalent private insurance by $400-450 per participant per year, possibly more. But eliminating $80 billion of annual insurance company profits and overhead in a $2 trillion industry does not magically deliver free health insurance to Americans. (Topic 23)

- Employers presently pay about $880 billion annually in insurance premiums for their employees, which is 20 percent of the nation's entire health care bills. Employers pay over 80 percent of total premiums under their group plans. A rational and cost-effective reform of health care must retain as many of those premium dollars as possible.

- Part III explores various models for multi-payer hybrid systems to expand the federal role in health care while still retaining various levels of individual and employer contributions. (Topic 25)

> It is possible to provide basic health care and college education for all with a balanced budget, but will voters approve of the major tax increases?

- Liberating states of their share of Medicaid costs under a fully-funded national health insurance plan would relieve state budgets sufficiently to underwrite resident tuition at most public colleges and universities. In that manner, a novel "Two-Fer" could be funded by a well-designed plan to finance universal basic coverage. To stimulate deeper thinking and discussions, Part III includes discussion of the politics and economics of the kind of national plan that would be required to provide "Basic Health Care and Public College Education for All *with* a Balanced Budget." (Topic 25) Whether voters would ever support such a grandiose generational policy shift, readers can ponder or dismiss as pie-in-the-sky.

- A final section in Part III explains several supply-side policies that can help reduce medical costs by (1) expanding the supply of doctors and trained medical professionals who are now in short supply and (2) fighting inflated drug prices by requiring royalties and profit-sharing in exchange for research grants now awarded to drug research startups that capitalize on federal funds and then later hit the jackpot. (Topic 26)

Part IV: Infrastructure

- Most Americans understand and agree that much of the nation's physical infrastructure needs repair and in many cases replacement. We have all seen the media coverage of old, failing bridges that pose a safety hazard to drivers. Many of our airports and transit systems are outdated and shabby. Myriad dams and levees on our waterways need reinforcement, and rising sea levels pose new risks that require sea walls and other solutions. Stormwater systems are inadequate in flood-prone regions. The American Society of Civil Engineers (ASCE) estimates that nationwide, the U.S. needs to spend $4.5 trillion on infrastructure upgrades by 2025.

- Because the U.S. government is perennially running budget deficits, the federal share of all infrastructure spending, other than highway projects, is now funded entirely by new federal debt.

- To properly fund a $1 trillion federal infrastructure spending initiative, Congress would need to raise taxes by roughly $50 billion annually and refrain from tax rollbacks for 30 years in order to pay off the debt. Any number of tax reforms discussed in Part II can underwrite a program of double this magnitude, but they must be sustained and not rolled back by a future anti-tax Congress. To address all the structural deficiencies cited by the ASCE, a comprehensive but controversial fiscal plan would be required, consistent with the outline discussed in Topics 20 and 25.

> For our nation, capital investment in core infrastructure is needed and worthwhile, if Congress can come up with a responsible plan to pay for it.

- As a nation, capital investment in core infrastructure is easily defensible, if Congress can come up with a way to pay for it. Unlike annual spending for social programs and income re-distribution, capital spending can legitimately be financed with long-term bond issues to spread out the costs over the projects' and taxpayers' lives. There is an asset to match the liability, as long as taxes can cover the debt service. In this era of federal deficit finance and tax ceilings on states and local governments, most infrastructure must hereafter be financed through user charges wherever possible.

- As to who pays for governmental infrastructure projects, the American system of federal government is unlike that of most other countries. Our national government "owns" federal buildings and major waterway infrastructure, but roads and bridges are typically built and maintained by states and their political subdivisions. Highway funding comes from statewide fuel and motor vehicle taxes along with federal taxes on gas and diesel. Airports and transit facilities are typically built and operated by local special-purpose districts. School buildings are typically funded locally by property taxes and state-shared revenues from income or sales taxes.

- State and local governments face serious constraints on their ability to fund new and replacement infrastructure. They lack the power to print money, so they cannot fund projects "out of thin air" through the nation's central bank, the Federal Reserve system. Relatively few local governments, including school districts and special districts, can raise taxes to pay for infrastructure debt service without voter approval. Most states and almost all local governments are prohibited by law from running an operating budget deficit by borrowing money through general obligation bonds. These are important impediments for any major federal infrastructure initiative that requires state and local funding or matching funds.

- In addition to direct expenditures funded by federal borrowing, the U.S. has several "debt management" tools available to it to incentivize state and local government capital expenditures on both a long-term permanent basis and as part of a shorter-term, counter-cyclical strategy. Topic 29 includes innovative strategies to cut their borrowing costs.

- An effective long-term, bipartisan fiscal federalist plan for infrastructure finance must include: (1) a long-term commitment to fund infrastructure projects that modernize the American economy with jobs-creation a secondary priority, (2) incentives for states and localities to complete land acquisition and rights, and prepare "shovel-ready" engineering and project plans that can be quickly accelerated and implemented in a recession, (3) policies to reduce the cost of state and local government bond issuance and (4) rigorous conditional funding requirements that ensure timely infrastructure replacement in the future through user fees where feasible.

> As electric vehicles proliferate, the benefits of transportation facilities must be funded by those who use them, when they use them.

- New technologies will disrupt the traditional model for financing highways and bridges, as electric vehicles become more prevalent, making traditional motor fuels taxes insufficient to fund construction and replacement of congested roads and bridge replacement. As vehicular automation and 5G telecommunications technology advances in the coming decade, cars and trucks must pay through micro-payment systems that automatically capture the revenue needed to replace the facilities they use. The benefits of transportation facilities will increasingly and eventually have to be funded by those who use them, when they use them.

- In recent decades, numerous "public-private partnerships" (P3) have organized to build and operate facilities for public use. Part IV describes the conditions where privatization and semi-privatization are feasible.

The Appendix provides an easy-to-reference table showing the relative annual dollar magnitude of various federal expenditures and political campaign proposals, along with the corresponding revenues that can realistically be collected through proposed new or reformed taxes. It provides a "Pinocchio fact-checking and smell-testing" scorecard with cross-references to the appropriate topics that provide contextual background.

PART I:

Fiscal Facts of Life – The Federal Budget, Deficits and Debt

....

Que será, será
Whatever will be, will be
The future's not ours to see
Que será, será

Doris Day, 1956

In simplest terms, fiscal policy is "the budget." It's taxing and spending by the national government. It's federal revenues vs. expenditures. It's how we fund the nation's government by taxing ourselves and borrowing from anybody willing to lend it money.

Very few Democrats, Independents, Millennials and collegians are financial experts, and most are not fiscally literate. It's not anyone's fault: no school or college teaches this stuff using real numbers in the present tense. This book is both an ice-breaker and a "home-study class in public finance" all under one cover.[1] Unlike a college textbook, it is written for Democrats and Independents, by an Independent Democrat

---

1 One professor, a prominent dean in Public Administration, calls this book's contents "encyclopedic" for its comprehensiveness.

who once served on the Governmental Accounting Standards Board and worked for decades in the financial and investment industries as a qualified financial expert. The book's audience also includes all Millennials and collegians regardless of their party affiliations, because their generation will soon inherit the unforgiving fiscal mess now brewing in Washington DC. With so many younger Americans strapped with college debt, and facing huge health insurance premiums that did not exist when the Baby Boom generation was their age, it is no wonder that younger voters are looking for their wealthier elders and especially the One Percenters to "pay up" for the cost of a lopsided economic order they are inheriting. Readers of all stripes with a strong social conscience and a sense of economic injustice must know enough about public finance to stand up to *status-quo* Republicans who are much more likely to have taken a class or two on business finance. In the process, all readers will also become better equipped to challenge cheesy and baseless campaign claims by candidates across the political spectrum, going into both the 2020 convention and the general election.

> We face the fiscal equivalent of Global Warming and rising sea levels. Who will be the passionate champion of fiscal sustainability?

Yes, the terminology is specialized and unfamiliar. The fiscal experts all speak in bureaucratese and use acronyms like GDP, TCJA, FICA, AGI, AMT and CMS.[2] The numbers are huge. The government itself is so big and complex that the average person is intimidated. So this Introduction starts by explaining the big chunks of revenues and expenses in basic categories that do not require a CPA or MBA to

---

2 A Glossary of acronyms is provided at the back of this book.

understand. It sizes up the annual budget deficit that every year requires the government to borrow even more to pay its bills. After that, readers take a quick look at the pile of debt that has accumulated in the past century, what it costs to pay the interest, and today's rate of growth in both debt and interest costs. That provides a foundation for understanding what happens if the federal government keeps doing what it is doing now, which is financially unsustainable.

What would be the fiscal equivalent of Al Gore's environmental movie, *An Inconvenient Truth*? Where is the passionate champion for fiscal sustainability in Washington, DC? Our government's coming fiscal cliff is the financial equivalent of Global Warming, with an eerily similar timeline to the point of irreversible harm. The inevitable consequences of doing nothing (what pundits call "kicking the can" down the road) will be described in simple, understandable terms that do not require a college degree in finance or economics.

The U.S. economy is huge, over $20 trillion in annual activity. The federal budget is about $4.7 trillion for fiscal year 2019, representing a bit less than one quarter of the economy. The annual budget deficit is now running at a rate of $1.1 trillion annually, and the accumulated federal government debt is $22 trillion. The idea that a trillion dollars is 1,000 billions is something students learn in elementary school, but there is nothing tangible about a trillion that average citizens can relate to.

> The current U.S. budget deficit annually exceeds the market value of all property built in New York City over the past four centuries.

To put a trillion-dollar budget deficit into perspective, the current market value of all real estate in our nation's largest city, New York, the financial capital of the world, is approximately $1.3 trillion. So every year, the federal government budget spends more than it collects by the entire property value of all New York real estate. Said another way, if Uncle Sam could somehow confiscate and sell all the real estate in New York City, which was built up by its inhabitants *over the past four centuries*, that would pay for only one year's worth of U.S. budget deficits. Next year, the Treasury secretary would need to sell all properties in Los Angeles and Chicago. The following year, it would take seven more entire cities. This adds up: the accumulated "national mortgage" that Americans collectively now owe for our federal government's unpaid bills exceeds the combined value of all urban land in metropolitan center cities throughout the entire country.

We hear campaign talk these days about a Wealth Tax. The federal budget deficit is a "Wealth Tapeworm." It's a generational tax on every adult American's children, nieces and nephews, and grandchildren. For Millennials and collegians, the federal deficit is a generational fiscal tapeworm handed down to them by their elders. As a politician once said, "Blessed are the young, for they shall inherit the national debt." But this debt is not just a deadweight burden for younger adults: Older citizens must now worry about the great risks to their own retirement security that will be squandered by runaway federal deficits, if corrective fiscal action is not taken in the coming decade.

There is another way to think about the size of this problem in terms that we can all relate to more personally: The outstanding federal debt now equals about two-thirds (2/3) of the value of all residential housing in the U.S. Over the years, Congress has mortgaged our nation to a level where each household's share of the national debt is two-thirds of today's value of our homes. In ten more years, that national debt will exceed the value of all homes. Every homeowner has both the mortgage company and our governments' bondholders holding a claim on their future.

In a nation where most families with college students cannot pay for their tuition without borrowing, and accumulated student loan debt now exceeds $1.5 trillion, most Progressives, Millennials and collegians consider that a crisis. The federal debt pile is 15 times that student debt number. Many swing voters will ask why is it that voluntarily indebted college students are so special that they deserve the next trillion of new tax dollars and not the rest of the country? Is the tail wagging the dog here? This chapter will ask and answer some tough questions that Progressive and Liberal candidates and voters will confront as they approach the general election in 2020.

Just to put the *annual* federal budget deficit into balance, every American household would need to contribute $8,500 in cash from its family pocketbook *every year*. If translated into what we personally consume, it would require a national tax of 7.5 percent of everything we buy, from automobiles to haircuts to fast food, insurance, cellphones, college tuition, dentists, groceries, vacations, movies, electricity, rent and house payments.

When confronted with numbers this large, most Americans shrug their shoulders. Intuitively many voters feel in their hearts that we are passengers onboard a fiscal *Titanic*. They just pray that somehow it will work out in the future, so we must live for today. *Carpe diem* and *Que sera sera* have become the implicit national mottos of American public finance.

Democrats have a unique opportunity to re-frame the national debate and the party's image with centrist voters by entering the 2020 elections with a plan to match their new spending with equal reductions of the budget deficit, funded by the tax reforms described in Part II. By attacking the GOP for its complete failure to install fiscal discipline, Democrats have an unprecedented opportunity to prove themselves to be the only adults in the room during the televised Presidential debates and door-to-door canvassing. It should not go unmentioned that the last balanced budget was delivered by a Democratic President, Bill Clinton.

SYNOPSIS

"We must not let our rulers load us with perpetual debt."

Thomas Jefferson, 1816 (who had sold bonds to finance 80 percent of the Louisiana Purchase)

Like a bad plaster cast on an untreated broken arm, the federal budget is now set in a widening structural deficit. Ongoing spending for military and social programs, combined with artificially low and deficient tax rates, have produced the largest peacetime full-employment budget deficits in our nation's history. The Trump Tax Cuts, known officially as the Tax Cuts and Jobs Act (TCJA) of 2017, have bled the federal treasury of revenue that must be reinstated in order to begin rebalancing the federal budget. Tax increases and revenue-generating tax reforms are both necessary and inevitable. Although everybody wants economic growth, we cannot grow our way out of the deficits by wishing it to happen. There was no truth in the unrealistic blue-sky and black-magic promises by GOP ideologues that unregulated economic growth would mystically produce surging tax revenues. Consequently the deficit and the debt are now worse, and will swell in coming years even without a cyclical recession. Throw in a garden-variety recession at some point along the way, and the annual deficit will rival that of the Global Financial Crisis in 2008-9 with no end in sight.

> Although everybody wants economic growth, we cannot grow our way out of the budget deficits.

Contrary to the habitual claims of the anti-tax lobby, the total tax burden in the United States is comparatively lower than many other developed countries. By cutting taxes to unsustainably low levels that do not pay the bills for today's expenditures, the Trump Tax Cuts took a festering problem and made it worse. The TCJA was fiscal malpractice, despite the sugar high it gave to Wall Street where corporate tax cuts translated directly into higher profits which converted directly into higher stock prices.[3]

Responsibility for today's mounting federal debt is not just a GOP failure. Both parties have contributed to this problem, and many incumbent Democrats have dodged budgetary discipline just as much as Republicans. If the Liberal and Progressive wings of the Democratic party insist on new, unfunded social spending, without also taking on the deficit monster, they will be just as complicit as their Tea Party adversaries across the aisle in Congress. If the Millennial solution to student debt is to simply refinance it with new unfunded government bonds, that is no better than Baby Boomers' unfunded Medicare prescription drug deal. There is plenty of blame to share, although the root of the problem goes all the way back to Ronald Reagan, whose strategy was to "starve the beast. " Reagan foresaw that if taxes were

---

3 Incredibly, the incumbent President now claims that the stock market will crash if he is not re-elected. Another contrived crisis of his own making? Have artificially inflated stock prices become a hostage for political ransom?

kept low enough long enough, there would no longer be any money left for social programs after paying for national defense, Social Security, the most rudimentary government functions like the Post Office and national parks, and interest on the national debt.

Failure to put our fiscal house in order will risk putting America on the same sorry path that preceded the demise and breakup of the Soviet Union's empire. It will affect both our future quality of life and our national security. For those worried about Chinese military ascendency, the words of George Washington should haunt every adult American:

"Avoid accumulations of debt by vigorous exertions in time of peace to discharge the debts, . . . not by ungenerously throwing upon posterity the burden which we ourselves ought to bear."

Farewell Address, 1796

The central point of this opening chapter is to explain to all Democrats (and especially their candidates, campaign teams and supporters) that their noble aspirations to improve the human condition in the USA cannot be built on a fiscal house of cards. As laudable as it is for political candidates to provide a taxing plan to pay for new spending such as universal health care and public college education, these incremental measures will be meaningless if the current deficits are not also resolved. By the mid-2030s, any major new spending programs coming out of the 2020 election will have to be scuttled because the existing unfunded commitments to Baby Boomer retirement security and the mounting interest on federal debt will suck up all available revenue, including every dollar from the piecemeal tax reforms that candidates are now pitching. The only choices after this approaching point-of-no-return are between (1) dramatically higher taxes on everybody (not just the One Percenters), (2) draconian budget cuts for education, housing, environmental and welfare programs, or (3) a corrosive inflation that robs every pocketbook, every senior citizen, every retirement fund and every savings account.

> Borrowing more and more to pay interest on the national debt is a doomed policy of inaction. It will result in higher interest rates, inflation and economic stagnation akin to the 1970s, only this time entirely because of Congressional neglect.

Politicians in both parties have ignored the risks to our economy that interest on the national debt and the underfunding of Social Security and Medicare will pose in fifteen years if not sooner. Borrowing to pay interest on the nation's credit cards is a doomed strategy. Eventually, this will require higher interest rates for consumers and homeowners, and a stagnant economy that loses its global advantages.

Inflation is what results if Congress does nothing, and that is not a painless outcome. History has shown repeatedly and without exception that government debt cannot be financed magically by printing money and expanding the money supply to fund escalating deficits. One of the most dangerous ideas now advanced by some on the socialist fringe of the Progressive wing is the concept of "Modern Monetary Theory (MMT),"[4] which purports that all the nation's accumulated debt

---

4 MMT includes the misguided and unfounded belief that federal budget deficits don't matter, and government can better allocate resources than private investors. The political economy of MMT holds that federal policymakers can operate a command (planned) economy more effectively than open, neutrally regulated markets. What MMT dreamers ignore is that the same Platonic powers to be given to their philosopher-king planners can be distorted perversely by an authoritarian or egomaniacal market-meddler like the incumbent President. The monetary part of their theory is that our central bank, the Federal Reserve,

is irrelevant because "we owe it to ourselves." Because our government owns the printing press for the world's reserve currency (the dollar) they naively believe that the debt can be paid off easily by issuing more greenbacks. But honestly, how can we owe it to ourselves if every family's share of the national debt is 15 times the median household savings in the U.S.? We will owe it to unforgiving lenders who will extract their pound of flesh in the form of higher interest rates. What the MMT disciples conveniently ignore is the irreparable harm that the inflation that results from printing money would do to the economy, the retirement security of tens of millions of pensioners and frugal savers who are now too old to work for more dollars. The end-game of MMT is a budgetary disaster and national economic malaise. Higher interest rates on federal debt will only deepen the deficit and the interest costs that crowd out social spending. The inevitable self-defeating impact of an MMT inflation on federal interest costs will be discussed later in this chapter.

Most adherents of MMT never lived through high inflation like the American middle class suffered in the 1970s when the money supply was mistakenly inflated to create "petro dollars" when oil prices surged from the Arab embargo. MMT ignores what we all learned back then about inflation expectations and CPI indexing. Never mind that a 10 percent annualized money supply increase back then brought on 10 percent inflation, which in turn clobbered stocks by 46 percent, which crushed public and private pension funds (that now rely far more heavily on investment earnings to pay benefits to retirees that now outstrip contributions by active employees). Never mind that younger Americans

---

can dramatically inflate our money supply in order to fund budget deficits by issuing new dollars to buy Treasury bonds for its account. (The Fed actually creates money "out of thin air" by buying Treasury securities from private-sector securities dealers and issuing credits for their market value to the bond dealers' bank accounts. These "deposits" increase the banks' reserve accounts at the Fed, which enables the banks to then lend those digital dollars multifold. That is how we "print money" in the modern world.) The money-printing camp asserts that the U.S. dollar is the world's reserve currency, to which they attach magical properties. That works until the music stops.

were frozen out of homeownership by double-digit mortgage rates. Acolytes of MMT have never lived through the kind of hyperinflation that currency debasement has given to Venezuela and other Latin American and African countries in recent decades. Although conventional Keynesian macroeconomics does support strong fiscal and monetary intervention during depression scenarios, MMT has plausible policy value only in the darkest days of capitalist cycles, not otherwise. MMT would just wallpaper-over the widening cracks in the national fisc.

Some readers will wonder why the risk of inflation is worth worrying about now, when inflation is so subdued and sovereign interest rates overseas have gone negative? With superabundance of capital from wealthy sovereign wealth funds, the demographic slowing of growth rates in advanced economies in the G7 countries, and wage pressures abundant from globalization, some would argue that inflation is not the problem: deflationary forces are in control right now. That argument has its merits, and cannot be dismissed lightly. The issue here, however, is not about today's inflation and interest rates, but rather what will happen to them in 10 or 15 years when federal debt piles up, and tax revenues are insufficient to service ongoing deficits and government operations, as well as the outstanding bonds? At that point, the typical default action of national legislatures (after first raising taxes to the point that they would crush taxpayers and the economic engine) has been to let inflation run upward so that tax revenues increase as middle-class taxpayers are pushed into higher brackets, so that the debt is paid off with cheaper money and automatically higher average tax rates. That is the tipping point that must be avoided if Millennials and today's collegians are not to be left inheriting a fiscal mess from their elders. It is the fiscal equivalent of New Orleans, Miami and New York suffering storm surges from rising sea levels; it will not happen overnight, but the day will come if the causes are not addressed in time.

Lest the MMT advocates dismiss this entire book for its aversion to their magical thinking, the recession scenario and its monetary antidote is also taken seriously here. As explained in Part IV under Topics 27 and 29, the acceleration of state and local government construction projects during a recession could be prudently financed through federal borrowing.[5] Those bonds could well be purchased by the Federal Reserve as part of counter-cyclical monetary policy, when the short-run inflation risks should be negligible. Part IV of this book explains the unique opportunity to engage the Federal Financing Bank as an unprecedented new tool of counter-cyclical recession remedies. This is the special case where Keynesian economics, federalist public finance principles and MMT would agree. But it is the exception, not the rule.

This chapter will review four categories of federal spending, their predicted growth into the future as calculated by Congressional Budget Office and the General Accountability Office, and the key revenue sources to pay for expenditures.

> The four categories of federal expenditure are national security, entitlement programs, discretionary programs and interest on the debt. Escalating interest costs and entitlement payments will crowd out discretionary spending.

The four primary categories of federal expenditure are: (1) National security, the military budget, (2) Entitlement programs including Social Security, Medicare and Medicaid, (3) Interest on the federal debt and (4) Civilian discretionary programs, which includes all the other federal departments that provide services that must be cut if the first three categories overtake all the available revenue and borrowing capacity. Each

---

5 The Federal Financing Bank is a conduit agency well suited for this function, as described in Part IV.

category will be described from a fiscal-policy perspective, focusing on the numbers more than the subjective merits of the various ways that taxpayer money can or must be spent.

Not all of the national debt is "bad debt" in the sense that the federal government does have assets. Who can place a monetary value on the national parks? If navigable rivers were tollways, what price would they bring? How should we assess the value of offshore oil reserves that are federal property? What is the value of all the aircraft carriers, government satellites, nuclear submarines and military bases that our borrowed money has paid for? All that federal money invested since the 1950s in the interstate highway system and local subways and bridges did give us Americans some hard assets that have economic value as core infrastructure. State and local governments hold around $5 trillion of nonfinancial assets on their books at cost, of which a large percentage was federally funded infrastructure. Unfortunately, national income accounting does not differentiate operating deficits from capital expenditures to simplify quantification. Governmental accounting does not recognize current market value of these assets. What we do know is that in recent decades, federal spending for infrastructure has been about $100 billion annually in inflation-adjusted dollars. When added to what might be a comparable number for military fleet equipment (not armaments) based on a "capital vs. ordnance" share of the $150 billion military procurement budget, one could "guesstimate" that perhaps 15 to 20 percent of the federal debt has a corresponding tangible asset that was acquired. Beyond that, there is not much in the physical world to show for the nation's trillion-dollar deficits and debt. Much of it, unfortunately, is the sunk cost of foreign wars and the rest is from chronically over-spending the available revenues (with a few trillion of the debt attributable to taxing too little, for those with that point of view).

A key factor that cannot be ignored is the interest on the federal debt, which is mounting every year as annual budget deficits require ever-more new Treasury bonds (T-bonds) to be sold. Remember what

Einstein said about the power of compound interest. Einstein's "eighth wonder of the world" now has the potential to become America's greatest curse in 15 to 20 years. If today's low interest rates lurch upward to compensate investors for monetary inflation and an unstoppable flood of new government bonds to pay interest on interest, the game (of kick the can) will be up. An increase in T-bond interest rates from current levels to a more historically common six percent (where they traded from 1968 to 2000) would double the interest costs in our national budget, and squeeze out *all* funding for discretionary domestic programs. Outside of government, mortgage rates of seven percent or more would return, clobber home values and housing affordability, and put many owners underwater on their home equity.

Our military adversaries do not need to escalate their spending that much to rival us in 2040. They now need only wait for two decades, at which point the American military budget will be hamstrung by fiscal constraints. For those nemeses willing to play the long game, as lifetime autocracies can do, it is now only a matter of time (one generation at most) if Congress keeps kicking the can. That is a scenario that fiscally literate readers must comprehend for the geopolitical risks it poses to their best intentions and the welfare of our nation's children and grandchildren.

The subsequent chapter on Tax Policy and Tax Reforms will address the opportunities and challenges facing Democrats as they debate various ways to pay for new universal benefits programs that would only deepen the budget deficits and national debt if "pay-for" taxation is not included in their proposals.

Fiscal overview of federal spending

The purpose and framework of this chapter is not to enumerate every expenditure program in the federal budget. Readers interested in how much the U.S. Departments of Education, HUD, or Agriculture, or the national park service, spend annually can readily find that information online. Fiscal literacy for the purposes of this book begins with a birds-eye view of the core components of the federal budget as they will play themselves out over the next 20 years. Liberals are usually keen to understand those categories, specific programs and pet policies that are near and dear to their hearts. But in order to be fiscally literate, they must first understand how and where they fit into the bigger picture of long-run financial sustainability.

It is not the role of this chapter to outline or recommend new ways to spend more or less for governmental functions already established under law. This overview section is primarily descriptive, from the standpoint of identifying and categorizing in the broadest terms possible where federal dollars are now spent, whether it be funded by taxes or borrowing. The discussion of deficits and interest costs will address the broader normative fiscal issues, not with an axe to grind on specific governmental functions, but rather with a candid description of what happens if we leave today's budget imbalances to run on autopilot.

TOPIC I: National Defense and Military Spending.

··

"In the councils of government, we must guard against the acquisition of unwarranted influence, whether sought or unsought, by the military-industrial complex."

Dwight Eisenhower's Farewell Address

Military expenditures (aka National Defense) are not the largest component of the federal budget, but national defense is arguably the first priority of any nation-state. Until such time as *homo sapiens* evolves into life forms that all co-exist peacefully on the same planet without resorting to violence to gain territory, plunder, revenge, or holy grail, then national governments must maintain a military defense. By a long shot, the U.S. spends more on national defense that any other country in the world. In fact, American military spending exceeds the combined total of China, Saudi Arabia, India, France, Russia, United Kingdom and Germany (in that order). Think about that: If they all lined up against us, we would still be outspending them! Like it or not, America is unquestionably the world's Superpower in military spending and global reach. The traditional American policy formula has been that Preparedness through Superiority equals Deterrence, although that has sometimes proven to be aspirational and unrealistic in wars against terrorism and other non-conventional theaters (such as the Vietnam guerilla war).

> Democrats looking for ways to save money on national defense have few viable options for major cost cuts, absent breakthrough diplomatic solutions with global adversaries.

The official annual budget for defense is now approximately $670 billion, which represents about 14 percent of total federal spending. But that overlooks defense-related and -supporting line items in other cabinet departments that bring the overall total to almost $1 trillion, closer to 21 percent of the federal budget. Whichever number one cites, 14 to 20 percent has been the general range of the defense department budget share in the post-Vietnam era. Of this, a record $200 billion[6] is now proposed for Overseas Contingency Operations (OCO) which are essentially the "war budget" and potentially a giant Defense department "slush fund" in the eyes of some critics. The department's 2019 remaining base budget is what we might otherwise consider the nation's "peacetime defense budget."

The Defense department budget is approximately the same size as the Medicare budget, at least for now. As the American population ages, the Medicare budget, even without anything like "Medicare for All," will likely overtake the military's base budget. For national security hawks, therein lies a problem, so there has been heavy lobbying within the defense establishment to build up fleets in what is characterized as rebuilding and modernization.

Nobody in Washington DC wants to weaken our national defense, although the voters' appetite for costly distant wars has receded since 9/11. Democrats looking for ways to save money on national defense have few viable options, politically. One strategy is to diplomatically seek more cost-sharing by our allies in NATO and elsewhere, but without all the drama of the incumbent Administration's antagonistic antics. The civil approach to burden-sharing is what one might call the "Calmer Global Leadership" strategy: a pitch to voters that political grandstanding and gamesmanship by the leader of the Free World is counterproductive, and ultimately more costly than a cooperative diplomatic approach. As a campaign theme, this is unlikely to resonate with the Trump political base, but it may get more of the remaining 60 percent of the electorate out to the polls if the White House overplays its cards. The Silent Majority could become a Democratic majority this time around.

---

6 In the latest White House budget for 2020, including offline support for OCO in other departments. A sceptic might ask why the Administration has suddenly reclassified $100 billion of presently "base" defense budget expenditures now as OCO. Could it be a ploy to give the President more executive discretion to end-run the Congress on border interventions and other political grandstanding?

The other approaches to cost-cutting are much more politically sensitive and risky to politicians: military base closures and weapons procurement. Although there are hard-core military hawks for whom every military base and weapons program is an asset, many Progressives and Liberals would agree that there is some fat to be trimmed. Weapons procurement represents about a third of the defense spending, with much of it devoted to ship-building and aircraft that arguably are capital assets on the federal balance sheet. The political problem is that one voter's wasteful spending is another community's economic foundation and another's defense contractor, both of which provide gainful employment and sales taxes in their Congressional district. Nobody in Congress was ever re-elected on a platform of vocally advocating a base closure in their district.

Could $100 billion be trimmed from today's annual Defense department budget over a period of time? Perhaps, but Progressives and Liberals will face strong opposition from Eisenhower's dreaded military-industrial complex, partisan general election opponents, constituent mayors, radio talk-show announcers, and national security hardliners. This makes defense cutbacks a treacherous path to budget-balancing. That said, it will be less politically painful to cancel announced White House plans to escalate spending on ships and planes by $100 billion annually in this decade, before those plans take on a life of their own and acquire their own constituency. Sensibly reining in the Trump team's full-throttle military build-up procurement plan is probably a theme that can resonate center-left. And the 2020 White House budget's OCO slush fund recategorization clearly deserves closer Congressional scrutiny and oversight.

The most worrisome geopolitical risk in the long run is that entitlement programs and interest on the national debt will eventually crimp the nation's ability to fund essential military operations to deter ascending bad actors overseas and terrorists on our own soil. We must revisit that longer-term issue in the later discussion of deficits and debt.

TOPIC 2: Entitlement programs: Social Security, Medicare and Medicaid.

. . . .

The largest single component of the federal budget is what most analysts call "entitlement programs." The definitions for this category are muddy, overlapping and can be disputed. Most fiscal professionals agree that Social Security and Medicare are entitlement programs, because all citizens are entitled to earn benefits that they receive upon attaining old age. They are the largest entitlement programs, so the nit-picking over terminology begins with the third largest entitlement (or mandatory) program, which is Medicaid.

Some politicians, bureaucrats and recipient constituencies throw around the term "mandatory," and that term is used in many White House budget documents. (To most Beltway insiders, Mandatory means that an expenditure is immune to sequestration, which is an automatic budget cut if Congress is deadlocked.) For our purposes here, we will include Medicaid in the entitlement category, because of both its size which is similar to Medicare when state contributions are included, and because the basic criteria for eligibility are formulaic: If one's income is below or near the poverty line, the household is entitled to Medicaid. But Conservatives could take issue with this treatment, because recipients did not "pay forward" into the system; it is purely a federal subsidy.

As a reminder to all, Medicare provides health insurance coverage to the elderly as its primary mission. Medicaid provides health insurance coverage to lower-income citizens regardless of age, if they meet certain means tests. As with Medicare, Medicaid is administered at the federal level by an agency called Centers for Medicare and Medicaid Services (CMS). However, unlike Medicare, the participant-level interfaces for

Medicaid are each of the states, which collectively contribute 38 percent of its costs under various matching formulas. The states have various levels of control over certain eligibility rules, making Medicaid participation less uniform than Medicare.

Two other federal programs are technically entitlements: workers' compensation and unemployment insurance, which both collect premiums; their net total costs to the Treasury are negligible. From a fiscal standpoint, they are not especially relevant to federal deficits and debt. Both are dwarfed by the "Giant Entitlement Spending Trio" of Social Security, Medicare and Medicaid. But their insurance-premium funding base technically qualifies them as entitlements.

In the final category that this chapter will present, called "Domestic Discretionary Spending," there are included a gaggle of other federal programs that now like to call themselves "mandatory." That terminology is arguably a convenient hiding place for program advocates, bureaucrats and lobbyists. In the Department of Health and Human Services (HHS), there are four welfare programs which are administered by the states under various formulas. In the Department of Agriculture (USDA), there are food stamps, farm subsidies and crop insurance programs that comprise 60 percent of its entire agency budget. They have acquired their status as "mandatory" through legislative language that attaches a formula to their distribution of funds. As long as there are appropriations, the payments become "mandatory." Few of us would call these entitlement programs, and most would agree that in a harsh budget-cutting scenario, these mandatory programs would have to be reconsidered and their formulas revised before cutting the defense department in a time of war, or reneging on Social Security and Medicare payments to our elderly. For our purposes, and without disputing the importance of any of these pet programs in the minds of their promoters, we will discuss them later in the section on discretionary spending. If they are now truly entitlements that have mutated into irreducible mandatory spending obligations of the United States government, then the fiscal problem is worsened for Liberals and Progressives who advocate new spending elsewhere.

TOPIC 3: **Social Security.**

. . . .

When Franklin D. Roosevelt pushed the Social Security Act of 1935 through Congress, it had three primary components: (1) It would be funded universally as a social insurance program to which all workers and their employers would contribute through a payroll tax, not an income tax, to avoid the stigma of "socialist" income-redistribution. (2) Eligibility for the full retirement pension would begin at age 65, except for disability and widow benefits. And (3) the tax rate was set at one percent of the worker's first $3,000 of income (equivalent to about $56,000 today, adjusted for inflation), to be paid by both the employee and the employer.

In some ways, times have not changed too much since FDR's time. Social Security is a financial lifeline for most elderly citizens. It is a central fact of their lives. For one-quarter of the elderly, Social Security is all they have. For 36 percent, it provides 90 percent of their income. For 65 percent of the recipients, Social Security is their primary source of cash income. As retirees' ages increase, and they spend down their personal assets, these numbers go higher and higher. Social Security for these people is not "gravy" or "mad money for retirement indulgences."

However, times have changed both the benefits and the taxes. Over the years, the program benefits were expanded, to provide more income for the elderly. The tax rate has escalated over time, to now require 6.2 percent of the first $132,900 of workers' earnings, which is paid by both the employees and the employers.

When Social Security was enacted, average life expectancy was 58 years. Benefits have not been adjusted sufficiently for longevity.

What hasn't changed very much, is the retirement age. When German chancellor Bismarck introduced the world's first national retirement pension plan in 1881, average life expectancy was 40 years, and the retirement age was set at 70. (It was reduced to 65 in 1916.) When the American Social Security act was passed with age 65 for retirement, the average life expectancy was 58 years. Only those who outlived their normal life expectancy by more than seven years were expected to receive full benefits.

Without any Congressional action, what has indeed changed over time is life expectancy, which has increased by 20 years to age 78 at the time of birth. Males who survive to age 65 can expect to live another 18 years, and for women that number is 20 years. Yet the retirement age for full Social Security benefits has been adjusted only by months and not years, to age 66 for early Baby Boomers and rising a month at a time until it reaches age 67 for those born in 1960 or later. As a result, a system that was originally intended to benefit only a fraction of the population now must provide substantial retirement income to a growing population for an average of 18 to 20 years. By 2030, the number of old-age recipients will increase by 50 percent from 48 million to 73 million, as the entire Baby Boom generation qualifies for benefits.

The Social Security trust fund will be depleted in 2034 unless Congress quickly enacts a sound financing plan. Topic 12 explains the options.

What has also changed over time is the Trust Fund, which was originally designed to operate like an insurance company's reserve account and provide actuarially for the assets needed to pay benefits for all retirees without requiring additional payments from the next generation. As all readers know, that idea failed dismally because of repeated Congressional reluctance to raise the payroll tax rates sufficiently over time to match the benefits improvements. The Trust fund will be depleted in 2034, according to the latest trustees' report. This does not mean that benefits will stop, but it does mean that the system will be actuarially unfunded, essentially becoming a pay-as-you-go system of income-transfer in which younger generations pay for the benefits of their elders and pray that their children and grandchildren will do the same. Those incoming payroll tax contributions are projected to cover roughly 79 percent of the promised benefits to all recipients if no changes are made to the tax rates, eligibility ages and benefit formulas. Whether that would result in benefits reductions, or more deficit finance, or cross-subsidy from other taxes, is both uncertain and unknowable.

Liberals and Progressives all have their own ideas about how to reform Social Security and bolster its solvency. Part II of this book addresses some of those ideas from the side of tax reform, including one bill sitting in Congress that seeks to address both revenues and benefits. On the benefits side, it goes without saying that any additional benefits increases for Social Security recipients will drive the budget deficit deeper and hasten the depletion date, unless financed by additional payroll taxes or new revenue sources. A relatively modest but politically unattractive 2.2 percentage-point increase in payroll taxes could solve the funding problem, as can other measures contained in various bills that have been introduced in Congress. But we have yet to hear a single Presidential candidate pitch that idea, in the last six election cycles.

One obvious candidate for reform is the normal retirement age, which is clearly too low to be sustainable in light of modern longevity.

The problem for most Democrats is that many workers who perform manual labor lose productivity and struggle physically as they attain age 62, and for them a suitable and sufficient retirement income floor is needed, despite general population longevity. Many in this occupational category enter retirement with worn-out bodies and very limited savings, reflecting the lower end of the income spectrum. How to craft a non-reduced benefit for that group without awarding a free ride to others is a riddle that fiscally literate Liberals must solve. With such a provision, it should become more palatable to raise the normal retirement age incrementally from 67 to 70 over a decade, without ruining the lifelong financial plans of those already in their 60s. The current schedule for age escalation is clearly too timid, and can be accelerated at a more aggressive rate without causing undue harm to most workers born after 1960.

Some readers on the Left would instinctively propose means-testing of Social Security benefits so that wealthier citizens receive lower benefits or possibly no benefits whatsoever. Whether that solves the larger funding shortfalls in any meaningful way is open to question, given that the more-affluent recipients already must pay top-bracket income taxes on this category of income, even the Fat Cats who enjoy various loopholes. The actual dollar savings is reduced by those offsets at both the state and federal levels, which together can represent a 40 to 45 percent offset already built into tax law. As a percentage of Social Security recipients, the One Percenters are likewise one percent of the elderly subpopulation, so the savings to government budgets is about $6/10^{ths}$ of one percent (aftertax) if Congress kicked them all entirely out of the benefits pool immediately. Existing retirees in this subpopulation would undoubtedly file a class action lawsuit to recapture foregone benefits from previously deferring their distributions until age 70 under alleged "fraudulent misrepresentation." That recapture could be as much as $150,000 per person, thus wiping out half the potential net savings. Compared to a 21 percent funding shortfall coming in 2034, a means-tested exclusion is truly a drop in the bucket. For those in the upper-middle income brackets, a ceiling on benefits may be workable, but care should be taken to avoid alienating the popular base of citizen-voters whose support is needed to swing elections. If Social Security becomes a pure income-redistribution scheme, FDR might turn over in his grave.

TOPIC 4: Medicare.

....

The nation's health insurance program for elderly citizens is administered by CMS, the Center for Medicare and Medicaid Services. As with Social Security (and unlike Medicaid), the Medicare program also has a trust fund which is funded by payroll taxes, presently 1.45 percent of earnings with no limits, paid by both employees and employers. Taxpayers with earned income over $250,000 also pay an additional Medicare tax of 0.9 percent on earnings over that level. In addition to the payroll tax, Medicare is also funded by an income surtax that was instituted in 2012 under the Obamacare (ACA) statute. This 3.8 percent tax on investment income for taxpayers with incomes over $250,000 (joint returns) applies to their interest, dividends and capital gains but not to earned income, although the earned income is included in the totals that trigger the tax. (A married couple with earned income of $250,000 plus investment income of $10,000 would pay 3.8 percent on their investment income only, or $380, for this additional "Net Investment Income Tax.")[7]

---

7 If this same couple earns more than $250,000, they will also pay an additional 0.9% Medicare surtax on their earnings. As a result, the upper middle class is already paying more in taxes for Medicare than most readers realize.

The Medicare trust fund is in even more trouble financially than Social Security, with depletion expected in 2026. Despite efforts under the Obamacare legislation to shore up Medicare's finances, the costs of health care continue to escalate faster than actuaries predicted. Adding prescription drug coverage (known as Medicare Part D), without an actuarially based tax increase, completely blew a hole in the program's fragile financial structure.

> The Medicare trust fund will be depleted in 2026, just one Senate term from now. Medicare is not free health care, as many naively believe. "Medicare for All" will become a cruel hoax, if it is built on a financial house of cards.

One of the ironies in the current debate about Medicare for All is that that the existing program is already in financial trouble, yet politicians clamor for more benefits, not fewer. Fiscally literate Democrats must all face up to the need to legislate the additional revenues needed to sustain the existing Medicare program first, and then design any additional benefits carefully with a funding plan that realistically covers costs.

Many supporters of Medicare for All now mistakenly believe that today's Medicare is free and fully funded. They wrongly assume that Medicare for All would likewise be free as long as "somebody else" magically pays the taxes. Almost none of them realize that for those who retire with less than 7.5 years (30 quarters) of credited payroll contributions, the premium for Medicare Part A (hospitalization only) insurance is more than $430 monthly. And that is the just tip of the iceberg: They overlook the more-important reality that almost all retirees pay a monthly Medicare "Part B" premium, and that income-based premium surcharges are already part of its billing structure. Retirees with upper incomes now pay as much as $537 monthly for their individual Medicare Part A and Part D (prescription) benefits, regardless of how much they may have already contributed into the program. Medicare also pays only 80 percent of most medical bills, so participants are still responsible for 20 percent co-payments. Supplemental insurance under so-called Medicare Advantage (Part C) programs typically cost up to $200 monthly for recent retirees to insure for this 20 percent participant responsibility under today's Medicare, and those premiums escalate with age. Medicare is anything but free health care, even for retirees and especially for those with less than 10 years of credited prepayments.

This does not mean that expansion of the Medicare system is a bad idea. After a brief outline of Medicare finances, this book returns to the issue of national health care reforms in a comprehensive discussion in Part III (Topics 23-25), as well as a section within Part II that explains potential Social Security and Medicare tax reforms that will be needed to re-balance the books (Topic 12).

Americans spend $4 trillion annually on health care, including insurance coverage. That works out to $13,000 for every adult and child. Of this, Medicare insurance represents only $670 billion, or 17 percent. An equal amount is insured by Medicaid once the matching contributions from all the states are included. Together, these public programs represent one-third of the total cost of health care in the U.S. To provide Medicare for All, if that is to mean free health care for everybody, it would take $2½ trillion each year to fund it. Uncle Sam's personal income tax collects $1.8 trillion, so that tax would have to more than double for everybody even if rates were first returned to levels under Obama. Even if the current funding sources from everybody who now pays insurance premiums and out-of-pocket deductibles and co-pays could somehow magically be left to the consumer, the additional cost to taxpayers would be $1½ trillion. That again is a number that cannot be funded reasonably by an income-tax increase and piecemeal tax reforms. It will take a huge pile of new taxes on top of existing taxes to fund Medicare for All or something close to it, and that does nothing to solve the nation's current and escalating budget deficit. Instead of being under-taxed relative to other developed countries, the USA would be taxed above-average on a comparative basis.

> There are viable policy options to achieve basic health care for all, but they are not as simple and oblivious to arithmetic as the single-payer model suggests. There is not a single tax reform that can pay for Medicare for All.

Progressives and Liberals need not despair, however. There are viable public policy options, but they are just not as simple and oblivious to basic middle-school arithmetic as the "single-payer" model would require taxpayers to underwrite. First, it is entirely feasible to make the existing Medicare program available to all citizens *at cost,* without spending a dollar of new federal money. This means that for each age group and family status, the actuaries could calculate a monthly insurance premium for that household on a non-profit basis. Younger people with no children would pay less than families and older citizens whose medical bills are typically higher as they age. There would be no insurance-company profits, plus lower overhead and marketing costs, which could probably cut the cost of such insurance by $400 per person per year, holding everything else equal. Employers could also elect to buy Medicare at Cost for their employees, often with similar savings.

With some reasonable tax reforms, Congress could also extend the current Medicaid system to include more people who are presently uninsured and under-insured. And beyond that, Medicare itself could be expanded to include basic care policies with taxpayer-subsidized premiums that are income-based -- similar to today's Medicare premiums for retirees, but at a higher price for younger enrollees. Such a "taxpayer-subsidized multi-payer" system would still allow private insurance companies to compete with Medicare, offer group policies to employers who want to continue their current benefits plans, and offer supplemental insurance policies similar to today's Medicare Advantage policies.

Part II of this book, which follows later, provides a panoply of tax reform and revenue options that could fund various levels of Medicare/ Medicaid expansion and a path to universal health insurance without adopting a single-payer government takeover. It even provides an unprecedented federal revenue strategy to fund basic health care *and* public college education for all citizens. Part III explains how to design a cost-effective multi-payer system, by putting together various health care policies and the revenues needed to support them, as well as other essential and important governmental functions. For those readers who become discouraged by the Fiscal Facts of Life in this chapter, please hang in there: the darkest hour is just before dawn. Tax Reform in Part II is your sunrise and Health Care finance in Part III is your high noon.

As with Social Security, the number of retirees receiving Medicare benefits is escalating rapidly as more Baby Boomers complete their working careers and claim their entitlement to subsidized health insurance. Mandatory spending on Medicare will double from 2019 to 2029, according to projections of the Congressional Budget Office.

One small finger in the dike to manage costs will be to age-link the Medicare eligibility age to Social Security. This would have several benefits to American taxpayers. Medicare costs would be lower, even if the program allowed an "early retirement surcharge" for health insurance premiums charged to those who retire at 65 rather than 67, or later as the Social Security requirements are raised to reflect longevity. For employers like state and local governments that have pension plans that permit earlier retirement ages for police, firefighters and teachers, any delay of Medicare eligibility will dramatically improve their actuarial funding because many of their employees will work longer and draw pension benefits for fewer years, if they must wait for Medicare at age 67. For those with defined contribution plans (401k and 403b) this is even more true. Even though many of them will bear higher health insurance costs during active employment, most employers would prefer to see a later Medicare eligibility age, and the overall economy would benefit significantly from the longer productive career periods that result.

TOPIC 5: Medicaid.

. . . .

In some ways, Medicaid is the least-understood and perhaps most underappreciated federal social safety-net program. 75 million Americans are enrolled in the Medicaid program, which provides federal and state-subsidized health insurance to households with low incomes. That is 22 percent of the U.S. population! Children are a major beneficiary group in the Medicaid program, with 39 percent of all Americans of age 18 and under now enrolled in Medicaid. Children represent over 40 percent of the needy subpopulation that now receives Medicaid benefits, because their parents simply do not earn enough to afford private insurance premiums.

There are exceptions and variations, but the simplest formula to understand is that Medicaid provides health care assistance to those with incomes below 133 percent of the federal poverty guideline. (133% x $25,750 for a family of four in 2019 = $34,200 as a rough proxy). Given the high costs of private medical insurance, even at $6,500 annually per capita for average working-age households, the income tests for Medicaid qualification are "medically indigent" by anybody's definition.

Total government spending for Medicaid exceeds $600 billion annually. Of this, the states contribute about 38 percent and the rest (over $400 billion) is paid by the federal government. The states spend more of their own tax dollars on Medicaid than they do on higher education or transportation. Unlike Medicare, for which workers and their employers contribute payroll taxes, Medicaid insurance is funded for the most part by general tax dollars and deficit spending.

> Medicaid expansion could provide coverage to the 30,000 Americans who are uninsured, but those who now pay for their insurance will be highly resentful and expect the same deal, which then becomes much more costly.

To extend health insurance coverage to the 30,000 Americans who are now uninsured, one possible strategy would be to expand Medicaid coverage. This would leverage the existing program infrastructure, and states could be required to share in the cost burden. When Obamacare was implemented, mandates took effect and the federal government began paying partial subsidies to the state insurance exchanges. As a result, the number of uninsured Americans declined by one-third. Undoubtedly, a federal subsidy at less than full cost could help bring down the number of uninsured and underinsured even more. However, the availability of government subsidies will also induce some people and employers) who now pay for insurance to seek out the subsidies that they see others getting, which will actually increase the cost of Medicaid expansion more than simple arithmetic would suggest. Just as farm price supports induce growers to switch crop plantings to collect federal subsidies, Medicaid expansion will siphon off some premiums now paid by consumers and employers, if the program is not skillfully designed and managed.

Part III includes a section that describes the economics of Medicaid expansion as one possible strategy to make health insurance more universal while keeping taxpayer costs as low as possible, by retaining the multi-payer system in which employers and individuals contribute as much as possible to premiums.

Part III also describes why and how universal health care would require a new, broad-based tax to provide sufficient federal funding to relieve states of their Medicaid cost share, but that could make it possible to provide free resident tuition to public colleges and universities.

Without quick and repeated successes at the ballot box, however, the handwriting is on the wall for Medicaid longer-term. Even though it is viewed by many as an entitlement program, and by others as a mandatory spending program because of its formula nature, Medicaid would be the first of the three major programs to be cut if (or when, if nothing is done soon) federal spending and interest costs outstrip all available revenues. The grey panthers and AARP lobbyists will prevail over medically indigent vote-less youth. One of the reasons that Republicans have proposed a "block grant" funding approach to Medicaid is that it will simplify the budget-cutting process in the future. Block grants are treated as discretionary spending, which makes them more expendable when revenues are insufficient. Fiscally literate Progressives and Liberals will need to keep an eye out for new funding sources to maintain Medicaid, if their goals are to move forward and not backward in their fight for affordable and universal health care.

TOPIC 6: Interest.

There is an old fable about how to boil a frog in a pail of water. If the water is scalding hot, the frog will instinctively jump out immediately, to avoid a quick death. But if the frog is placed in a pail of lukewarm water that is then gradually heated to a boil, it will fall asleep and perish. Interest on the federal debt is America's calescent water pail. It is the fiscal equivalent of global warming and rising sea levels.

> The next Treasury Secretary should begin selling many more 20- and 30-year bonds to reduce economic risks. Topic 6 explains why.

Consumers who borrow on their credit cards to pay for everyday expenses, and make only the minimum payments, will eventually run up against their credit limit. Credit-card spending is essentially what Congress and the White House have been doing for decades, but our national credit limit is now coming within sight without the need for binoculars. The horizon of the first fiscal cliffs are now only 10 years out because of Baby Boomer retirements and skyrocketing interest costs. The greatest single threat to Liberal political causes is the financial pressure on domestic program spending that these promised retirement benefits and escalating interest costs will cause if today's budget deficits are not reined in soon.

Total federal debt today is about $22 trillion. Of this, about $6 billion is owed "internally" to various federal agencies including the Social Security and Medicare trust funds. But as we know from the preceding sections, both of those two trust funds will be depleted in coming years, with Medicare running out first in 2026 followed by Social Security in 2034. Right now, those two trust funds enable the U.S. Treasury to rob Peter to pay Paul and camouflage the deficits and the interest costs: The interest payable to the trust funds is an asset of the trust funds, which partially offsets the annual shortfalls of those two programs which now spend more on benefits than their payroll taxes bring in. But when those trust funds are depleted (and they are nothing but bookkeeping entries, not real investment accounts with independent assets like a pension fund), then the Treasury will have to borrow even more from other investors. So even though the official outstanding debt of the U.S. Treasury held by the public and other governments is $16 billion today, the ultimate debt accumulated to date is actually the $22 trillion.

> By 2025, runaway interest costs will exceed almost all other categories of federal expenditure. This is the foundation of a house of cards.

So that $22 trillion is the debt on which the interest is owed. Right now, the White House budget projects the interest costs for 2020 to be $470 billion, although the nonpartisan Congressional Budget Office (CBO) uses a lower number for 2019 that conveniently ignores intra-governmental interest payments. Either way, this is roughly what the U.S. spends on Medicaid benefits. By 2025, immediately after the next Presidential term expires, runaway interest costs will exceed almost all other spending categories outlined in this chapter. And the problem, the big hairy problem, is that CBO already projects interest costs to escalate to over $900 billion in 2028 even without a recession before then. Even subtracting out inflation, that is almost double what these interest payments are costing us today; and higher, normalized interest rates could triple the annual cost.

To help understand the interest rate structure of the U.S. debt, and the reason this rapid growth of interest costs is such a frightful prospect, it helps to understand how the U.S. Treasury borrows money. Unlike a revolving credit card, it borrows for specific time periods and then repays those debts with the proceeds of new borrowings which are greater each time around because of accrued interest and continued budget deficits. The due dates range from 13 weeks to 30 years. About 12 percent of all government debt has been sold as bonds with maturities of 20 to 30 years, more like mortgage payments. These bonds today have an average interest cost slightly less than three percent, lower than the interest rate on a 30-year fixed mortgage, because investors trust that Uncle Sam will repay the debt even without collateral. The rest of the debt is much shorter in term, with 70 percent or so due for repayment in five years or less. (More debt is typically due within one year than what is payable beyond 20 years.) These "T-notes and T-bills" today carry interest rates below two percent. Overall, the average interest rate on all marketable U.S. Treasury debt is about 2½ percent.[8]

The fiscal problem for American citizens is that these are very low interest rates by historical standards. The only reason that our national debt has not already become a hair-on-fire crisis already is that interest rates are so low worldwide, reflecting low inflation rates here in the U.S., central-bank accommodation in Europe and Japan to fight deflation there, and a global superabundance of institutional and sovereign (mostly petroleum-state) capital looking for "risk-free"

---

8 Current market yields on Treasury securities are lower than the corresponding yields on outstanding obligations that were issued previously when market interest rates were higher. Cynics would say that Trump's trade wars have hurt the global economy so much that rates now reflect a self-inflicted global slowdown. See the tariff tax discussion in Part II (Topic #21). The lower market rates today will provide some temporary budget relief in the Treasury's interest costs, but those are likely to be transitory over the coming decade.

government-bond interest rates. So, in today's world of 2½ percent interest rates on outstanding debt of $16 trillion held by the public, the Treasury's official annual interest costs are still running about $400 billion annually.

> If there is any one certainty in this universe, it is that federal government interest costs will escalate dramatically in the coming decade unless budget deficits are reduced. If interest rates go to six percent, federal interest payments in 2032 will exceed today's income tax revenues. How will other national needs be funded?

If there is any one certainty in the financial universe, it is that this subdued interest cost will not last much longer. Remember what Einstein said about compound interest, and then supercharge that exponential factor with annual increases in the "base" (outstanding debt). With annual budget deficits of $1 trillion or more, which Trump is perpetuating, the official CBO projection of outstanding debt by 2029 is $29 trillion.[9] Applying today's 2½ percent average interest rate on that clearly foreseeable future principal balance gives us an annual Treasury interest cost of $700 billion after the trust funds are depleted. And that is the good-cop version. The bad-cop version is that higher interest rates with an average Treasury interest cost of five percent would double that number to $1.4 trillion. Even taking into account the longer maturities of those bonds that won't mature and roll over,

---

9 The CBO optimistically assumes that Trump Tax Cuts expire before 2029, providing more revenue, which is why their number is below $30 trillion. CBO further assumes there is no national economic recession during its entire 10-year forecast period that would automatically balloon the annual deficits and mounting federal debt.

the best possible case in that scenario is an annual interest cost of $1 trillion by the end of the 2020s. If rates go to six percent or higher, the annual interest costs skyrocket to $1.7 trillion or more. By 2032 that will exceed all the income-tax revenue that the IRS collects from individual taxpayers today. And these estimates blindly assume that there will not be an economic recession in the next decade, which will add even more red ink to the federal deficits and national debt.

As they now say in bond-trader academy: "There is a lot less distance from two percent to zero, than there is from two percent to infinity." As legendary Federal Reserve Chairman Paul Volcker (who is credited with rescuing the U.S from rampant monetary inflation and stagflation of the 1970s) proved, it can take double-digit interest rates and a painful recession to cure an inflation malaise once it sets in.

> Modern Monetary Theory offers a false panacea. It guarantees future inflation and with it, the destruction of home values and retirement nest eggs.

This is the dynamic that advocates of "Modern Monetary Theory" just don't address with honesty. No one can dispute that the U.S. can issue more debt to refinance its maturing bonds when they come due. Likewise, no one can dispute that as a reserve currency used for international transactions, U.S dollar debt enjoys a unique privilege in bond markets. Our federal debt can be "monetized" by expanding the money supply globally through our central bank, the Federal Reserve. Sophomore students of collegiate macro-economics are taught that already. But what the MMT crowd simply ignores is that money-printing and monetary expansion ultimately compounds the problem. Investors, especially foreign bondholders, are not going to sit meekly on the sidelines, watching their dollar-based T-bonds go down the drain in value. They have any number of alternative "hard" assets to purchase instead, ranging from gold bullion to offshore real estate to rare art. To buy those hard assets, they dispose of dollars, undermining our currency both globally and domestically. Foreign creditors will no longer accept the dollar as the world's reserve currency. They can sell longer dated bonds and move into short-term paper that at least matches inflation without losing purchasing power. Interest rates will surge higher just in order to attract investor capital every time a Treasury bond, note or bill matures and must be re-financed. And when -- not if -- inflation eventually follows the monetary expansion, rates will move to correspondingly higher levels. In the 1970s, one-year Treasury bill rates skyrocketed from four percent to 10 percent as the money supply was inflated along the very lines that the priests of MMT would advocate. A commensurate increase in this decade would take us well above six percent, totally consistent with the bad-cop scenario described above. Federal interest costs would then triple, with frightening ramifications.

MMT advocates lack historical perspective. Their theory is that inflation hurts capital, and thus capitalists, more than it hurts ordinary people who don't own a lot of assets. They presume that workers will eventually see their salaries and wages catch up with the inflation, so they will be OK. Just ask any working-class homebuyer or home-seller how that worked out in 1982 when the interest rate with sellers' points on a conventional VA mortgage was 17 percent. And they have no comprehension of what high inflation will do to state and local pension plans and retirees. The retirees' cost-of-living allowances (COLAs) are typically capped at three percent, and most of these pension funds are cash-flow negative, meaning that they depend on investment income to pay the bills. Many workers' and retirees' 401k and IRA accounts would lose half of their market value if interest rates triple. Home values and financial assets will suffer mightily if inflation returns to even high single digits, let alone double digits. This quickly becomes a middle-class problem, not a billionaires' problem.

> With low-taxation budget deficits in a full-employment economy, Trump has run the greatest Ponzi scheme in world history.

To insulate our future budgets from this kind of risk, previous administrations have tried to lengthen the maturity structure of the U.S. debt. The more that federal debt consists of long-term bonds, the less damage a short-term inflation shock can cause to the federal budget itself, and the various markets in the private sector. But there is a catch: higher Treasury bond (T-bond) rates could have a quick and negative impact on 30-year mortgage rates. Few Administrations are willing to take that heat from their realtor and homeownership constituencies. Add this to the incumbent President's statements that he is "a fan of low interest rates" and he "loves debt," it is hard to imagine a leveraged real-estate tycoon in the oval office biting the bullet to extend maturities at higher rates. Clearly, the Trump strategy is to play the Congress and the country for suckers by running low-taxation budget deficits during his presidency, and leave the mess for his successor to clean up and take the fall -- just like Obama took the fall for the global financial crisis in 2008. Mr. Trump can then resume his reality TV personality and pontificate to his base about how he Made America Great Again -- by running the greatest Ponzi scheme in world history. In retrospect, Bernie Madoff was just a Little Leaguer.

This is actually one area where the next U.S. Treasury Secretary can lawfully implement a sensible foresighted fiscal management plan by unilaterally locking in longer maturities on new T-bond issues while interest rates and inflation are still low.[10] Even more such 20- and 30-year bonds should be sold if a recession were to arrive on the national scene and drive "risk-free" bond yield temporarily lower. In the light of depressed yields on Treasury securities brought on by fragile economies overseas, which have been aggravated by the Trump trade wars with our trading partners, this would be an ideal time to begin issuing longer-dated T-bonds with a view toward mitigating the risks of rising interest costs in the coming decade. There is ample demand for long-dated maturities,[11] especially in recession periods, and these will generally not impact home mortgage rates that price off of the 10-year bond. Those who have enjoyed the Broadway musical "Hamilton" can be sure that our first Treasury Secretary would approve. Fiscally literate readers, and especially those who advise today's and tomorrow's Washington politicians, please take note.

TOPIC 7: Domestic discretionary spending and projected "crowding out"

· ·

This brings us to the last category of federal spending, often labelled as "domestic discretionary." It includes all the other federal programs and functions. This grouping includes all the Cabinet-level education, agriculture, energy, housing, transportation and environmental agencies, plus many others too numerous to list. Depending on how one

---

10 30-year T-bonds typically have a commonplace ten-year "call" feature that enables Treasury to redeem the bonds at par at any time a decade or less before final maturity, in the event future interest rates are lower for any reason.

11 Corporate pension funds, sovereign wealth funds, and insurance companies all need long-maturity bonds to offset stock portfolio risks and long-term liabilities.

calculates the other categories, for which there is some overlap, the combined total of all these programs is approximately $700 billion in the current budget year. Some of these agencies and programs have budgets that include "mandatory" spending, which is formulaic and not subject to appropriations. For example, over one-half of the Agriculture department budget is now tagged as mandatory, for nutrition assistance, national crop insurance and farmer subsidies. But even those programs would be subject to the budget axe if or when Congress ultimately needs to trim expenses severely in order to pay for other "first priorities."

There is one additional source of potential revenue that could conceivably offset some, but not anything close to all, of this shortfall: The Trump Tax Cuts, like most Congressional tax laws, had a sunset provision for many of the tax breaks that will be discussed in Part II. To the extent that Congress becomes gridlocked throughout the next two presidencies, certain tax rates will revert to Obama-era levels. That will produce some additional revenue, but only in the range of a few hundred billion dollars per year at most. Not nearly enough to sustain $700 billion of domestic discretionary spending. And the annual deficits will continue to mount, along with the interest costs that go with them at a rate that outruns these hypothetical tax restorations.

Herein lies the rub for Liberals and Progressives, as well as all Millennials. For purposes of comprehension, put national defense spending aside for now, where budget reductions beyond $100 billion are extremely unlikely under any scenario. Combined with the additional interest on mounting federal debt, the inevitable growth of Social Security and Medicare spending for the Baby Boomer generation will consume more future tax dollars than all of these remaining departments and existing programs combined, probably by the end of the coming decade. Budgeteers call this "squeezing out." Without Congressional intervention, this inescapable fiscal arithmetic is not a matter of "if," but simply a matter of "when." It's like a game of musical chairs in which national security, entitlement programs, and interest expenditures all have reserved seats while the other chairs are removed, year by year. This will not happen overnight, so this is not a doom-and-gloom story about fiscal Armageddon, but the erosion of the funding base for discretionary social programs is as inevitable as every sunset that brings on the darkness of night. Reagan and his successors will have won: The beast will be starved. Big government will remain big, but only some oversized parts of it will survive, and that will not include today's discretionary programs.

> At some point, Republicans need to own up and cut defense costs, eliminate business and farm subsidies, and raise taxes to balance budgets. They are co-owners of the deficits.

But Democrats should not bear the entire burden of balancing the federal budget by starving social programs. At some point, Republicans need to own up and start managing defense costs the way they cut costs in corporate America, eliminating subsidies and raising taxes to reduce deficits.

TOPIC 8: Implications of the Fiscal Facts

An entire book can be written on the impending fiscal squeeze that is destined to crowd out discretionary social programs that are considered vital by many Democrats. Indeed, the subject of today's federal fiscal imbalances has been documented in both books and websites, so there is no point in beating that poor horse to death here. Readers who want more information, including vivid charts that show the year-by-year projections of current expense categories in juxtaposition to the revenues, can visit the bipartisan Congressional Budget Office (CBO) or General Accountability Office (GAO) websites with a keyword browser search, using the term "fiscal sustainability." Those craving for even more compelling information can visit the website of the Peterson Foundation, a bipartisan nonprofit with business leaders and stellar advisors from both parties that keeps pounding this drum in the hope that eventually, Americans will wake up and listen. Every Millennial regardless of political orientation should take just one hour of free time someday to scan those websites: it is your future staring you right in the face.

> Middle Americans may not have all the answers, but they know there is a debt problem and it makes them suspicious of runaway Tax-and-Spend policies.

Readers who remain uninterested or unconvinced that these problems should be addressed or even considered in the course of the 2020 election are entitled to move forward with their personal or tribal agendas. If nothing else, you are now aware of the magnitude of these issues, and the risks that will remain if a new layer of government spending is piled on top of today's unbalanced budget. At the least, you will be fiscally literate, even if you remain agnostic to this part of the discussion. Please keep in mind that these concerns are front-row to Centrists in both parties. Middle Americans may not have the answers, but they know there is a debt problem and it makes them anxious about Tax-and-Spend Liberals who ignore the elephant in the room.

Those readers who "get it," but find themselves overwhelmed by the magnitude of these fiscal imbalances, can take heart that solutions are indeed possible. Readily feasible Social Security reforms, mentioned previously, are described in greater detail in the next section of this book (Topic 12). If nothing else, modest incremental payroll tax increases along with longevity-based eligibility ages will make a huge difference in the long-term solvency of both Social Security and Medicare. Medicare-at-cost is a fiscally sound policy proposal with modest budget impacts as the next step in making health care more affordable. Medicaid expansion for many who are now uninsured is achievable with one or two overdue tax reforms to fund it. A truly comprehensive multi-part budget-and-tax reform policy, as described later, could address the current budget deficit and the loftier ambitions of many Liberals and Progressives who favor a path to more-universal health insurance and college education funding. Whether the American voter is ready for such a generational change is open to question, and that could be what the coming and following national elections will be about.

As suggested previously, Democrats will be wise to include a promise and a plan to match their new spending plans with a pledge to reduce the current budget deficit, dollar for dollar. This will require tax increases and tax reforms. There is no better strategy to secure the support and ballots of centrist voters, who will most likely determine the 2020 elections.

Now that you, the reader, are fiscally literate on the deficit issues, we can now hunt for the money: Tax Reform is the next subject.

PART II:

Federal tax policy and funding options

....

Louis XIV's finance minister Jean-Baptiste Colbert said that "the art of taxation is to keep plucking the goose to obtain the most feathers possible until it hisses." In modern America, the problem for Congress is that the wealthy have trained their geese to hiss louder than a venting steam engine whenever a tax of any kind is proposed, no matter what its magnitude or for what cause. So it's now impossible to avoid hissy-fits from the right wing in any tax debate. On the other end of the political spectrum, the democratic socialist camp's rhetoric suggests they would be delighted to pluck the goose until it nearly dies from exposure.

Somewhere between these two extremes, the next Congress must begin to dig itself out of a $1 trillion annual budgetary deficit. Meanwhile, many if not most Democrats are also inclined toward some kind of governmental backstop for struggling middle-class Americans. That ambition will require new tax revenues, whether it be for affordable health care, higher education cost relief, retirement income, or manageable housing costs. Politically, this runs the risk of being branded by opponents as "Tax and Spend Democrats." This chapter is devoted to the practical politics and the economics of tax reform, which requires understanding basic parts of the U.S. tax system, the revenues it now generates, and all of its weak spots, in order to fix it.

SYNOPSIS

The next Congress will face unprecedented challenges to re-balance the federal budget, and piecemeal tax reforms alone will not be sufficient to accomplish that task. Substantial new revenues can be collected from several of the tax reforms that are explained and quantified in this section, which is the intentional purpose of this section. But none of them alone would produce sufficient revenues to both overcome the current budget deficit *and* finance new social programs like universal health care, free college tuition, and income redistribution through tax credits. Even if today's progressive federal income tax rates were to be *doubled*, there would not be enough money --and that over-reach would result in an unachievable and uncollectable 75 percent tax rate for the top bracket, which would be utterly confiscatory when combined with state and local taxes in such Blue state bastions as California, New York, Hawaii, Connecticut and Minnesota. Even with the best left-wing demagoguery, voters will never buy into that slippery slope. And even if they did, a mass national outmigration of wealth and talent would result in a self-defeated, shrunken tax base. Only a pragmatic combination of multiple tax reform measures, skillfully constructed and negotiated, can deliver on the laudable aims of existing and proposed social programs that so many Democrats cherish and advocate.

> International comparative data reveal that Americans are not over-taxed. The question is what don't we get for the taxes we pay, that other countries do?

Tax reforms and tax increases would not be responsible options if the U.S. were overtaxed as we often hear. International comparative data reveal that the American tax system is actually below median for developed countries, making the opposition claims of over-taxation subjective, not objective. Nonetheless, the stigma of runaway taxing and spending is sure to be raised in a general election, which may require a "lockbox" assurance to voters and taxpayers that their money will not be wasted. (The lockbox concept will be explained later.)

The most ambitious taxation strategy discussed in this chapter would be a new value-added tax (VAT) to fund both universal health insurance and public college tuition relief. The economics and politics of a national referendum to ratify a major new tax on all citizens as a "*New New Deal*" or a "Better Deal for America" are discussed in Topic 20.

Topic by topic, this section puts realistic numbers on each potential tax reform category and relates it to relevant spending programs. Major and minor revenue sources are clearly identified and placed in appropriate perspective. For minor revenue sources, each narrative explains where and why tax fairness and progressive taxation principles would be more important and achievable than the funding of new social programs. Diligent readers will become fiscally literate and well-equipped for political discussions and debates. Each Topic in Part II reveals the shallowness of some politicians' grandstanding claims that one or another tax reform will magically pay for their big-ticket spending plans. Each segment tells it like it is, and explains clearly how and where the math works. Readers will learn more about the core principles of pragmatic progressive taxation, and the obscure nooks and crannies of the current tax code, than what they knew before reading this book.

TOPIC 9: The politics of tax reform

"Every proposal for a specific tax is sure to meet with opposition."

Alexander Hamilton, 1782

To win the 2020 election, Democrats will need to galvanize a voter base, unite their factions, and energize them to get out the vote. As aspiring party leaders, and as champions of the working class and middle-income families in particular, Democrat candidates will be spinning their themes during primaries to appeal to voters and polling audiences. Their talks about taxes will be rhetorical, not technical. They will all complain that the Trump Tax Cuts (formally, the Tax Cuts and Jobs Act, or "TCJA") were really just a giveaway to the rich.[1] Before the party convention, they will pitch tax reform in sound bites that appeal to the party's base, which is left-of-center nationally.

During the primary season, and leading up to the party convention, voters and caucuses will be picking candidates and delegates who span across a spectrum of ideologies, beliefs and proposals. The purpose of this chapter, and this book as well, is to give all those involved in this process something more than rhetoric on which to base their decisions and their political support. This book is about how to translate campaign sound-bites into actual fiscal policy legislation. Part II is about how tax-reform slogans must and can be converted into tax reform policies that address both tax fairness and the need for federal tax revenues to fund both existing and proposed social programs. The

---

1 Most polls show that most Americans did not think they really got a noticeable tax cut or didn't know how much. Many households got smaller refunds, even if their paychecks got a small bump in take-home pay. The word "negligible" is applicable here.

Appendix in the back of this book provides an easy-to-read summary of the various tax policy options and the revenues they each could generate. (That is why it's called the Pinocchio Fact-Checking and Smell-Testing Scorecard.)

> Democrats need the electoral energy of the party's left wing, and the swing voters in Middle America. One without the other is a loser in 2020.

When it comes to tax reform, the fringe socialists and the Progressive wing of the Democratic party have captured the imagination of younger voters and those who resent the growing economic inequality of recent decades. Thirty to forty percent of American households are struggling financially without enough savings to cushion themselves from even a single financial challenge such as childbirth or college expenses. With that many households living paycheck to paycheck, the Progressive wing represents both an ideology and the objective economic interests of most its followers. This book respects the classic "trust-busting Teddy Roosevelt" legacy of Progressives' focus on using government power to make large institutions and companies play by the rules. In today's Democratic party, however, most self-identified Progressives also lean left of Liberals on fiscal matters. Activists in the socialist fringe of the Progressive camp posture in terms of class conflict. To them, it's workers against greedy capitalists. It's the 99 Percent against the One Percent, and it's time to retrieve what the Fat Cats have taken. Trump and the GOP are villains, and the good guys need to take back the country. Wall Street and Big Banks are monsters to be tamed. Their implicit goals are to redistribute wealth and income. Scandinavian socialism and egalitarian economics are models that many Progressives consider to be more worthy than the libertarian-conservative mantra of economic liberty under free-market capitalism.

For Progressives, higher taxes are the price that everybody must pay (and especially the rich) in order to fund universal benefits like health care, free college, Medicare and Social Security. One Progressive candidate's proposal would replace FDR's "a chicken in every pot" with a $6,000 check (tax credit) for every family making less than six figures annually.[2] Corporate taxes are now far too low. Trump Tax Cuts for corporate America were their spoils of war, and It's time that We the People reclaimed control of the tax code. Most Progressives see no reason that income from capital should be taxed at a lower rate than salaries and wages. To them, that is the second step in tax reform, after they first raise the upper-income tax rates, even to levels above those in the Clinton and Obama years.

Budget deficits are a secondary issue for this camp. Raising taxes is about funding new spending like Medicare for All and free college education, and helping out America's struggling lower-income households. It's not about shoring up the already-gaping revenue shortfalls for Social Security and Medicare, or trimming the mounting interest on the national debt, which they deem to be problems for voters tomorrow but not today. To conjure up the money for yawning budget deficits their new spending would only worsen, some of the left-leaning intellectuals now promote inflationary Modern Monetary Theory as their panacea.[3]

---

2 For the record: The Census Bureau says there about 90 million U.S. households making less than $100,000. At $6,000 each, that totals more than $500 BILLION annually. The federal budget deficit would expand by 50 percent from current levels, just for that one proposal. To put this into "tax reform" perspective, the total revenue gain from taxing capital gains and dividends at ordinary tax rates all investors is just a quarter (25 percent) of what this contrivance would cost. Alternatively, federal income tax rates would have to increase by *one-third* for ALL taxpayers, even including almost half of those who would receive these checks, just to finance this one income-redistribution scheme. Not only would this proposal rob Peter to pay Paul, it would rob Paul to pay Paul.

3 MMT includes the misguided belief that federal budget deficits don't matter because we are simply "borrowing from ourselves" and the U.S. government can print more money at will regardless of interest costs and inflation rates. MMT ignores the impact those inevitable

Today's middle-class struggles are more important than balancing today's federal budget, even when the economy is running at full steam.

Whether one agrees with them or not, Progressives have become an electoral force to be reckoned with. No matter how much many Liberal and Centrist Democrats would disagree with some Progressives' worldviews, the raw political math is that the party's left wing holds a vital key to the 2020 election. Without strong and energetic voter turnout in November from the Progressive base, no candidate heading the Democratic ticket can win the election if they stay home, unless Trump's runaway id defeats his own campaign team. Tax reform and health care reform bills will be dead on arrival for four more years.

Enlightened, progressive public finance requires *sustainable* funding that includes deficit reduction.

Although some Progressives may infer a hidden agenda to rebut their beliefs, the underlying goal of this book is not to alienate those who are fed up with politics as usual. The primary goal is to inform and illuminate, where indisputable fiscal facts run contrary to populist mythology. The genuine purpose of this compendium of Tax Policy options is to inform readers of all persuasions of the various revenue sources and funding opportunities that are not widely understood by most citizens. In simple math, it also explains the limitations of various tax reform proposals. Enlightened public finance requires that the aspirations of the Progressive wing must be channeled effectively to accomplish lasting social change. That cannot be accomplished if their party's standard-bearer is defeated by voter backlash, or if their enacted

---

results have on the general economy including retirement savings and mortgage rates. The subject was discussed in Part I and will not be repeated here, to avoid redundancy.

legislation is promptly rolled back after a midterm reversal. A replay of the 1972 Nixon vs McGovern landslide election outcome is the disaster to be avoided, as would be a Tea Party II backlash.

Today's Liberal wing of the Democratic party, to the extent it can be distinguished from the Progressives, takes a slightly softer tone in its rhetoric. The champions of the modern American Liberal tradition focus more on meat-and-potatoes issues and coalition-building. Liberals' instincts are that money may not grow on trees, but there are plenty of bushes where it can be harvested. Unlike their colleagues on the far left, the Liberal core of the Democratic party talks in terms of reform and not revolution. They see income inequality as an inevitable condition in any market economy or societal meritocracy, but agree with the Progressives that gaping income inequality and wealth disparity is now completely out of control. However, they would rather pluck the goose that lays golden eggs than kill it. They believe a rising tide lifts all boats, that the best way to give out bigger pieces of pizza pie is to bake a larger pizza. Just give us some more dough, and we'll make it all bigger and better for everybody.

Some prominent Liberals come from families with money (think back to John Kennedy, and today of Al Gore). Some of them have been successful captains in business themselves, but are generous enough to care about those less privileged (think of Michael Bloomberg, regardless of party). Most Liberal politicians will listen closely to what labor union leaders tell them when it comes to lunch-bucket issues, while also keeping a door open to large employers that operate in their jurisdiction. With a few exceptions, they are willing to accept campaign contributions from large donors, so they try not to bite the hand that feeds them to the point it severs an artery.

Tax reform to a Liberal is now more a matter of reversing the direction of the pendulum, which has now swung way too far to the right. Classic Liberals believe that the wealthy should pay their fair share, and higher-income taxpayers should pay higher tax rates. They see the Trump Tax Cuts for corporations as giveaways that underwrite stock buybacks for Wall Street investors and dole out crumbs for workers. They agree with Progressives that the corporate rates are now too low, but many would stop short of reverting the corporate tax cut entirely because of the impact that will have on the economy and the stock market (which is important to pension funds and employee retirement accounts). Liberals will look for any new or expanded tax revenue they can find, but they will stop short of punitive or confiscatory tax rates. Most would instinctively say that tax rates under Clinton and Obama were about right, and that we don't need to overshoot those to achieve tax reform.

Liberals in Congress would gladly vote to cut Trump's estate tax exemption in half in order to tax more mega-millionaires, and raise the estate tax rates to at least 50 percent for the filthy rich. They also understand that billionaires would much rather take a tax deduction for charitable contributions during their lifetimes than pay an estate tax on half their empires. But many Liberals would buy into a policy reform that extends the capital gains tax to first take a cut from those double-dipping billionaires whose deductible charitable donations are made from appreciated stock acquired for pennies a share. They would favor a reasonable tax on corporate stock buybacks and a stiffer minimum tax on the wealthy.

Liberals uniformly believe in tax fairness and the concept of tax progressivity, just as a matter of principle, even if it affects their own families. They also believe that the people's elected representatives in legislatures know better where to spend the marginal tax dollar than does the taxpayer who involuntarily contributes that dollar (which is what fundamentally and sharply distinguishes Liberals from Conservatives). That is to say that if given the chance, Liberals will righteously spend other people's money -- and their own -- to benefit the those less fortunate. They prefer social programs over tinkering with tax rates and tax credits at the paycheck level. They like to earmark money to show what good they have done while in office.

> None of the centrist Democratic candidates dare campaign overtly for a balanced budget, but they do understand that deficits will ultimately crimp federal spending for the social safety net.

The Centrist Democrats include those at the core of the party's 2018 Blue Wave in re-capturing control of the House of Representatives, by winning in historically Red congressional districts. Centrists[4] are more moderate, pragmatic and most would say, realistic. They may include successful professionals, firefighters, lunch-bucket union members, independent contractors and some of the small business owners who built from the ground up. They lean left of most Republicans, but understand that money does not grow on trees and bushes, and that budget deficits do matter. They wonder where the all revenue will come from in the future for our entitlement programs even at today's benefit levels, given the demographics of an aging populous with limited immigration. They privately doubt the idea of Medicare for All as a nice aspiration but unrealistic. None of the centrist Democratic candidates are trying to win the 2020 Presidential nomination by campaigning overtly for a balanced budget, but they do understand that deficits will ultimately crimp federal spending on the social safety net. As they look down the road, they see America's social programs heading into a financial wall, and realize that Congress cannot spend our way out of it. Centrists would be attracted to a tax reform plan that matches every

---

4 Readers should feel free to comprehend the broad labels "Centrist" and "Moderate" interchangeably. This book will not split hairs to formulate a definitional difference, although there are partisans who do.

dollar of new spending with a dollar of deficit reduction,[5] as would many Middle Americans.

Centrists privately hate it when Progressives low-ball the annual costs of their unfunded "universal" programs in one interview or speech, and then cite lofty 10-year projections of their pet tax reform revenues as the solution in their next appearance. How those on their far Left plan to pay for the second, third and tenth year of their big-ticket spending is something that the Centrists want to ask, but dare not attack too vocally, if their candidates hope to win primaries and the 2020 nomination in Milwaukee. When debating, they need to politely point out the facts of life in public finance, to foster an intelligent and informed debate that is grounded in reality and not just magical thinking and wishful economics. But they cannot alienate the Left and still win the nomination and then mobilize the energy and voters they need in the general election.

To Centrists, "Politics is the Art of the Possible."[6]

Centrists would rather shore up Social Security and Medicare first before launching unaffordable new social programs that will only worsen the deficits. Their ambitions for tax reform are typically incremental, although they are keen for new solutions that cause less tax drag on the overall economy. They will support efforts by those on their left to take back many of the Trump Tax Cuts to help balance the budget, and they will be open to new revenue sources as described in this section, if done purposefully and thoughtfully. However, they are more inclined to focus first on (1) budget-balancing, (2) finding some new tax revenue to subsidize affordable health care options without nationalizing health care, and (3) funding infrastructure, before they would support Robin Hood income redistribution. They would probably support a national

---

5 Thus, two dollars of new tax reform revenue, channeling a dollar each to these two competing priorities.

6 *Evita*, 1976, lyrics by Tim Rice.

referendum to let voters decide if they would mandate a value-added (national sales) tax to fund universal health care, but they would not impose a new broad-based tax on their constituents by political fiat.

Centrists are far more likely to work across the aisle in Congress to get a tax bill passed, even if it is imperfect when it clears both houses of the Congress. The Centrist Democrats alone openly recognize that a Senate GOP minority can roadblock any of the Progressives' idealistic tax talk. They would say that half a loaf is better than none. That said, they are not keen to defend GOP tax policies and will support or even take the lead on reasonable, even aggressive reforms if their party consolidates behind them enough to sweep the election. Middle-of-the-road and targeted ("One Percenter") tax proposals discussed in this part of the book will be palatable to Centrist Democrats, whose engagement and support is essential if the Progressive wing hopes to ever see enactment of major tax reforms in this election cycle.

There is little doubt in most political analysts' minds that the further to the left the Democratic party swings, going into and out of their convention, the better the chances that Donald Trump will squeak by in the November general election.[7] And even if Trump loses the White House over non-economic issues, the inevitable GOP campaign rhetoric about a "Socialist-Liberal" in the executive branch will surely scare enough Republican voters and swing voters to re-elect incumbent GOP members in the Senate. There, the numerical advantages of staggered terms still remain with the Republican party in the next Congressional session, if only for purposes of impeding a popular wave that FOX TV would dub a runaway legislature.

---

7 By painting a more clear-eyed picture of the realistic options available for tax reform and the finances required to underwrite populist public spending initiatives, this book's availability in 2020 may help prevent a replay of the anti-McGovern backlash that gave Nixon his second term.

On the other hand, Democrats need to energize their base, and get out the vote in the general election. Centrist slogans and decency won't be enough unless Trump blows himself up politically, and that alone does not produce a landslide in the Congressional races. If the Progressive wing stays home, as some did in 2016 when Hillary Clinton lost, then Trump will find a familiar path to a majority in the electoral college, and GOP senators in pivotal states will win re-election. Clearly the party's tax reforms, those that Centrists can support with enthusiasm, must also appeal to the party's primary base which is left of them. The party clearly needs to fire up voters' animosity toward Fat Cats, Trust Fund Brats, and Wall Street. The good news is that this can be done without losing the center, if its leaders and candidates play their cards well. But it likewise cannot be achieved without the center.

> The GOP has enough safe seats in the Senate in 2020 to obstruct major tax reforms if Democrats don't reduce deficits as part of their plan.

Which brings us now to the other political party. Unless Democrats can somehow pull off an overwhelming landslide up and down the national balloting, which seems dubious, meaningful tax reforms will need to overcome the inevitable resistance that a GOP minority can still mount. Any talk of taxation runs the risk of reincarnating the inveterate label of "Tax and Spend Democrats" in both the election and its aftermath. In the Senate, it takes more than just a simple majority to pull off a generational tax reform package. And right now the math, the safe seats in the Senate in 2020, and the fractured electorate do not likely add up to Democrats achieving a filibuster-proof Senate majority. Although the procedural rules for budget reconciliation could conceivably provide Democrats a path for adoption of ground-breaking tax reforms in both houses on a simple majority, that scenario is remote at best.

All this said, Republicans also have an obligation to "play ball" to reduce federal budget deficits. If they lose the White House, the GOP will no longer be the Party of Trump and traditional "Chamber of Commerce" fiscal conservatism will rise again in their caucus. Democrats can take the lead after they re-take the White House, but without GOP cooperation, they will struggle to unilaterally cut defense costs, trim business and farm subsidies, and raise taxes to reduce the budget deficits. Senate Republicans will "dig in" if Democrats take an unbridled, steamroller approach to tax reform. Without horse-trading or shirtsleeve compromises, or a second sweep in 2022 to regain working control of the Senate, Democrats will be stymied.

Even if Democrats were to win both houses in Congress in the 2020 elections, the hard fact of life is that every major lobbying firm in Washington DC will be pressuring members to strip away support for tax reforms that gore the oxen that they represent. Democrats taking office will be hounded by wealthy constituents who will tell them that tax reform was OK on the campaign trail, but just not for their particular situation when it comes to writing tax code. Special interests will surface all over Capitol Hill, and those emotional, dramatic calls to "Tax the rich and feed the poor, 'Til there are no rich no more"[8] will soon fade away.

The classic book in this field is the deceased political scientist Murray Edelman's *Symbolic Uses of Politics* (1964), which explains how the transient and shallow hunger of unorganized voters for symbolic reassurance is easily satiated, and will typically succumb to more-powerful organized economic interests. Tax legislation, and especially loophole-crafting, is the paradigm example.

---

8 *I'd love to change the world.* Ten Years After, 1971.

> Smart Liberals will not overpromise what tax reform will buy on the expenditure side. That will just assure voter disenchantment and midterm election losses in 2022.

For real Tax Reform to actually materialize, Democrats will need to first win a clear mandate and then bring tax experts to the table with them after the election. That requires more than just slogans and demagoguery. Going into the general election, voters will need to understand what Tax Reform means to them and to the Fat Cats, in terms they can understand and believe in. The idea that voters can give a new President the authority to jack up everybody's taxes to fund single-payer national health care, free college for everybody, and expanded entitlements forever -- that is a pipedream, even with a partisan Congressional majority. Many middle class and especially younger voters want the One Percenters and Wall Street to pay up. But that alone will not pay for all the spending initiatives that are arriving at the upcoming party convention. Smart Liberals will not overpromise what tax reform will buy on the expenditure side. That will just assure voter disenchantment and midterm election losses in 2022.

To be successful even if they win, Democrats cannot promise the moon like Trump has.[9] The Moderates will posture that "We'll see where that gets us and come back again in two and four years to show what we were able to accomplish." That's a message that can work, but convention delegates and voters will want to know at least generally what that means. What follows is "meat on the bones." These are all achievable tax reforms, and they add up to enough revenue to shore up our entitlement programs and deliver on some (but not all) of the liberal-progressive

---

9 Admittedly, a double standard. Sustained, fundamental change cannot be founded on deception.

promises for more-affordable health care and public college tuition, without raising taxes harshly on Middle America.[10]

A final requirement for success in tax reform is the level of sophistication that Democrats in Congress must achieve in writing tax code. Republicans typically enjoy the benefit of technical expertise in their camp when they re-write tax laws that favor businesses and investors. Capitalists hire tax lawyers; workers do not, so the partisan expertise is always lopsided. Democrats must not only enter the process of tax reform with purpose and resolve, their Congressional delegation must secure the technical and financial expertise to navigate the subtle and complex issues described in each of the narratives that follow. The opposition is crafty, and "it takes fire to fight fire" when loopholes and tax preferences are on the line.

TOPIC 10: Progressive taxation: theory, history and reality

"Another means of silently lessening the inequality of property is to exempt all from taxation below a certain point, and to tax the higher portions of property in geometrical progression as they rise."

Thomas Jefferson, letter to James Madison, 1785.

---

10 The one exception below is the Value Added Tax (VAT) for which Topics 20 and 25 describe a national referendum (a democratic plebiscite) to ratify Congressional legislation to fund universal health care at an affordable level with income-based premium-surcharge tiers similar in structure to those already now applicable to upper-income Medicare members. Income-based premium surcharges would be necessary in order to make the numbers work, and would be both appropriate and sufficient to retain progressivity of the entire program.

A reader need not consider oneself a Progressive to believe in a progressive tax structure. There are many (although perhaps fewer nowadays) Republicans who understand the rationale for, and believe in, a progressive tax system at the federal level. In public finance, the term simply means that the percentage of income (or wealth) paid for taxes should increase at successively higher levels of income. The rationale is simple: Poor people have very little money, and need all of it for basic subsistence. Shelter, food and clothing, transportation and medical costs exhaust the budgets of at least a quarter of the population, even without counting middle-class expenses like entertainment, vacations, weekly restaurant meals, music lessons, obstetricians and college tuition. Wealthy people, and those with high incomes, do not require all of their resources to pay for necessities, and are able to save and invest, sometimes large sums of money. They are better able to pay more to support essential governmental functions.

> A progressive tax system sets increasing rates for higher levels of income and wealth.

A progressive tax system therefore sets increasingly higher rates for higher levels of income. Sometimes this can be accomplished with a simple tax structure that applies only to upper level incomes, so that the average tax rate starts and increases from zero and approaches the specified percentage when the numbers get big. (The estate tax is an example, with a large exemption before the high rates apply to the taxable wealth.) In the case of the income tax, the tax table provides a stair-step of progressively higher marginal tax rates, which apply only to income levels above a given threshold. For example, the current U.S income tax schedule has successive tax rates of 0, 10, 12, 22, 24, 32, 35 and 37 percent for "ordinary" income such as salaries, wages, investment interest, self-employment and rental income, and lottery winnings. The zero rate applies to all income below the level of the standard deduction, which for 2019 is $24,400 for married filers. Income above that is taxed at 10 percent on the first $19,400 of taxable income, and then at successively higher rates until taxpayer income exceeds $612,300. The 37 percent rate then applies to all taxable ordinary income above that level. The 37 percent rate is called the *marginal* tax rate at the upper tier, because it applies only to the marginal dollar *in excess of* that threshold.

The concept of marginal tax rates is very important for fiscally literate readers to understand. It is the rate paid on *every next* dollar subject to tax. Mathematically, it is not the same as the *effective* or *average* tax rate, which is the percentage of total income or wealth that is taxed. In a progressive tax system, the average rate will always be lower than the top marginal rate. That is because at least some of the wealthiest taxpayers' income, specifically those portions subject to lower rates, are subject to the same lower rates as everybody else. Arithmetically, this means that their average or effective rate must be somewhere in between. For the very rich, of course, the average rate comes closer and closer to the top marginal rate, on taxpayers with incomes in the millions of dollars.

Aside from the estate tax, which applies to only a very small fraction of all deceased taxpayers, and after a very large exemption which is tax-free, the federal income tax is our nation's most progressive universal tax structure by design. In practice, however, the overall national system of taxation is less progressive than the income tax tables alone would have us believe. First, there are major loopholes and exceptions in the federal income tax that result in upper-income investors paying far lower tax rates than what the official schedule would suggest.

As readers will all see below, capital gains and other forms of investment income are subject to much lower marginal rates than many middle-class taxpayers pay. As a result, the richest taxpayers typically do not pay the ordinary tax rate on most of their income, but instead pay a flat 20 percent tax rate on investment income at all levels,[11] which is shamefully lower than the marginal tax rate paid by a married couple with taxable wage and salary income of $80,000.

To put the concept of progressivity in perspective, readers must first understand that only one-half of U.S. government revenues come from individual income taxes. Thirty-six percent (36%) of our federal revenues come from payroll taxes for Social Security and Medicare. And the payroll tax is not progressive; in fact it is regressive, technically. This is because it applies a single flat tax rate on an employee's earnings up to the wage base ceiling for Social Security,[12] which was $132,900 in 2019 (escalating for inflation each year). This means that for all taxpayers below that level, they and their employers all pay the same flat tax rate as a percentage of their earned income. For those earning more, however, the marginal rate is zero, and the average tax rate on their pay stub is lower and lower as their earnings go higher. For incomes above the wage base limit, it's the exact opposite of progressive taxation.

So with a moderately regressive payroll tax, and with so many regressive exemptions and loopholes now written into the individual income tax, it is no wonder that Progressive politicians on the left wing of the Democratic party are up in arms about restoring progressivity to the tax code. And they are right, in principle. The debate for Democrats to resolve is how far to take this battle, going into their national convention and then into the general election in 2020, and where should the progressive tax features begin if they succeed in their campaign? Which geese should be plucked, how many feathers are even available for plucking, how many should be taken, and when to stop before the golden geese die of exposure?

---

11 Plus a 3.8 percent Medicare surtax on investment income, for taxpayers with incomes over $250,000 (not inflation-indexed).

12 Medicare now has no ceiling on payroll taxes. All earned income is subject to Medicare taxes, plus the 3.8% tax rate that now applies to investment income under the Obamacare legislation.

> Efforts to remove the wage base ceiling on Social Security will rapidly undercut the broad popular support this program achieved. FDR knew exactly what he was doing, when he opted for a limited payroll tax and not an income tax. But the wage ceiling can and should be eliminated on the *employers'* share.

Many Liberals instinctively think they can start by lifting that $132,000 wage base limit on Social Security. On the surface, it looks to some like a natural solution to just raise the limit. But there is a problem with that idea that warrants a history lesson and some modern political savvy as well. When President Franklin Roosevelt and his fellow Democrats succeeded in pushing through the Social Security Act in 1935, there was already an income tax law in effect. They could have funded Social Security with a progressive income tax, but they did not. Roosevelt was a pragmatist who knew that without widespread national support, the program would be killed or seriously diluted the next time the Republican party regained control of power in Washington DC.[13] He and his Brains Trust team therefore sold the entire nation, including many main-street Republicans, on the concept that Social Security was to be a national *social insurance* program, not a scheme for income and wealth redistribution. The rich were not targeted to pay progressively for Social Security in FDR's time. The wage base was capped at $3000, which was a lot of money for most laborers in its time. But in 2019 dollars it works out to $56,000. So it can easily be seen that the wage base has more than doubled over the years, adjusted for inflation. Meanwhile, the tax rate has gone up from 1 percent to 6.2 percent of

---

13 Imagine the GOP campaigns in an alternate universe of the 1940s to "Repeal and Replace" Social Security if FDR had not been so popular with most Americans. By the time Eisenhower ran for office, it was too late: the social insurance model had firmly taken root in the national psyche.

covered wages for Social Security (plus what is now 1.45 percent for Medicare with no limit).

Roosevelt also argued[14] that in the New Deal, employers would pay an equal contribution, and also fund unemployment insurance, giving workers a three-for-one return on their wage tax. To him, that was progressive.

There is great concern among political centrists, and many fiscal literates in both parties, that any effort to remove the wage base ceiling on Social Security will rapidly undercut the broad popular support this program has achieved and retained over eight decades. First, it should be noted that the wealthiest Americans do not derive most of their incomes from salaries and wages, so they would not be paying the lion's share of the new taxes collected by removing the cap on the Social Security wage base. Instead, it would be the more-affluent professionals, technicians and managers, and the everyday self-employed business owners, freelancers, proprietors and sales professionals, who would bear the brunt of such a tax increase. For them, it would be the worst deal of their lifetimes. They would pay more and more in taxes, for which they get absolutely nothing of value to themselves. And most of those folks already feel that they have paid more into the system than lower-income wage-earners whose benefits are subsidized by their contributions. This issue is therefore one of those Third Rail conundrums for Progressive Democrats to think about more deeply than their impulses may lead them to believe. There is no faster way to lose suburban and young-professional voters than to eliminate the Social Security wage base cap. That just moves Blue voters to Red without actually solving the funding problem.

Where Democrats have completely missed the mark on the wage ceiling is their blind adherence to the FDR model of equal taxation

---

14 See FDR's 1936 election-eve speech at Madison Square Garden. His rhetoric then was arguably more passionate and fiery than most 2020 primary election candidates'.

of employers. There would be very little voter backlash from taxing employ*ers* at the 6.2 percent FICA-OASDI[15] tax rate on all earned income. Although this would raise the cost of doing business in the U.S. adversely for a few employers that compete globally, the impact would lodge primarily in high-paying service industries and not the blue-collar economy.[16] No company is going to lay off high-paid managers and executives because it must pay full FICA taxes on their salaries and bonuses. At most, their bonus checks might be shaved a bit. Self-employed taxpayers below the One-Percenter level could receive a limited credit to offset their "employer" share, just like the current system. This action alone would eliminate one-half of the regressivity of the Social Security tax, and help reduce the drain on its trust fund.

As explained in Topic 12 below on Social Security and Medicare taxes, however, there is a thoughtful proposal already under consideration in Congress, to revisit payroll taxes and the wage base limit. Rather than front-run that information here, readers are referred to that presentation, a few pages below.

Defenders of the investor class (who also oppose elimination of the wage base ceiling) will then readily retort, and with a grain of truth, that the Obamacare legislation of 2012 already compels them to pay a 3.8 percent Medicare surtax on their investment income, which significantly offsets the benefits they enjoy from the Social Security wage base limits. For those readers who are dead-set that the investor class should pay a yet-higher rate on their investment income, a more-comprehensive solution that "treats all money as green," whether the income is earned or unearned, is presented in Topic 18, which addresses the Alternative Minimum Tax (AMT).

---

15 FICA is Federal Insurance Contributions Act. OASDI is Old Age, Survivors and Disability Insurance, aka Social Security.

16 Six percent of workers earn more than the current FICA wage cap.

Taking into account the Social Security wage base and all its flaws, the Obamacare surtax on net investment income, and the individual income tax structure, there is a modest level of progressivity overall in the federal tax system when all its pieces are added together. However, it is not as progressive as the income tax schedule alone would suggest. Nor can it be called regressive at any specific income level. The combined marginal tax rates escalate steeply and progressively between zero and $133,000 of (joint) taxable income, then flatten in slope until the $300,000 level, and escalate again with more progressivity above that. That picture applies, at least, for taxpayers with substantial and predominantly earned income. Where the progressivity stops, however, is when investments are the primary source of income.

> The income tax can be made more progressive in the three or four upper tax brackets. But the annual revenue yield will not exceed $100 billion, about 1/10th of the Trump budget deficit.

There is no question that the income tax could and should be made more progressive for the three or four upper tax brackets. Where to draw the line is open to a fair debate that can only be resolved after an election, not during the campaigns. There are too many balls in the air for tax policy to be set that precisely in TV sound bites. Knowing as we do already from Part 1 that the budget deficits must be addressed sooner than later, it is inevitable that those upper bracket rates must and will be restored to Obama-era levels. That is simply an inescapable fiscal fact of life. Every pragmatic Centrist in both parties knows that the Trump Tax Cuts for those making over $250,000 in taxable income are simply unsustainable. And the Congressional staff bean-counters will tell their tax committees that increasing those tax rates back up to pre-Trump levels cannot even generate an additional $100 billion of annual revenues on their own,[17] less than even one-tenth the magnitude of the current Trump-era budget deficit. It would cover a puny five percent of the cost of single-payer Medicare for All.

Progressives need to better understand the boundaries on progressivity. In order to raise sufficient revenue to fund both the current federal deficit and major new social programs, from higher income tax rates, the income tax would have to double. Top-rate taxpayers would then face a 75 percent marginal IRS tax rate, in addition to their state and local taxes, which essentially confiscates their entire income. That fact remains true even if capital gains are taxed as ordinary income. Stated clearly, it would take a 100 percent increase in the income taxes now paid by every citizen to eliminate the current federal budget deficit, Social Security and Medicare deficits, and underwrite universal health care subsidies just for those who are now uninsured and underinsured.[18] And even that unimaginable tax-hike would not provide new funding for college debt relief or tax credits for households making less than six figures. Those are all pipe dreams that cannot possibly be funded on the backbone of even-the-most-progressive income tax that Congress can even theoretically design. The numbers just don't work.

As it turns out, the single most important step that can be taken to increase the progressivity of the federal income tax structure is not the ordinary tax rate schedule that most of us consider to be "the" schedule. It is rather the Alternative Minimum Tax (AMT), which is the fiscally literate Democrat's single best shot at improving the progressivity of the

---

17 2016 federal income tax data summarized by the Tax Foundation on November 13, 2018 attributed $840 billion of income tax receipts to the top 5% taxpayers, those with AGI incomes over $198,000. Pre-Trump tax rates with no other adjustments to TCJA tax brackets, would require an increase in taxes of less than ten percent, or $84 billion. This is not completely "apples-to-apples," but it provides a reasonable proxy for our purposes here.

18 Again, this begs the question of subsidies for some but not all citizens, and why employers would continue to offer health insurance benefits if subsidies are offered to those now outside the system. See Topics 24 and 25.

federal tax structure. And for anybody who gives more than lip service to the mounting federal deficit, it will take both to make a meaningful difference -- along with other important measures to be explained and discussed below. Each of the sections below describes some of the building-blocks that would have to be cobbled together to fund any major new spending programs, while also making more than just a dent in the ongoing budget deficit.

TOPIC II: Tax preferences: lower rates, deductions and loopholes

One reason that the federal income tax system is not as progressive as the tax tables would suggest is that Congress has carved out dozens of "tax preferences" and "tax expenditures"[19] in the form of special, lower tax rates for various categories of income. The most obvious and notorious of these tax preferences among Progressives is the lower tax rate accorded to investment income. Capital gains and qualified dividend income are taxed across all income levels at lower rates than the same taxpayers would pay on salaries and wages. Not only does this specific investment tax preference apply to the standard tax returns, but it carries over into the one tax provision that was supposed to level the playing field: the Alternative Minimum Tax (AMT). Although investment income kicks an affluent taxpayer into AMT taxation, the

---

19 A tax expenditure is a loophole in the tax code that exempts certain categories of taxpayers from a tax because of something they do. Capital gains taxes are considered a tax expenditure because the investor gets a lower tax rate than the general tax schedule for "ordinary income." Exemption of employer-paid fringe benefits from income taxes is considered a tax expenditure. Tax deductions and credits for fossil fuel exploration and solar panels are tax expenditures.

investment income itself is not subject to the higher AMT rate. This is a major defect that the later discussions of capital gains and AMT will address head-on. For now, it is simply noted that the estimated cost of capital gains and dividend tax preferences last year was $128 billion, if one assumes that this income could otherwise be taxed as ordinary income tax rates. That is the maximum size of the loophole, which is hardly enough to pay for major health care, or free tuition and college debt relief.

> The total annual tax revenue loss for capital gains and dividend preferences is $128 billion. That comes nowhere close to funding universal health care or college tuition. It is only one-eighth (1/8th) of today's annual budget deficit.

The other major federal tax expenditure and tax preference is one that many Democrats do not think about very often, and often ignore in their rhetoric. It is the tax exemption given to workers who receive employer-paid medical insurance. These "fringe benefits" are a form of labor compensation that completely escapes the federal income tax system. What most Democrats overlook is that this tax preference actually costs the U.S. Treasury more than the capital gains and dividend preference given to investors! The tax expenditure for employer-paid health insurance benefits is estimated at $150 billion presently.

Of course, this tax benefit has more value to high-earning workers than those whose income taxes are tiny, so it is not fair to draw a moral equivalence here. Given that the Five Percenters (at the top income level) pay 58 percent of income taxes, they also enjoy over one-half of this tax expenditure benefit, and the top 25 percent of taxpayers correspondingly derive 85 percent of this tax expenditure. So only 15 percent of this tax benefit is enjoyed by the bottom 75 percent of taxpayers, those with taxable income below $80,000.[20]

Nobody in the Democratic party is now proposing to modify the workplace health-care-insurance tax preference, but it will be important to keep it in mind when looking for ways to reform the nation's health care system. If some of today's employer-paid medical benefits are replaced eventually by an expanded Medicare system or option, then a portion of this tax expenditure can be devoted to a national solution. And to the extent that employers pay only for supplemental benefits similar to Medicare advantage or PPO options, then those premium benefits could be made taxable to redeploy the current tax subsidies to help fund basic coverage nationwide.

The third largest tax expenditure is also worker-friendly on its face, namely the tax benefits from contributions and earnings on defined contribution (401k, 403b and 457) plans at the workplace. This tax preference has a cost equivalent to the capital gains and dividends preference, roughly $125 billion annually. As with the employer-paid medical exemptions, its benefits tilt most heavily toward upper-income taxpayers, but not as lopsided because of the cap on annual contributions, which limits its value to the One Percenters. On the other hand, a heavier share of total tax-deferred retirement account balances is held by the top Five Percenters, so the percentage of tax-deferral benefits accruing to America's upper-bracket taxpayers is disproportionate.

Here's an insight and a takeaway for fiscally literate readers, on the topic of tax-deferred saving plans: The Congressional Budget Office and IRS scoring of tax expenditures for retirement accounts ignores the absolute certainty that the IRS will eventually collect ordinary income

---

20 Data source: Tax Foundation summary of 2018 federal income tax data, November 13, 2018.

taxes on these savings accounts later in participants' lives,[21] unlike the way capital gains are treated. So the Congressional scoring of tax expenditures reflects near-term tax deferrals, but not the eventual taxes of those nest eggs when employees (or their beneficiaries) must ultimately redeem their accounts and pay ordinary income taxes. As later discussions of the capital gains and estate tax will explain, wealthy investors now avoid capital gains taxes on appreciated assets held during their lifetime and left in their estate. Meanwhile, all the money held in retirement savings accounts (including IRAs) will be taxed at the higher ordinary tax rates through "required minimum distributions." The middle class bears the brunt of this inequity, which will be addressed later.

> Loopholes and tax breaks for real estate depreciation, appreciated property given to charities, and fossil-fuel extraction *all* require reform.

Besides these tax preferences for individual taxpayers, there are scores of tax exemptions, deductions and loopholes that apply to businesses. Although the TCJA did make some worthwhile efforts to clear out some of the underbrush of tax preferences enjoyed by businesses and partnerships, most of the larger loopholes were retained.[22] Of these, four are noteworthy, for different reasons: accelerated depreciation. fossil fuel depletion allowances, tax breaks for real estate developers

---

21 The one exception is Roth retirement accounts, where the income taxes are paid up-front but the principal, capital appreciation and income are tax-free upon distribution. For those expecting that all of us will face higher tax rates in the future, the Roth is likely a preferable vehicle for those now in the middle-income tax brackets.

22 Mind-numbing lists and tallies of these tax expenditures are available in the President's annual budget package submitted by the White House, and the Congressional Budget Office reports. For one example, see https://www.whitehouse.gov/wp-content/uploads/2018/02/ap_13_expenditures-fy2019.pdf

including the new Opportunity Zone bonanza, and tax deductions for appreciated assets contributed to charities.

Accelerated depreciation is a tax gimmick that enables a company or business owner to write off the cost of capital equipment faster than normal accounting rules would allow. It enables the taxpayer to avoid more taxes on its current income than a "straight-line" accounting would allow. In the Trump Tax Cuts law, the grand-daddy of all accelerations was included so that large amounts of capital equipment (even the popular "heavyweight" SUVs used by savvy realtors) can be expensed immediately to reduce taxable income in the first year. Obviously, the business community loves these tax breaks, which flow directly to their bottom line by sheltering income. Some of these short-term "sugar-high" gimmicks will expire purposely and "coincidentally" after 2023. Consequently they are unlikely to rise to the level of Presidential political debate, but the general concept is nonetheless worthy of mention. Almost $50 billion of tax expenditure was attributed to accelerated depreciation in recent income tax analyses.[23] In balancing the budget, these plums would be low-hanging fruit for tax reformers.

The second corporate tax preference worth a quick mention is fossil fuel extraction incentives, which include various tax credits and "depletion allowances."[24] The dollar amounts here are not material to any major budgetary or deficit issues, but Progressives and Liberals who vocally address climate change may want to take note of the 10-figure federal subsidy package now enjoyed by companies and partnerships engaged in petroleum extraction. This topic is addressed more fully in the subsequent chapter on corporate taxation. Just be forewarned that there is not enough revenue here to fund a Green New Deal -- but there

---

23 Joint Committee on Taxation, summarized by Tax Foundation *ibid*.

24 A depletion allowance is a tax deduction for the value of natural resources that are extracted and sold, which are not treated as income but rather the consumption of an asset.

could be enough to fund some meaningful research and development (R&D) for alternative energy technologies.

The third specific category of tax preferences and loopholes is centered on the real estate development business. Tax laws have favored developers for decades, and there is little doubt that some White House insiders have enjoyed many of the subsidies that Congress has granted to their industry. Without engaging in diatribe about White House occupants, let it suffice that the next Congress could be enlightened if its tax committees take a long hard look at the multiple tax benefits given away to real estate developers and their partners, which might possibly include some very prominent public officials. One of the most glaring is what was once aptly called "promote," which is a share of project profits given to the developer by the investment partners. This is typically a risk-free reward for managing the project on a profitable basis. From a tax standpoint, this form of compensation has been accorded preferential tax treatment at capital gains tax rates. Topic 16 on Carried Interest will address this issue.

Real estate developments and their owners enjoy the benefits of depreciation expensing to incur paper tax losses, which can then shelter taxable income from other sources. Along with actual capital losses on failed projects that carry forward to offset future profits, depreciation enables many developers to avoid federal income tax for extended periods. Without going into every available and conceivable way this is done, readers can explore for themselves the ins and outs of this realm by perusing the informative report on Donald Trump's tax returns as reported by the *New York Times* on May 7, 2019, and judge the veracity of those reports and the subject's claims for themselves.

A final category of Congressional giveaways was part of the Trump Tax Cuts of 2017, and even lured in some unwitting Democrats who thought they were doing a good thing for poor communities. Investors in real estate developments who locate their projects in state-designated

Opportunity Zones are able to defer capital gains from prior investments, eliminate taxes on some of those previous gains if invested for seven years, and then enjoy complete amnesty from capital gains taxes on the new project if the property is held for ten years. The well-meaning part of this law was the concept that opportunity zones would all be low-income areas. The statute itself set some guidelines to focus investment in census tracts that meet certain standards. However, there are numerous qualified zones that look nothing like the inner-city or rural-poor demographic that many sponsors were expecting. Some of them adjoin elite colleges where the low taxable income of full-time students weighs down the averages.

To exploit the new law, real estate developers and fund managers are scouring over the maps of eligible census tracts to find projects that were already proceeding through the permitting process for development. For them and their investors, this tax break is a pure windfall. Only time will tell how many structures will ever be built in Opportunity Zones that would not ever have been built without this tax break. This does not discredit the entire law, but it does scream out for reforms. For every legitimate center-city office building erected in Oakland and startup business incubator built in Compton, California, there will be many other structures that have nothing to do with bootstrapping blighted communities.

> Depreciation recapture is a giveaway to Opportunity Zone real estate developers who can have their cake and eat it too.

According to the trade press [25] it appears to tax professionals that the Opportunity Zone legislation and the ensuing IRS tax regulations have opened the barn door wide open for these investors to enjoy a completely unintended and unjustified tax break. Investors in these zones can claim depreciation on the structure as a rental property for ten or more years, reduce the tax basis of the structure as they go along, and then avoid the (otherwise mandatory) recapture of this accumulated depreciation when they later sell it, once they meet the ten-year test. Everybody understood that if the property were sold in the future for a profit from appreciation of the physical structure, that would be tax-free, but so far nobody has revealed the hidden secret that depreciation on these buildings will apparently become a complete giveaway. By dodging any depreciation recapture, opportunistic real estate investors get to have their cake and eat it too. Clearly, any new tax bill needs to outlaw such double-dipping. [26]

Finally, this section would be incomplete if it failed to mention a sacred cow of the investor class: the income tax deduction received from appreciated assets contributed to charities. To be clear, the author has no axe to grind with charities. But there is a gimmick embedded in the tax code that benefits only those investors who are able make contributions of appreciated assets to charities, avoid capital gains taxes, and get a full income tax deduction on the entire gift. In olden days, this was commonly done by giving appreciated stock or real estate to the charity which would then sell the asset for its treasury. (This paid for a lot of churches and hospitals.) Nowadays, these gifts are typically made to a charitable foundation that the donor controls. Several investment companies have even figured out how serve as intermediaries to receive the appreciated securities, sell the assets to buy into their proprietary

25 *Investment News,* February 15, 2019.

26 Senator Cory Booker (D-NJ) was a supporter of the Opportunity Zone provisions in TCJA, and he is encouraged to lead an appropriate technical corrections effort.

investment funds tax-free, and then give the donor rights to make grants to qualified charities from the commingled fund.

This tax loophole begs to be plugged, at the time of the charitable contribution of assets. If the property has appreciated in value, it should be taxable for the capital gains (to the donor) prior to the transfer. This does not require an immediate payment to IRS, as the full value of the charitable contribution would still be an income tax deduction. But the capital gains tax rate should apply to the amount of capital appreciation since the donor acquired the asset. The investor-donor's capital appreciation should not become a tax shelter for other income! Although fewer and fewer Americans now itemize deductions, the value of charitable contributions deducted is now estimated to be approximately $200 billion annually (down from $236 billion in 2016 because of the new standard deductions), and of that it is reasonable to assume that ten to 25 percent of this total is appreciated property. Applying a 20 percent capital gains tax rate to the capital gains within this total, and then backing out an offset for donors who would reduce their giving or contribute just cash, it is unlikely that this one tax reform would generate more than $5 billion of new revenue annually. But for those who chafe at the "free lunch" now given to capitalists who exploit this loophole, it would be a matter of both principle and (taxing the appreciated) principal.

TOPIC 12: Social Security and Medicare Taxes

As explained earlier in this book, the nation's two most popular entitlement programs, Social Security and Medicare, are running on fumes. At current rates, their primary funding sources, which are payroll taxes, are chronically insufficient to actuarially fund the benefits already promised. The latest projections by the federal trustees show that prepaid reserves[27] for Social Security will deplete entirely by 2034. For Medicare it is even worse, as its reserves will run out in 2026. A recession will accelerate the depletion dates. It is a mathematical certainty that the winner of the 2024 Presidential race will immediately face a Medicare funding pothole unless the victor in 2020 provides adult, bipartisan leadership to get ahead of this dirty little secret.

> It is a mathematical certainty that the winner of the 2024 election will face a Medicare funding shortfall, unless the next Congress takes decisive action.

When Social Security became law in 1935, the original tax rate was one percent of each worker's first $3,000 of payroll income paid by the employee and a matching one percent paid by the employer. Workers and their employers now pay 6.2 percent for Social security up to the wage ceiling, and 1.45 percent of all earnings for Medicare. Over the years, Congress has increased the "wage base"[28] ceiling for Social Security to $132,900 in 2018 (which is about 2.5 times the national median household income). In 1993, Congress removed the wage cap for Medicare, so that the Medicare payroll tax applies to all earned income without a maximum limit. Taxpayers with earned income over

---

27 The reserves for both programs are not cash in the bank. They are simply an IOU from the Federal Treasury to the two trust funds. In essence, the trust funds own Treasury bonds, which are nothing more than a promise from the federal government to pay the trust funds from its own borrowing. It's essentially robbing Peter to pay Paul. When the trust funds are fully depleted, the Treasury debt will still remain outstanding, with investors then holding the debt.

28 The wage base includes all earned income, whether wages, salaries or overtime. Self-employed workers pay both the employee and employer share of their net earnings (income minus business expenses) on their annual federal income tax return, although they are allowed a tax deduction for one-half of the employer's share when they file.

$250,000 also pay an additional payroll tax of 0.9 percent on earnings over that threshold.

To put the full burden of the payroll tax on workers into perspective, think of it this way: For unmarried employees who earn less than $100,000, the payroll taxes paid by them and their employers are more than the IRS collects from them as individuals from the income tax on their earned income.

Annually, these payroll taxes now raise a total of $1.2 trillion, with a capital T. (That is $1,200 billion.)[29] The budget problem is that annual expenditures for Social Security ($945 billion) and Medicare ($600 billion) exceed these combined revenues by more than $300 billion each year. As fiscally literate readers already know, the gap is growing annually because 10,000 Baby Boomers retire every day and start drawing benefits for which they no longer contribute taxes.

Political Centrists would stop the reader at this point and ask, "Why are we proposing new social spending programs that would only escalate the budget deficit, when we have not even provided the necessary funding for Social Security and Medicare solvency?" Americans are already $300 billion in the hole annually for these two entitlement programs, which remain chronically underfunded. The answer, of course, is that they are the Third Rail of politics: there is no political benefit to either party to take this bull by the horns. In the world of Trump, budget balancing is for sissies because debt is the other guy's problem. Lenders are suckers.

Even with unlimited Medicare taxes on all earned income, Congress has long been aware that retiree medical care expenses are swiftly outrunning the revenues received from the payroll and

---

29 To help readers appreciate the cost of single-payer health care, the payroll taxes we personally pay now will cover only 40 percent of what it will cost to eliminate insurance companies and rely on taxes instead.

self-employment taxes. To put a small finger in the dike, the Affordable Care Act ("Obamacare") of 2012 instituted a new investment-income tax (NIIT)[30] on higher-income investors that is presently raising a little more than $20 billion annually. This represents less than 2 percent of the revenue from payroll taxes, which is a drop in the bucket in the grand scheme of things, and certainly not enough to ever bring Medicare into budgetary balance.

For wealthy investors, it is worth noting that their effective tax rate on capital gains and dividend income is already higher than the 20 percent rate that most politicians ascribe to them. They are now paying a marginal tax rate of 23.8 percent on this preference income, because of this Medicare surtax.

To balance today's Social Security and Medicare deficits with a higher tax on investment income, the current 3.8 percent NIIT rate would have to be 15 times higher, which would require a ludicrous 57 percent tax rate on the affected taxpayers' net investment income, plus their 20 percent capital gains tax rate, for a total 77 percent federal tax rate on upper-income investors. Obviously, that is confiscatory, but this extreme example illustrates the difficulty of trying to solve the nation's serious entitlement funding shortfalls simply by Soaking the Rich.

As the subsequent sections of this book will clarify, there is simply not enough low-hanging fruit in the Fat Cat Taxes orchard to solve the current entitlement funding problem, let alone new proposals for universal social benefits such as Medicare for All and tuition-free public college education.

---

30 The Net Investment Income Tax (NIIT) applies to taxpayers whose gross income exceeds $250,000 (married). Above that level, investment income is taxed at a 3.8 percent rate without limitation. (The portion of investment income included in the exempt $250,000 exclusion is not taxed.)

> A combination of policy proposals can be crafted that would address the nation's serious entitlement funding crisis, but it requires action in the next Congressional session, not a decade from now.

This does not mean that the situation is hopeless. A combination of policy proposals can actually be crafted that would address the nation's serious entitlement funding crisis, but it requires action sooner than later. The longer our politicians kick the can, the more costly, painful and ultimately dangerous the future shortfalls will become.

This section describes just the tax side of the solution. Benefits adjustments for the affluent (who are already taxed at the higher ordinary income tax rates and now pay Medicare premium surcharges), and higher retirement ages that reflect rising longevity, will undoubtedly be an essential part of a long-term solution. But even with such reforms, more revenue is needed and higher taxes are inevitable.

Unless a new tax, such as a Value Added Tax, is to be imposed to fund Social Security and Medicare, the only two viable revenue sources are the income tax and the payroll tax.

An increase in income taxes to balance out these two entitlement programs (and nothing more) would presently require an increase in the effective tax rates of 20 percent (one-fifth) of what all income taxpayers now pay. A married couple with taxable income of $80,000 would see their top marginal tax rate increase from 22 percent to 26 percent, and top-bracket taxpayers would pay 44 percent rather than 37 percent on their high-bracket income. Capital gains and dividend taxes would have to be increased by 4 percent of such income to 24.4 percent plus the 3.8 percent Medicare (NIIT) tax which would have to increase to 4.5 percent for a total rate of 29 percent. Readers should note that these hypothetical tax rates are materially higher than they were before Trump took office: they are higher than the income tax rates under Obama and Clinton.

Sadly, without prompt action by the next Congress, these hypothetical income tax rates are almost inevitable. And delay will only worsen the problem and require even higher rates.

The other alternative is to begin immediately to raise the payroll tax rates in small annual increments. The exact formula is debatable, and would require thoughtful financial modeling by the Congressional Budget Office. But the direction is clear, and it is only a question of magnitude and the rate of escalation that require calibration.

Fortunately for Democrats, one of their colleagues in Congress has already introduced a bill that follows this template. This book is not designed to propose or support specific legislation, but the model embodied in Representative John Larson's (D-CT) "Social Security 2100 Act" does follow the general template for a viable solution. That bill would raise the 6.2 percent Social Security payroll tax in small 0.1 percent annual increments for 24 years to an ultimate higher level of 7.4 percent. [31]

> A bill in Congress with 200 co-sponsors would make serious headway in solving the Social Security funding problem. It does not fix Medicare, however.

---

31 Notably, the trustees' latest report implies that an 8.4 percent Social Security tax rate would be required for long-term actuarial balance, which is much higher than this bill proposes.

The bill also attempts to address the regressivity of the current Social Security payroll tax wage base limit, by also applying the payroll tax to earned income over $400,000. This is called a "donut hole" tax model, which does not apply the tax to income between the wage base ($132,000 in 2018) and $400,000 where the tax would kick in again. The reason for this design is to avoid crushing middle-income taxpayers with a new and high additional tax rate on their income above the current wage base limit, while still collecting more revenue from the One Percenters. Remember, however, that most One Percenters receive most of their income from sources exempt from payroll taxes, which would not be captured in this model. A modification of this design could apply a lower rate (such as three or four percent) to earned income over the current wage base cap, but that requires some complications for payroll processing systems used by employers and may be better administered through the annual income tax returns instead, just like the existing Medicare investment income surtax (NIIT).

Where Larson's bill falls short is that it only addresses Social Security, while the more-immediate and equally problematic funding shortfall is Medicare. Another increase in Medicare tax rates will be required to bring that system's revenues in line with current and future spending for retirees' medical care. Some of this might magically be addressed and cured in the nation's health care reform debate, but the unavoidable fact of life is that Medicare will exhaust its dwindling reserves in 2026, which means that a tax increase is inevitable. The demographic problem is that by 2026, well over two-thirds of all Baby Boomers will have retired from full-time employment. The bill for their Medicare will fall entirely onto their children and grandchildren unless individual premiums and co-pays are increased significantly, or a new tax is imposed.

To his credit, Representative Larson has gathered 200 co-sponsors, which puts him on a possible path to getting his bill onto the House floor. The bill itself contains numerous other provisions that are not essential to this chapter's discussion, but are worthy of Congressional debates and committee deliberations. Only time will tell whether this fiscal solution can be enacted in a bipolar Congress. Absent a miraculous bipartisan compromise, if a long-term solution is not enacted before the Milwaukee party convention, Democrats would be wise to address the issue and fine-tune their spending and taxing proposals accordingly.

Where Larson's bill could be improved is the employer side of the Social Security tax. Since FDR's time, employers have matched the employee contributions dollar for dollar, also subject to the same wage cap. But there is no magic to that formulation. Following just half of the formula for Medicare taxes, where there is no wage limit, Congress could easily tax *employers* at the full Social Security tax rate on all earned income, while leaving the workers' tax base intact. This would remove one-half of the regressivity of the Social Security tax, and also make a meaningful contribution to long-term actuarial solvency. For self-employed taxpayers below the One Percenter level, a tax offset for their "employer" share of the self-employment tax above the wage ceiling can provide them parity with other workers. This is low-hanging fruit in the orchard of tax reform, a clear opportunity for Progressives. Those who carefully read FDR's 1936 campaign speeches will quickly see his logic come to life here.

To put this "fix" in perspective: Annual new revenues on the employer side only would be approximately $35 billion. That alone won't rebalance Social Security, as it represents only five percent of total FICA[32] payroll taxes, and a fraction of the system's annually increasing revenue shortfall. But it is more than double what the estate tax now collects.

Before this chapter concludes, readers must be alerted to a dirty little secret that is Democrats' cross to bear: the state and local government

---

32 FICA is the Federal Insurance Contributions Act, the law that requires mandatory payroll contributions.

"carve-out" from Social Security. When Social Security was enacted in 1935, there was an unresolved Constitutional concern that states could not be taxed as employers, and FDR wisely crafted an exemption for states and their municipalities. Many of the teachers, police officers and other public servants already had a pension plan, so it was expedient to just leave their retirement security to the states as their responsibility and authority. Over time, many of the excluded employees asked to join the federal system because its benefits were actually better than the modest pensions provided at that time, so legislation was passed to allow them to "opt in." Later in the last century, the Constitutional issues were resolved by the Supreme Court in favor of federal authority, so this exemption no longer reflects a federalism dispute. Nonetheless, today we still have about four percent of the U.S. workforce (several million such employees) who do not contribute to Social Security at their primary jobs. Oddly, some of these workers still qualify for Social Security through outside employment or jobs they hold before or after their public service. Because Social Security benefits are progressive, favoring small earnings for which the taxes are paid, public pensioners who moonlight or retire early will capture a windfall from the system as double-dippers if they pay in enough to earn the required quarterly credits. Firefighters are notorious for this strategy, as are teachers who work during summer recess and police officers who moonlight as private security guards.[33]

> Democrats need to own up to the inequity of allowing many state and local government employees to avoid paying their fair share of Social Security's social welfare costs.

---

33 No disrespect is intended to hard-working public employees who earn outside income; the only issue here is the taxation inequity with respect to the portion of FICA we Americans all pay for the benefit of the poorest retirees, the disabled and survivors who are subsidized.

Here's the inequity: The total payroll taxes paid into Social Security are 6.2% x 2 = 14.4%. That is far more than what it costs to actuarially fund equivalent benefits for a public pension plan for a new employee now entering service.[34] So the rest of the money that these exempt employees and their employers are paying instead into their pensions is buying extra benefits that nobody else gets from their Social Security. It's called the FICA Free Lunch.

Public employee unions sometimes try to rebut that there is a compensatory "windfall reduction" of Social Security benefits paid to double-dippers who earn a public employee pension *and also* collect Social Security benefits from their separate private-sector or non-profit employment, but that is actually a sly diversion that has nothing to do with this *contributions* issue. The Federal system is losing almost $15 billion of payroll tax revenue by failing to collect the embedded social-welfare subsidies that all other workers nationwide contribute to the Social Security system, to provide ongoing poverty-level income to 15 million fellow American retirees who would otherwise be destitute. These "Four Percenters" go scott-free. (To put this non-trivial issue in perspective, this FICA Free Lunch causes more federal revenue loss than all the GOP-led reductions in the estate tax this entire century.) The actuaries estimate that mandatory coverage would reduce the entire system's long-term funding deficit by 11 percent, which can no longer be swept under the carpet.

The solution is not difficult: eliminate the exemption for new hires and bring them into the federal system. However, any suggestion to compel existing workers who are now exempt to join Social Security (on top of their locally required pension plans) mid-career is a political

---

34 Sadly, many public pension plans have higher costs because of past contribution and investment shortfalls that must now be amortized at taxpayer expense, but that has nothing to do with this issue. It is almost universally true that the *normal* actuarial cost for most new employees starting service in a public pension plan, including their disability insurance, will be lower than the equivalent cost of Social Security taxes at their pay level.

non-starter and a hornets' nest for public employers. Instead, a federal "make even" payroll tax rate of two percent for this subgroup of hold-outs would be equitable, instead of the 6.2 percent that other workers and their employers must all pay.[35]

As a matter of principle, Democrats must eventually face up to this one tiny skeleton in their closet. Progressives and Liberals cannot rationally promote tax reforms, universal health care and universal college education, yet fail to require universal participation in Social Security --just because their party has a pet bloc of municipal-union members who are milking a special deal at everybody else's expense. What is good for the goose must be good for the gander.

TOPIC 13: The Estate Tax (now tarred as the "Death Tax")

· ·

The modern federal estate tax first appeared in 1916 to help finance America's costs of World War I, although there were precursors as early as 1797 (a stamp tax on bequests, repealed in 1802) and for short periods in 1862 and 1898. Taxation of an estate was, and is still, viewed as a tax on accumulated wealth. The 1916 tax law introduced the concept of progressive tax rates that were higher for larger estates, and started with a top rate of ten percent which rose quickly to 40 percent in the 1920s but then reverted to 20 percent under Coolidge. During the Great Depression and World War II, the top estate tax rate was jacked

---

35 This would still be a fraction of the total revenues lost to the Social Security trust funds. Administratively, a pragmatic five-year step-up and a 20-year sunset provision would be recommended for this "make-even.".

higher four times, ultimately reaching 80 percent for the largest estates. That top rate continued until the Reagan tax bill started a three-decade downward ratcheting of the estate tax, accompanied by successively higher exemption levels.

In addition to the federal estate tax, several states levy inheritance or estate taxes at various rates with a broad spectrum of minimum and maximum estate sizes subject to those rates[36]

The most recent revisions of the estate tax were enacted with the Trump Tax Cuts (TCJA) in 2017. The most important change under that law with respect to estate taxation was a doubling of the size of estates now exempt from taxes. Presently, the first $11.4 million of each decedent's estate is exempted from the federal estate tax. (Thus, a married couple can exclude $22.8 million from estate taxes, with careful legal work.) Prior to 2019, the exemption was $5.5 million. The top rate for the estate tax remained at 40 percent under the new law.

Over the past two decades, the Republican Party has railed incessantly against what they successfully branded and tarred as the "Death Tax." Note that this moniker was assigned long before Donald Trump became a Presidential candidate, but the labelling was right out of his playbook. Nobody likes death, and nobody likes taxes, so the worst of all worlds has to be a Death Tax. Who could possibly be in favor of that? The GOP mantra was consistent: they clamored that the dreaded Death Tax forces family farmers and the heritors of family businesses to sell the family jewels in order to pay these awful taxes. Although there might have been a kernel of truth to that claim a generation ago, the exemption was raised dramatically over past decades, from $300,000 to $600,000 in 1997, to $1 million in 2002, to $2 million in 2006 and $5 million in 2011. From 2001 to present, the number of estates subject each year to the federal estate tax levy has shrunk from 50,000 to 1,900,

---

36 19 presently, at last count. The trend is downward.

a 96 percent decrease. As for the family farm myth, even back in 2013, when the exemption was half its current level, only a few hundred family farm estates nationwide were subject to paying the estate each year. Now that number is around 100. If ever there were a sacred cow in American politics, it has been the family farm in the estate tax rhetoric.

> The fiscal problem for Liberals is that the estate tax will never produce more revenue than the noise it generates. As a fiscal remedy, it lacks firepower.

The fiscal problem for Liberals is that the estate tax will never produce more revenue than the noise it generates. The total federal revenue from the estate tax under current rules is about $20 billion annually. Even if the rates were to revert back to 2001 levels with the exemption reduced to $2 million, the total revenue gain would be about $10 billion annually. In the context of a $4 trillion government budget and a trillion-dollar deficit, that number is little more than a rounding error. So even if the estate tax rates were doubled to levels above those that even the avowed democratic socialists now advocate, that would produce only enough new revenue each year to pay for three weeks of Social Security and Medicare operating deficits, or one week of federal budget deficits, or three days of single-payer national health care.

This is not to say that the estate tax exemptions should not be reverted to their prior levels or perhaps something midway, and the top rates raised back up to 50 percent,[37] as a matter of principle. But it must be clear to all who debate the issue that the rationale for such changes is not to balance budgets or pay for new programs. The estate tax is now more a matter of symbols and principles, not budgetary math.

---

37 In 2001, the top rate was 55 percent on taxable estates over $3 million.

The rationale for an estate tax is founded on the egalitarian ideal that America should not become an aristocracy in which a moneyed class rules the country and passes along its power and wealth from one generation to another. Regardless of one's beliefs as to what "all of us are created equal" meant to both the founding fathers and today's citizenry, it is widely believed that "equal opportunity" is preferable to a caste system in which the parents' economic status puts a lid on a child's opportunities. Very few Americans believe that the idle rich should enjoy the spoils of their grandparents without contributing to our society. This problem has been exacerbated by the *Citizens United* court decision that gives wealthy campaign donors disproportionate influence on civic matters. If income taxes are not an equalizer, if capital gains are given preferential tax treatment to encourage productive investment and reward risk, and if there is no federal tax on the wealth of living persons, then the only remaining device available to level the playing field and curtail economic inequality is the estate tax. Feeble as it may be, it is the one remaining policy instrument that prevents our country from reverting to archaic medieval social structures or devolving into plutocracy.

How did the estate tax become so trivial, as a solution to the modern disparities of wealth and income constantly cited as the worst in a century? How is it that a stiff estate tax cannot solve the nation's revenue problems, in some noble way that would level the playing field?

The first answer is simple financial math. The total value of taxable estates is around $100 billion each year. Of that, roughly a third of the assets go to surviving spouses who are not taxed, so the taxable base is limited and hardly sufficient to produce revenue sufficient to accomplish major social spending objectives. Even a 50 percent estate tax rate applied to the Obama-era tax base would generate little more each year than $25 to $30 billion in total, not even double the current annual level. The estate tax is a one-cylinder engine in a world of turbocharged V-8s and jet propulsion. As a fiscal remedy, it lacks firepower.

The second shortcoming of the estate tax is legal ingenuity: Wealthy families have an ample supply of creative and skilled estate tax lawyers and tax accountants, who have successfully crafted an entire gamut of tools to evade the estate tax. These folks are not the attorneys who prepare wills for John and Mary Smith in Middleville. They work for the richest families in the country. Imagine yourself an IRS tax examiner going up against the best tax attorneys and accountants that money can buy. And every time Congresses catches up to their latest estate-tax avoidance scheme, it takes only a year or two for these crafty technical experts to concoct yet-another workaround. It's a proverbial game of Whack-a-Mole for the IRS, which is sorely understaffed and outgunned (some critics would say "by design").

To be fair-minded, the tax laws have also given super-wealthy capitalists like Warren Buffet of Berkshire Hathaway and Bill Gates of Microsoft a strong incentive to donate their fortunes to philanthropic causes through a charitable foundation (usually in their own name but not always, as Buffet has shown). The Bill and Melinda Gates Foundation, and their Giving Pledge for fellow billionaires, does reflect humanity's better angels and they deserve our respect where credit is due. But it should not go unnoticed that capital assets contributed to a charity during one's lifetime benefits the donor immediately through the income tax deductions they receive, and there is no capital gains tax on the appreciated assets.[38] The foundations then earn investment income tax-free as long as they meet the annual minimum spending tests which apply. Not only does the donor enjoy these tax benefits, these pay-forward foundations also reduce the taxable estate.

This does not belittle their charity, but it does point out how the current system works, for those wealthy enough to "give back" to society and still leave a few chips on the table for the heirs in their families. The difference is that the donors have a far stronger say in how their money

---

38 See preceding discussion of this loophole in Topic 11 on Tax Preferences.

is spent than they and their heirs would if the money instead were paid out as estate taxes to be spent by Congress. That is why Conservatives favor tax incentives for charitable deductions over estate taxes, as a matter of principle and their donors' self-interest.

> Reforming the estate tax will not raise a sufficient amount of revenue to pay for any new major social programs. The rationale for estate tax reform is social justice and deficit reduction.

Even with all this as background, there is no reason that trust-fund babies and silver-spoon heritors should continue to enjoy a "free ticket to paradise," simply by virtue of birth. There are viable tools available in the progressive taxation toolkit, if Congress decides to "follow the money" and close a few loopholes with some reasonable estate tax reforms. Such reforms would begin with reverting the exemptions and estate tax rates closer to Obama-era levels. As noted already, this produces a modest revenue gain that is unlikely to exceed $10 billion annually.

An equally important and new reform that can be achieved in the estate tax is to eliminate the "step-up" of capital (investment) asset valuations at the time of death. Presently, the executors of an estate are allowed to "step up" the tax basis (essentially the purchase cost) of property [39] to its current market value. This enables the estate to completely avoid paying capital gains taxes on assets that have appreciated in value

---

39 Property includes financial assets like stocks, precious metals, art and jewelry, real estate and equipment. For real estate, the tax basis also includes the cost of improvements, but equally important to wealthy families, it includes a cumulative depreciation adjustment. The step up ignores all the past benefits of depreciation claimed by the decedent, and simply re-values the property at its current appraised value.

during the deceased's lifetime. For family dynasties that have passed property down from one generation to the next, the original tax basis is often a mere fraction of its current value, and the intergenerational step-up in basis totally circumvents capital gains taxes. For many years, members of the wealth class, their lobbyists and ideological apologists had argued that it is impossible to keep track of all those property values. Given the mess in the attic, or the flood in the basement, who knows what Grandpa paid for his IBM stock or the third-generation corn farm or the personal capital put into the family held company? For financial assets, however, much has changed in the past decade: Financial institutions are now required to keep track of the cost basis of their client's financial assets. And valuing non-financial assets with a reasonable proxy for their historical value is not that difficult. Specialized appraisal firms do this all the time when they conduct fixed-asset inventories where records are lacking. The wealthy use appraisals all the time to minimize their taxable estates; eliminating the step-up is simply "good for the gander." When in doubt, there are general inflation and property-valuation indexes that can be applied in the absence of any other method. Comparable sales by other investors or buyers during the same time period are also discoverable if the dollar amounts are material.

Proponents of the step-up also argue that, if nothing else, it gives the estate credit for inflation. That is a flimsy argument unless ALL capital gains are to be inflation indexed. On that broader point, scholars and lobbyists can differ, as noted in Topic 15, later. We will review capital-gains taxation more broadly in that section. The point here is that the estate valuation step-up is a loophole whose rationale is becoming increasingly flimsy, especially if capital gains were to be inflation-indexed.

The best locus for administering and collecting this capital gains tax is the decedent's final annual tax income return. (Every executor or personal representative files a final 1040 form on behalf of the deceased taxpayer.) Only those assets that will transfer to a beneficiary other than the surviving spouse would be subject to this final "catch-up" on the capital gains tax. It would not be paid by the heritors. Only those with large incomes would be subject to AMT taxes, otherwise the lower capital gains rate is appropriate for modest middle-class taxpayers. For the surviving spouse, the tax basis should remain unchanged. This means that if the spouse then sells an appreciated asset, the capital gains would then be taxed at the time of sale, using the decedent's tax basis. For assets held in trust in which the spouse remains a primary beneficiary (or transferred into such a trust at the time of death), those assets would likewise retain the decedent's tax basis. Then, upon the death of the surviving spouse, that final tax return would become liable for the capital gains tax on those remaining assets.[40]

> Wealthy inheritors of capital gains should no longer escape taxation. AMT reform can cure this.

As with broader estate tax reform, this modification of the step-up rules will not produce a huge financial windfall to the U.S. Treasury. The ballpark order of magnitude of new tax revenues to be realized is $20 billion[41] annually, not $100 billion nor $1 billion. If capital gains taxes are assessed in the decedent's final income tax return, then the remaining value of the estate will be lower, so tax experts must account for an offset to the estate tax projections. Nonetheless, with the estate tax now collecting only 17 percent of taxable estate values, it is clear that a capital gains tax at a 20 percent rate (plus the 3.8 percent Medicare surtax in many cases) would produce net new revenue for the U.S. Treasury. Applying the AMT rate for larger portfolios would of course raise the

---

40 As noted elsewhere, a special rule for smaller farmers and family owned businesses can allow for installment payments of this capital gains catch-up.

41 See Topic 18 for the calculation.

income potential somewhat, and that higher rate would apply only to One Percenters.

Finally, there is a strong argument that principal distributed to beneficiaries and heritors who are not the decedent's spouse should be subject to a minimum tax if their annual or lump-sum bequests are large enough to push them into the One Percenter category. Rather than previewing the logic and details of how and why the Alternative Minimum Tax (AMT) should apply to those who enjoy oversized silver spoons, munificent trust fund allowances, and similar gifts from the grave that just keep on giving, this chapter will simply reassure most Progressives that "we're not done here."

In summary, there is a clear argument for reforming the estate tax, moving the pendulum back closer to the exemptions and rates that prevailed before Trump and TCJA 2017. Also importantly, the tax-basis step-up of appreciated assets should be revised significantly to close that loophole. And finally, a stiffer AMT, to be discussed in Topic 18, should capture some of the distributions received by One Percenters who enjoy big checks from trust funds and other beneficiary arrangements. None of the incremental revenues gleaned from these tax reforms will fund a major new social program, or even close the gap in current budget deficits by a material amount. So let's stop using them as an "answer" to the legitimate question of "How are we going to pay for all these great ideas?"

TOPIC 14: Corporate taxes

Despite the argument posed by some economists that "corporations don't pay taxes, people do," the corporate income tax has played an important role in the U.S. tax and budget scheme since adoption of the

16th Amendment which authorized an income tax in 1913. Although corporate taxes produce only 14 percent of the revenue that individuals pay to the U.S. Treasury, they are the second largest source of revenue for federal government operations because payroll taxes are entirely devoted to the Social Security and Medicare trust funds.

The Trump Tax Cuts of 2017 (TCJA) reduced significantly the percentage of total federal revenues derived from corporate taxation, from 9 percent to 7 percent.[42] Previously, the corporate rate ranged from 15 to 35 percent, and the TCJA established a flat rate of 21 percent. Total revenue projected from corporate taxes is now roughly $250 billion. It is essential that readers appreciate the magnitude of that number, if only because it establishes the limitation of this source of income for expanded social programs. Even if the corporate tax rates were restored to Obama era levels, the resulting revenue increase would not likely exceed $75 billion annually. That is not insubstantial, but it is a drop in the bucket compared with the annual price tag of universal health care or free college tuition.

And here is Trump's poison pill: When the GOP cut corporate tax rates, they fueled the coinciding stock market rally for which the White House is constantly taking credit. Not because the economy was made stronger, but because the profits of U.S. corporations after taxes were significantly increased by that $75 billion that companies now get to book as profits. The market math is not hard to understand. If profits increase by $75 billion because of corporate tax cuts, and the average price/earnings (P/E) ratio is 22:1 on the S&P 500 companies, that translates into a $1.6 trillion increase in the value of corporate stock prices. Investors pay for higher profits, and Wall Street ebullience over this political victory pushed the P/E ratio higher so the results were

---

42 That statistic was quoted in the Administration's 2019-20 budget. Brookings data suggest that the actual revenue reduction for corporate taxes was closer to 40%, in line with the reduction in the maximum rate. Reality is probably somewhere in between those two extremes.

exponentially magnified. Take that candy away, and guess what happens to stock prices, including the value of public pension funds that invest heavily in the stock market? It comes as no surprise that our incumbent President has the hyperbolic nerve to claim that if he is not re-elected, the stock market will "crash like never before." That is essentially a ransom demand. Trump has created another self-fulfilling prophesy. So any efforts to restore a higher tax rate on corporate profits must now be done very carefully, on an incremental basis, lest well-intended tax-reforming Democrats be blamed for what their opponents will call "irreversible damage" to pension funds and workers' personal retirement accounts if markets re-calibrate stock prices to reflect a return to tax rates more common internationally.

> Corporate tax reforms can increase rates by a factor of 20% over four years without a stock market crash. A moderate 7% surtax on stock buy-backs should make company directors and CEOs work harder to grow their businesses and payrolls.

With that precaution, there are two viable strategies for tax reform in corporate America, that will not bring down the house. First, a modest, incremental corporate tax rate increase over a four-year period is both feasible and fair. Second, Democrats should claw back the corporate tax breaks that have been used for stock repurchases rather than dividends, productive investment and employee compensation.

Start with the tax rate: One of the major arguments in favor of the lower corporate tax rate was international competitiveness and consistency of tax treatments. Proponents of the corporate rate cut pointed to the high 35 percent top federal rate on U.S. company profits and compared that with much lower rates overseas. What they swept under the carpet was the actual effective average rate of U.S. corporate income taxes which was previously closer to 27 percent because of loopholes and allowable deductions. And what was the worldwide average GDP-weighted corporate income tax rate in 2016? It was 29 percent![43] Even allowing for state-level corporate taxes,[44] the U.S. average was hardly a standout; it was just unevenly distributed across different industries. Where the tax-cutters' arguments did ring true was the wide dispersion of effective tax rates in various industries which have each lobbied successful for their own special rules and tax breaks. So there was a defensible rationale for establishing a lower, "flat" corporate tax rate, although the level is certainly debatable.[45] The TCJA rate of 21 percent could be ratcheting up incrementally to a higher level, perhaps in the range of 25 percent over a four-year period. This would ultimately produce an incremental annual revenue yield in the range of $50 billion by 2025, and still position the U.S. competitively in the mainstream of advanced economies.

In addition to this tippy-toe strategy, Democrats of all persuasions have an opportunity to unite on a common theme with respect to corporate stock buy-backs. Although the Trump Tax Cuts for companies were widely "Trumpeted" as a source for employee bonuses and pay hikes,[46] the more-prevalent trend on Wall Street has been to return capital to shareholders indirectly through stock buy-backs (share repurchases). Although there have been celebrated examples of companies

---

43 Source: Tax Foundation report on corporate rates worldwide, August 18, 2016.

44 The U.S. average for state income taxes on corporations is approximately 3.5 percent at the top level, which is relevant to international competitiveness.

45 One problem with flat and ostensibly uniform tax rates in the corporate sector is that they almost inevitably get "carved out" by lobbyists for specific industries who sneak exemptions and deductions into future tax bills. Over time, today's 21 percent corporate rate could become the maximum rate of a new, lower range, as the TCJA begins to look like a slice of Swiss cheese.

46 According to one news report, as many as 750 companies issued announcements that they would award bonuses or pay increases shortly after the TCJA was signed.

that used tax-cut income to increase wages, those have been the exception not the rule. Needless to say, this has irritated labor unions and Progressives, making the buy-backs a lightning rod for complaints of unfairness.

Until now, however, Democrats have been toothless barking dogs on this issue. That need not be the case. There is a way to address this issue through tax policy, again without bringing down the house: a modest but effective surtax on corporate stock repurchases. A feasible tax rate would be seven percent of the corporate cash spent on these buy-backs. The objective of such a surtax would be to compel corporate directors to think twice about returning capital to Wall Street investors rather than re-investing in their business, expanding their operations, improving their productivity, distributing immediately taxable dividends to investors, and improving workforce compensation. The surtax would make a societal statement to corporate directors, at the same time that it ensures that the IRS collects revenue on capital distributions now and not decades later, when an investor's grandchild (or their trust fund) ultimately sells or bequeaths the appreciated stock.

Corporate stock buy-backs exceeded $1.1 trillion in 2018. A seven percent surtax would probably generate around $30 to $50 billion annually, after taking into account the corporate-boards' conscious re-deployment of surplus capital in favor of other productive uses of idle corporate cash, to sidestep the buy-back surtax.[47] Any increase in dividend distributions, employee compensation and investment expenditures to expand business capacity will generate additional income tax revenue, which will show up elsewhere in the tax returns. All new tax dollars are green, as far as the revenue projections in this paragraph are concerned. Those indirect, derivative income tax receipts are potentially as large as the revenue gain from both the buy-back surtax and a viable

---

47 Corporate shareholder meetings will become even more interesting if directors must defend paying the surtax.

increase in the corporate income tax rate itself. Altogether, these tax reforms in the corporate world could increase federal revenues by as much as $100 billion annually if implemented skillfully. The obvious takeaway for fiscally literate Liberals here is that a blunt instrument will cause unnecessary economic trauma that can be avoided by using a laser rather than a dull knife.

The other tax reform that warrants mention here is the suggested elimination of Social Security payroll tax caps on the employer side. This will impact the companies, not the employees, in most cases. For those earning more than the $132,900 wage ceiling subject to FICA-OASDI taxes, the companies would be subject to a 6.2 percent tax on all of those employers' incomes including salaries and bonuses but not stock-option profits. Although there may be some cases when bonuses will be trimmed to offset the company tax payments, it is unlikely that most corporations will blink an eye about higher payroll taxes on their highest-paid professionals, managers and executives. The U.S. Chamber of Commerce and conservative think tanks may squeal bloody murder, but they cannot legitimately claim material economic damage and job losses if the FICA ceiling is removed only on the employer side of payroll. The additional revenue to the Social Security trust funds would be approximately $35 billion annually, with well over half of it paid by corporate America.

Before moving on to personal income-tax reform topics, however, a few brief paragraphs on the fossil fuel industry's tax breaks are appropriate here. Corporations, pass-through partnerships and Fat Cat investors annually enjoy a few billion dollars of tax breaks for tax credits, accelerated depreciation and expensing of capital outlays, and oil depletion allowances. The dollar amounts are therefore relatively trivial in the grand scheme of federal finances. However, there may be a message that Progressives in particular would consider important in their quest for a lower-carbon world in the future. A carbon tax has been discussed by some in their wing of the Democratic party, although the Green tide has been unsuccessful in the ballot box at the state level even in the bluest of Blue states on the west coast. As time goes on, a robust carbon tax could become necessary on a worldwide basis, to curb greenhouse emissions that threaten our planet and many forms of life thereon. For now, however, a broad-based carbon tax proposal in 2020 would simply be political suicide for Democrats, given all the special interests it would awaken in opposition. Rather, it may be wiser to "start small" with a rollback of the fossil fuel tax incentives now given out to the oil and gas exploration and production industries. That would not kill the industry; it just avoids over-building of a capacity that our nation is unlikely to need in 20 years. A punitive tax on industrial greenhouse emissions is also feasible politically, with proper design and political posturing.

America's energy independence is a worthwhile development that has resulted from the industry's innovations in shale petroleum exploration and extraction. Our nation's immunity from political and economic ransom from the OPEC cartel (which precipitated the inflationary ruin of our economy in the 1970s) is a welcome development. Putting aside the environmental issues of horizontal drilling and hydraulic fracturing impacts on groundwater, bedrock and soils, "fracking" has made America energy-independent. Fortunately, for American consumers and those outside of the fossil fuel industry, the technology and economics are now so favorable for the exploration companies that their business is more of a mining operation than a risky wildcat business. Natural gas production is so abundant, and the market price is so low, that many drillers wastefully burn it at the wellhead (which sadly contributes to global warming).

> There is no rationale whatsoever for continuing any tax subsidies for fossil fuel producers.

So now is a perfect time to re-evaluate why the American taxpayer should subsidize fossil fuel production. A rollback of the dozen or so federal tax incentives now given out to the oil and gas industry would be a timely topic for a Democratic Congress, if the party succeeds in 2020. That would send a political signal to accompany the market signals the petroleum industry is receiving already from Millennial investors and progressive pension and endowment funds, who are now putting their capital into renewable energy sources -- rather than fossil fuel exploration companies and pipeline infrastructure that may become obsolete or subject to punitive carbon taxes by 2035.[48]

Even if U.S. petroleum production volume eventually declines a bit without its tax subsidies, the price that Americans will pay alternatively for increased renewable energy is not too high for consumers to afford. A $10-15 increase in the prevailing peacetime price range for a barrel of crude oil is sufficient for the shale industry to thrive in the major production regions that cover several states and not just Texas. For gasoline, that works out to less than one dollar per gallon of raw feedstock, which will not bring American consumers and truckers to their knees. Prices might return to 2007 levels, but not higher in peacetime. At that price level, renewable energy infrastructure for solar and wind power becomes increasingly competitive without federal subsidies. So a modest deceleration of the rate of domestic hydrocarbon exploration would actually be beneficial to American interests in the long run. Remember that "The first rule of Holes is to stop digging." If oil and gas investors want to "Drill Baby Drill," they certainly do not need financial encouragement from federal taxpayers.

---

48 A similar "family discussion" needs to be held within the Democratic party, but preferably after the 2020 election, as to whether it makes any environmental and fiscal sense whatsoever to subsidize corn-based ethanol production, which has a very heavy carbon footprint. Even if Iowa is the first-caucus state.

A carbon tax is politically unachievable in 2020, so an escalating industrial greenhouse emissions tax is where to start, ASAP.

Rather than devoting an entire section to the prospects and revenue potential of a carbon tax, this section will dismiss the concept and legislative prospects as politically premature, and fiscally lightweight. Although a compelling case can be made that climate change and global environmental alliances will eventually overwhelm the political clout of the domestic fossil fuel industry and agricultural users, the carbon tax has been a political loser even in Blue states. When the day comes that the nations of the world finally formally agree that collective action on carbon emissions is a global human imperative (as they did decades ago with a chlorofluorocarbon CFC ban to protect the ozone layer), the U.S. will have no choice but to join in. But international political groundwork must be laid, including negotiations with India and China -- whose posture is that they are playing economic catch-up so the affluent countries should take the lead in carbon cutbacks. Both countries anticipate accelerated hydrocarbon consumption as their massive middle classes expand. We need treaties, not tariffs, to secure their cooperation.

Substantial revenue potential is available from global carbon taxation, but that will probably be a 2028 debate as to whether such revenues should be devoted to promotion of renewable energy capacity, tax relief for impacted consumers and workers, or instead to balancing the budget. As for the order of magnitude for carbon tax revenues, there is little doubt that it could raise $100 billion annually nationwide in early years, but less over time. At current levels of U.S. petroleum consumption, a product-based carbon tax rate would have to be almost equal to product prices to move the needle significantly higher than $100 billion in annual revenue. At that point, consumption would decline markedly -- which of course is the environmental purpose of the carbon tax. So its success atmospherically would eventually be its downfall as a revenue generator. The takeaway here: Don't count on a carbon tax to cure a festering U.S. budget deficit.

Nonetheless, one variation of the carbon tax is completely defensible and feasible immediately: A punitive tax on industrial air pollution emissions. These are what economists call "negative externalities." Those are costs that the producer imposes on others, but pays no price for that damage. Industrial emissions taxes can include levies on hydrocarbon-burning electricity generation stations, for which the emissions tax should be implemented incrementally and increase annually. This way, the managers and investors in such plants have clear incentives to convert to the lowest possible carbon footprint (e.g., switch from coal to natural gas). A tax on gas-flaring by drill and refinery operators would be the most obvious and achievable example of an emissions tax that should be implemented in full force after a one-year notification and implementation period. There is simply no excuse for the general population to allow private companies to pollute the airshed with natural gas burnoffs. A stiff tax on this practice will drive the polluters to cleanly capture and process those fossil fuels, which represent about 3½ percent of the world's natural gas output. The "flaring tax" revenue can be devoted to renewables or deficit reduction, and the benefits are both environmental and fiscal in this specific case. The Congressional Budget Office has estimated that a carbon emissions tax could generate as much as $100 billion annually, but that apparently includes non-industrial emissions. It seems more likely that companies would take actions to avoid the tax, and thus reduce the revenue stream; the reduction of negative externalities is the foremost benefit of this tax strategy, with fiscal impacts less measurable but noteworthy: $50 billion annually, possibly less and declining over time, seems like a more realistic order of magnitude for an industrial greenhouse emissions tax.

As to the use of carbon tax proceeds, Democrats must decide whether to favor a "carbon dividend" that returns revenue from carbon taxation to impacted taxpayers,[49] or devote the proceeds to a specified public purpose. Interestingly, several leading firms in the fossil-fuel industry are looking forward to the potential global establishment of a carbon-tax regime, and have proffered the concept of a carbon dividend to demonstrate their good faith in the climate debate.

Beyond these four reasonable tax reforms in the corporate world, it may be wiser to focus more on the Fat Cats themselves, rather than their businesses proper. For those who believe that in the long run, corporations don't pay taxes, but people do, then the better way to address tax equity in the corporate sector may be to focus on the distributions of corporate earnings to individuals. That is where progressive capital gains and dividend taxation, with a keen focus on One Percenters through the Alternative Minimum Tax, may be a better playing field.

Now, back to the building blocks of Tax Reform.

TOPIC 15: Capital Gains and Dividends Taxation

Like many other developed countries, the US taxes certain qualifying investment capital gains and dividends at a preferential, lower tax rate. For those in the top brackets, the benefit is greatest: Ordinary income at the top rate is taxed at the marginal rate of 37 percent, whereas the top rate on capital gains is 20 percent before the 3.8 percent Medicare investment income surtax is applied. Because almost all investors in the top

---

49 Lower-income households could be impacted disproportionately, according to most economic models.

tax bracket pay the Medicare surtax on net investment income (NIIT), their true effective tax rate is 23.8 percent vs. the top marginal rate on salary income of 37 percent, That represents a 35 percent tax savings.

For most middle-income taxpayers, a 15 percent rate on capital gains is applicable, which compares and corresponds with ordinary income tax rates of 22 percent to 32 percent. Those in the lower half of this range would generally not be subject to the 3.8 percent Medicare surtax because their total income would not exceed the NIIT surtax threshold. There is no reason for Democrats to go after these people.

These preferential tax rates for capital gains apply only to investments held for a period of at least one year, which qualifies them as "long-term" gains. The idea that 366 days is a long-term investment holding period is itself debatable. That time requirement has bounced around over the past 50 years, with three-year and five-year periods prevalent under various Presidencies. The discussion of holding periods will resume later in this chapter. Also noteworthy is the relatively recent treatment of qualified dividends[50] as equivalent to capital gains. For many years, it was only capital gains that received the preferential tax rate, but the business lobby finally convinced Congress that dividends are comparable to capital gains as ways that companies and corporate boards reward shareholders. Since 2003, qualified dividends have enjoyed the lower preferential rate, and this rule applies to dividends regardless of the holding period. There are no long-term or short-term dividends, only qualified vs. ordinary dividends based on the criteria mentioned previously. The lobbyists successfully argued that a board decision to declare a dividend, especially a special (one-time)

---

50 For preferential tax purposes, qualified dividends must be issued by an eligible corporation that follows certain prescribed accounting rules, and typically does not include most so-called pass-through companies. The latter are now eligible for a separate tax break that will be discussed later in the "QBID" section of the AMT chapter. Non-qualified dividends include those of many foreign stock issuers whose shares are traded on non-US exchanges, real estate investment trusts (REITs), and master limited partnerships (MLPs) which are prevalent in the oil and gas pipeline industry.

dividend, should not be punished by a higher tax rate than a decision to buy back stock, which has the intended effect of raising the share price by shrinking the share count which usually or eventually facilitates a capital gain[51] *pari passu*.[52] The argument for a lower, preferential rate on dividends includes the indisputable truth that corporate earnings are taxed twice when a dividend is distributed, once at the company level when the profit is earned and again when the investor is paid. Hence, the tax code now assigns equal preference rates to both forms of investor compensation.

With that historical background to describe the lay of the land, the key questions for policy makers are: (1) why should capital gains and dividends receive a preferential rate, (2) if the preference were eliminated, what additional revenues would that generate and (3) what would be the side-effects or undesirable results if any? We will also take a look at a fourth question, which asks what is the logical holding period requirement to differentiate short-term capital gains and long-term capital gains? Finally, inflation adjustments to qualifying long-term capital gains will be given a fresh look, to the surprise of some readers on the Right who have made their case correctly. The remainder of this chapter addresses these questions one at a time.

---

51 Progressives who criticize company stock buy-backs will be interested in the discussion of corporate tax rates and surtaxes on stock buy-backs. From the standpoint of tax policy, the issue is better addressed at the corporate boardroom level, rather than an indirect strategy of punishing or rewarding the investor differentially. If directors face a tax on buybacks but not on dividends and employee compensation, the incentives and disincentives would be obvious and behavior change would be more likely.

52 To economists, *pari passu* means "all else being equal" or "on the same footing." From the Latin "with equal step."

> For the U.S. to prevail in a competitive global
> economy, a modest tax preference for capital
> investment is warranted.

The rationale for a lower capital gains tax rate starts with the premise that the investor has already paid tax on the capital now invested during the process of earning and saving that capital, so a tax on investment income is double-taxation. For some, this is true, but we have already shown that a substantial amount of inherited wealth was never earned or taxed in the first place. The tax code does not legitimize this rationale, because we tax all investors' interest income and short-term capital gains at ordinary tax rates, so obviously the double-taxation argument can only be persuasive in combination with other reasons. The second and more plausible rationale is that equity (ownership rather than lender) investors deserve the lower rate, to compensate the owner-investors for the risk inherent in entrepreneurial and competitive business activity. This risk-based argument is consistent with the federal policy distinction that interest and rent is taxed at the higher ordinary tax rate while capital gains and dividend income enjoy the lower preference rate.[53] For the U.S. to prevail in a competitive global economy, there is good reason to support business investment. Finally, there is the somewhat flimsy but at least pragmatic argument that "other countries give away this tax break, so we must as well" in order to avoid capital flight to lower-tax jurisdictions and tax havens.

Although some of these arguments hold some water, there are counter-points that warrant review. First, the previously taxed capital is not taxed again, only the profits and earnings on that capital. The principal is not taxed for capital gains, so the double-taxation argument

---

53 Later, we deal with the thorny but solvable problem of "capital vs professional risk" in the next chapter on "carried interest," which logically follows this discussion.

is specious on that score. Second, there is a gross inequity in how we reward tax-advantaged risk capital of the One Percenters and the fully-taxed risk capital invested in the most common vehicles used by John and Mary Smith -- which is their IRA and 401k accounts. Although the latter are not taxed when their ordinary income is put into the account, the entire value of the account must eventually be withdrawn at ordinary tax rates during their lifetime or that of their designated beneficiary. There are NO capital gains tax benefits for ordinary investors in their retirement accounts to equal those given to the One Percenters who enjoy preferential rates that save them at least one-third on their tax bills (and even more for their heirs if they take it with them to the grave).[54] All that John and Mary Smith get is the tax-free compounding of their investment income during their working lives, and the hope to pay lower ordinary tax rates in retirement than during their working years when they contributed to the retirement accounts. But ultimately the middle class gets hit with ordinary income tax rates on the back end of their tax savings plan, when withdrawn in their retirement years. Third, much of the dynastic family wealth passed from one generation to another was never taxed along the way. So the double-taxation argument is at best a half-truth, which makes it a half-lie.

In the context of these shades of gray in the "capital gains rate debate," there may be a better solution than the ordinary tax rate: something in-between might avoid an exodus to tax havens, and still give a defensible tax break to middle-class workers and professionals who are climbing the ladder of success as they aspire to become One Percenters and fulfill their American dream -- but still aren't there yet. A fair and logical solution to this conundrum would apply the Alternative Minimum Tax (AMT) with a stiffer top rate for the One Percenters, above 30 percent but below the 37 percent paid by high-income professionals.

---

54 Note: There is no capital gains step-up for estate taxes on IRA and 401k accounts; they are fully taxable at current market value.

> Capital gains and dividend tax rates for One Percenters are 30 percent too low. To avoid punishing middle-class investors, the best way to level the playing field is to include these items in an expanded AMT (Topic 18).

The second question is what does it cost the Treasury now to award these tax breaks to high-income investors, and what additional revenue could be gleaned if these preferences were reformed in one way or another? The first part of this question is relatively simple: The latest official estimates of the annual "tax expenditure" for capital gains and dividend preference rates were $128 billion, according to the Congressional Joint Committee on Taxation. That number implies that all such income would be taxed at ordinary rates without any adverse economic consequences. It is a lot of money, but it won't pay for Medicare for All, or free college tuition, or other populist and socialist spending plans. Other policy solutions, which may leave the tax benefits intact for middle-class taxpayers, or focus entirely on the One Percenters, or apply a blended "compromise" rate midway between the two polar extremes, would yield correspondingly lower revenue gains. An AMT on capital gains should generate somewhere between one-half and two-thirds of the current tax expenditure, depending on its calibration.

Importantly, the AMT could also apply to "carried interest" compensation of private investment fund managers who now dodge ordinary income taxes by claiming their zero-risk cut of clients' profits is a capital gain. Topic 16 below explains this issue and the appropriate remedial tax reform concepts.

As to side effects from tax-avoidance expatriation, the answer is probably "some but negligible." Undoubtedly there will be some international tax dodgers, just as there are New York mega-millionaires and billionaires who have now located in Florida to escape state and local income taxes now that the SALT tax deduction has been capped. Some high-profile, prosperous startup CEOs will move their digital stock certificates and their personal income tax domicile to offshore havens. Whether that number comes up to three or four percent of the total, nobody can say; but it seems highly unlikely that the tax-dodging ex-pats will number more than that. Far more additional revenue will be gained than what is lost, especially if all preference income is subject to AMT to avoid tax-shopping investors who tilt their holdings to the investment vehicles with the lowest U.S. tax rate.

Finally, to answer the fourth question posed in this section, the minimum holding period for long-term capital gains is hardly what any investment professional would call long term. Long-term investors are not near-sighted. They provide the solid base of shareholder capital that American corporations need in order to finance their businesses. No company can sustain itself if all its shareholders sell their holdings within one year of purchase; America's capitalist corporate model would collapse.

There is no magic number to guide tax policy here, but back in the 1960s, the long-term capital gains tax rate applied only to gains derived from investments made for at least three years. In the late 1930s the holding period was ten years. There was a brief interlude during the second Bush administration when a complex multi-year holding period schedule with a special 5-year rate was used; that model was advocated by Presidential candidate Hillary Clinton, but with no discernable following.

> Longer holding periods for tax preferences should be required. Long-term capital gains should be indexed for inflation. That would be a fair *legislative* compromise, and genuine tax reform.

As a matter of principal, Congress can easily justify raising the holding period requirement to two years immediately, and escalating it incrementally to three years thereafter. The additional revenue from this change would not be huge, probably in the ballpark range of $10 billion annually. But as with estate taxes, the principle is important here: Short-term trading is not an investment and does not deserve preferential tax rates. "Fast Money" traders should pay ordinary income taxes, much to the chagrin of the television show hosts, book promoters and brokers who pitch short-term trades to retail speculators on the false premise that market timing is an investment. Most successful traders are professionals, not part-time amateurs. If trading is a learned skill, as they promote, then it should be taxed as earned income, at ordinary tax rates.[55] And let's not forget that gamblers' winnings are taxed as ordinary income, so lucky part-time stock traders belong in this category also.

Before concluding this chapter on capital gains tax reform, it is only fair to revisit an issue that has been advanced repeatedly by conservative think tanks and the investor class they serve: indexation of capital gains. As a matter of principle, government should not profit from inflation. Here, it is time to give the devil his due, but only with respect to assets held a significantly long period of time, even longer than the holding period for long-term capital gains tax preferences. A better and simple tax paradigm would be to allow investors who hold assets for

---

55 The "prudent person rule," long used in fiduciary law says that investments are held "not in regard to speculation, but in regard to the permanent disposition of their funds, considering the probable income, as well as the probable safety of the capital to be invested."

five or more years to escalate their tax cost (basis) by an inflation index, so that capital gains taxes only apply to *real* appreciation and not just inflationary appreciation. For assets held for shorter time periods, the inflation factor is relatively negligible in the first place, and it is really the longer-term investments that were legitimately bought and held for the longer periods that deserve consideration.

Given that the incumbent Administration has proposed indexing by executive order, please note that the Constitution assigns the power to tax and to write tax law to the Congress, not the White House. Inflation indexing is a substantive tax deduction that cannot and should not be granted by executive edict.

TOPIC 16: Carried interest

One of the greatest tax-avoidance schemes ever devised in the United States is called "carried interest." It's how hedge fund tycoons, real estate developers and private equity fund managers have managed to avoid paying billions of dollars in taxes for the work they do, without ever investing a nickel of their own money. Instead of paying taxes for earned income, which is taxed at ordinary tax rates (now 37 percent at the upper end), these sharpies have figured out how to take a "cut" of the profits on the investment funds and projects they manage, and enjoy all the benefits of lower (20 percent) capital gains tax preferences without investing their own money. Nice work if you can get it. Especially because they don't have to pay 20 percent of the losses.

Only the investors who risk their capital are subject to losses of their investment principal.

The author will never forget sitting aside a lake in the Pacific Northwest with a friend of the family who does this for a living. When asked how he could justify the tax breaks he gets for what is essentially a management function, he tried to pitch it this way: "Essentially, for tax purposes, what we do is create a security (out of thin air) that has a zero cost basis so that it qualifies for capital gains. The security is a claim on the profits derived from future value of the fund." So if the investors put in $10 million of their actual cash, and the fund is later worth $20 million, he gets 20 percent of the $10 million profit, which in this case would be $2 million. Now, imagine how this works for a private equity fund that earns a 20 percent compounded annual investment return (which is the normal industry target, by the way) over 10 years. In that case, the $10 million grows to $60 million, generating a $50 million profit for which the manager receives $10 million. And that gets taxed at 20 percent, not 37 percent. So the tax benefit alone, for this carried interest, is worth $1.7 million. Again, nice work if you can get it.

> Carried interest is how high-fee money managers dodge 35 percent of their tax bills without risking a nickel of their own capital. It should be subject to AMT taxation.

Investors in his fund would each have to put in $2 million to start, in order to enjoy the same returns, for which they also get the same tax benefit. The difference is that they must risk real money in the game, and take a gamble with their capital that he never has to take. By comparison, he could have instead taken employment as a mutual fund manager who gets paid salaries and bonuses for investing in stocks or bonds. But those dollars are taxed as ordinary income and he would have paid well over $3 million in taxes on those "ordinary" earnings over the same 10 years (at least 50 percent more).

Now think about what the profits and the carried interest tax loophole looks like if the fund's initial investments are not $10 million, but $100 million or more, which is not uncommon in the world of private equity funds, especially those that collect pension fund investments. Even if the fund earns a lower double-digit rate of return, a billion-dollar investment fund can generate gazillionaire incomes for the managing partners.

What is particularly infuriating to average Americans is that middle class investors can't even play in this game with their own savings. The entry requirements for an initial investment in these private funds are far too high for most folks. The smaller deals are not readily available for an IRA or 401K account. Only millionaires are allowed to join most of these partnerships.[56] Pension funds do invest here, as part of their diversified portfolios, but that gets blended in with their 2 percent Treasury bond yields, and the retiree just gets a fixed annual payment from the fund, not a profit-sharing sliver. So this game is rigged for the upper class and the Wall Street partnerships that capture these tax benefits for themselves and their cronies. This playground of privilege will only get worse as private equity, especially in Silicon Valley where our nation's innovation economy is centered, has morphed into a breeding ground for what are called "unicorn" companies that don't go public until their market valuations are staggering, such as Uber in 2019. The unicorns now provide rich rewards to the private equity fund managers with carried interest, giving them megamillion-dollar and even 8-figure profits as a group, taxed at a 20 percent capital gains rate for

---

56 To enjoy exemption from S.E.C. regulations, these funds typically accept only "accredited investors." That automatically and systematically excludes the middle class.

their risk-free compensation as the fund managers -- a lower rate than a single worker with taxable salary income of $40,000!

In real estate development, it's the same game. There it's called a "promote" but it is still a sub-category of carried interest. Until recently, some of these real estate moguls enjoyed a zero-tax rate on certain qualified "promotes" but now they generally belong to the same category of tax preferences, including the new "passthrough" tax deduction that is discussed in the next chapter.

This is not to say that that these private fund managers and real estate tycoons don't invest their own money in their funds and their projects. Many do. They get the benefits of lower capital gains taxes on those at-risk profits also, but unlike the average retail stock market investor, they have full insider information about what is happening with their money while it's still privately held. They make their real money before a stock goes public on the stock exchanges, where retail investors get their hand-me-downs and second-hand shares.

Readers may wonder where the term "carried interest" came from. It goes all the way back to the Medieval times of the European ship captains and trade merchants who would raise royal and private money to fund an expedition. This was risky business. Ships laden with treasure and goods could sink for any number of reasons, including piracy. The financiers wanted some assurance that the captain wouldn't jump ship at the first sign of trouble, or yield control of the vessel to Jolly Roger and his crew without a fight. So they invented the novel concept of carried interest, which was the captain's 20 percent share of the profits on the cargo he brought back. It was in his direct *interest* to *carry* the goods home in good condition, and thereby arose the term. What is remarkable is that the 20 percent number has survived unchanged for an entire millennium (that's 1000 years since the founding merchants of Venice!) and persists to this day.[57] But nowadays most seafaring shippers have private insurance on their cargos, and carried interest is all about financial schemes and not marine transport.

There is no societal benefit from the tax preference given for carried interest. It's "earned income in drag." The money-manager's opportunity to earn income without risking one's capital is too good to pass up. The legal fiction of calling it a pseudo-security is a ruse. But there is an entrepreneurial aspect of these deals that can arguably justify giving a modest tax break to the people who devote every waking hour to maximizing their investors' returns on capital, which is why this book recommends that carried interest income be subject to the Alternative Minimum Tax, as described and explained below. In fairness, carried interest does reward these managers for their lost time, which they put at-risk if the expected profits don't materialize. That arguably warrants a few percentage points of tax preferences -- just not a 46 percent reduction in their tax bill. Like several other tax preference items discussed in this section, carried interest is a hybrid activity, so a compromise between capital gains treatment and ordinary tax rates is equitable and sensible.

That said, there should be one exception to the benefits of this hybrid tax rate that deserves mention, in deference to the labor movement: When profits and thus carried interest are earned by a fund or a project that deliberately puts people out of work, such as a leveraged buyout or a union-busting hotel restructuring, then the entire carried interest should be taxable at ordinary income tax rates. Giving tax breaks to capitalists who put others out of work is just bad public policy. Congress cannot outlaw their contractual share of these pseudo-profits, but these modern-day "captains" need to pay ordinary income taxes when they slash payrolls by restructuring and cost-cutting to create a profit for investors. Those affected workers don't pay income taxes on

---

57 Even though today's "captains" of 20 percent carried-interest deals never risk their lives to fight pirates!

their lost wages, so Uncle Sam suffers from these deals. No Liberal or Progressive or Centrist Democrat should disagree on this point.

TOPIC 17: Passthough business income tax deduction (QBID)

. . . .

The newest billionaire tax loophole, under the Trump Tax Cuts of 2017, is the "qualified business income deduction" (QBID), also known as the "passthrough" deduction for businesses that don't pay taxes as corporations. It's costing the U.S. Treasury $33 billion annually in lost tax revenue.

It's not hard to figure out who promoted this tax break, given that several officials in the White House have made their fortunes in real estate and business partnerships. Likewise for the Koch brothers, who are magnanimous campaign donors to pro-business causes, who just coincidentally head up a private company. In fact, the original version of this tax gimmick was targeted almost entirely at the big-money Fat Cats. Then the small businesses lobby (National Federation of Small Businesses) jumped onto the bandwagon as the 2017 tax bill was being railroaded through Congress. At least now it also provides some tax advantages to smaller sole proprietors, family farmers, independent contractors (such as realtors and Uber drivers) and eligible small businesses.[58] What started out as a "passthrough" deduction for the wealthiest partnerships and big private companies was ultimately re-named

---

58 To avoid going completely overboard and risking public outrage, the rules are restrictive for certain professions, so that most high-paid doctors, lawyers and accountants cannot duck ordinary income taxes on their professional fee-for-services income without setting up an elaborate investment partnership structure.

the Qualified Business Income Deduction in order to include sole proprietors and independent contractors who don't have all the legal shell companies and partnerships that this gimmick was originally designed to benefit.

> The passthrough tax deduction gives a needless 20 percent tax break to billionaire business owners. The "QBID" loophole *never* had a mathematical rationale that made sense. It should be capped, just like state and local tax (SALT) deductions

The QBID loophole gives these taxpayers a 20 percent tax deduction from their business profits, similar to the taxpayers' personal itemized deductions but in addition to those. So if Sally Realtor collects $80,000 in commissions and declares $15,000 in expenses (like her vehicle costs, dues and home office), her business income would be $65,000 and the QBID deduction would reduce that by 20 percent or $13,000. It's no wonder that the small business lobby pushed for this candy, and it's also no wonder that GOP politicians will be reminding small businesses, independent contractors, farmers and realtors that it was Trump's baby all along.

And wait -- There's more! Unlike the new GOP ceiling on personal itemized tax deductions for state and local taxes, which clobbered the Blue states' middle-income taxpayers, there is no ceiling on this QBID deduction! If a private company's business profits are $1 million or $100 million, the owners and partners get this 20 percent off the top on the entire profit without any limit. Do you see an irony there? It turns out that two-thirds ($33/$57 billion) of the new SALT-deduction-cap revenues were indirectly turned over to the QBID clan. For those readers now subject to the $10,000 annual SALT deduction ceiling, that's where your money went. Very little actually went to work for lower tax rates.

There is not a single wage-earner or salaried professional who wouldn't like to also get a 20 percent tax deduction for just showing up at the workplace. So how did this come to be?

The political and theoretical rationale for this tax break is what some have called "penis envy" from the private-company owners who considered it unfair that they don't get to enjoy a lower tax rate on their income the way a public-company shareholder does on their dividends, which are taxed at the lower capital gains rate (15 percent or 20 percent, depending on total income). For tax purposes, all of their companies' income is "passed through" to them as the owners and then becomes taxable at ordinary income tax rates.[59] Now mind you, the private-company owners never pay the corporate tax that applies to "C" corporations, which includes most of the stock-exchange companies. They do, however get to enjoy all the expense write-offs and benefits of depreciation allowances and private jets and such. But the Trump Tax Cut bill was cutting corporate tax rates down to 21 percent (from a top rate of 35 percent), so they really felt left out of this party. Then arose the crafty lobbyists who invented the "passthrough company" tax deduction. This new loophole was rationalized as the best way to provide comparable tax advantages to the privately held companies. They weren't thinking about the little guy when this was first proposed, but once the GOP realized the political bonanza they would garner by extending it to small businesses and farmers, it was unstoppable.

As a matter of public finance mathematics, all of this was actually hocus-pocus. Corporations now pay taxes on their profits at the new 21 percent rate, and their wealthier investors in turn must pay taxes

---

59 If they sell their company, they would of course be liable for, and pay capital gains on the appreciation. So this is all about taxes on operating earnings, the profits earned annually by companies whether public or private.

on dividends they distribute at a 20 percent rate. So top-tier corporate income is now double-taxed at a higher combined rate[60] that is the same as the very top private company owners' ordinary income tax rate of 37 percent.[61] Business owners and private partners in lower tax brackets already pay less in taxes than comparable double-taxed shareholders in public companies.

This tax perk is completely under the radar for most voters. Unless they are themselves an independent contractor, an Uber driver, realtor, small business operator or a farmer, and their tax advisor or tax software pointed it out to them before April 15, most Democrats don't even know that this loophole exists. And it's too esoteric a topic to rile up the crowd at a campaign rally or party convention. But as you can see, there is some big money involved here, which needs to be part of tax reform.

Although the QBID deduction is just plain-stupid tax math, Democrats will be even stupider to take this lollipop away from the small business and farm community as their first move out of the gate if they win in 2020. That is just political suicide. Even though these small fry were never part of the donor base or the intellectual rationale for the QBID deduction, it's now baked into their 2018 tax returns. There are 10 million self-employed taxpayers in this country.[62] That is a huge bloc of voters to irritate, alienate and scare away. Any roll-backs on the lower end of the income spectrum would need to be gradual and incremental.

---

60 This is actually the justifiable reason that dividend income is properly taxed at a lower rate than ordinary income.

61 Tax impact is multiplicative not additive. For the effective rate on corporate dividends, it's "1 minus [0.79 (the reciprocal of 21 percent) times 0.8 (the reciprocal of 20 percent)]" which equals 37 percent. That just happens to be the top rate on ordinary income. So QBID is mathematically a complete give-away, because private company owners' capital was **not** disadvantaged when all these tax rates were cut in 2017.

62 The number of freelancers is estimated to be 57 million, but only a fraction of them file tax returns as self-employed. However, as the "gig" economy grows, this number will escalate.

Although one can easily argue that the deductible percentage should be shaved from 20 percent to a lower number such as 10-15 percent over three or four years to make the adjustment gradual, that still does not address the gross inequity of the entire arrangement. The smarter way to achieve tax reform here is to cap the QBID and take it away from the One Percenters, which is where the giveaway is greatest, from a revenue standpoint.

So let's start with a cap on the QBID. Just as there is now a federal limit on the SALT deduction, Democrats could put a ceiling on the QBID deduction, if they sweep the election in 2020. Some might like to make it the same dollar limit as the SALT deduction, and use the reclaimed revenue to raise the SALT cap. That would probably end up with a number between $15,000 and $18,00 for both deduction ceilings, which would arithmetically cap out the QBID deduction for net business income (after expenses) above $90,000. In our previous example, Sally Realtor could still enjoy her $13,000 QBID deduction, since her net business income is less than $90,000. Every taxpayer now claiming a passthrough deduction could deduct up to that limit and no more. There is a certain symmetry and logic to this formula, on the basis that what is good for the goose is good for the gander.

A second remedial reform, and this doesn't need to be mutually exclusive, is to phase out (or even eliminate) the QBID deduction when calculating the Alternative Minimum Tax (AMT). That idea is discussed in Topic 18 below in much more detail: the preview here is that for taxpayers with the highest income, they should pay a minimum tax on all income. A reformed AMT would have few or no deductions and exemptions for income beyond the reach of the middle class. That way, we finally close the various loopholes that Fat Cats enjoy, including this one.

To illustrate, a combination of these two reforms could look like this: Cap the QBID deduction at $20,000, which cuts off the tax break for business income above $100,000 but leaves it intact for everybody below that level, including those earning or collecting more. That supports progressivity. Then, if the taxpayer's total income exceeds the levels where AMT kicks in, the deduction itself should be phased out in the AMT calculation, so that the minimum tax rate applies to all of the net business income. The phase-out will amplify the progressivity of these reforms. Small businesses, contractors, realtors, gig workers and farmers raking in less than $100,000 after expenses will not have anything to worry about, because neither the cap nor the AMT will affect them. They can remain the favored champions of Free Enterprise and Free Markets. The "Five Percenters" in this occupational cluster with six-figure incomes below a half million dollars will still get a tax break on their first $100,000 but nothing beyond that. In tandem, these two tax reforms focus only on the One Percenters.

So now, let's move on to that oft-heralded Alternative Minimum Tax. Some readers will find this topic technical and complex, but it's impossible to address tax reform intelligently without understanding AMT and knowing how to use it wisely, shrewdly and progressively.

TOPIC 18: The Alternative Minimum Tax (AMT)

· ·

The famous billionaire Warren Buffet of Berkshire Hathaway stated long ago that there is something wrong with a tax code that allows him to pay a lower rate than his secretary.

The best way to remedy this inequity is through the AMT. In fact, it is probably the only way. Every Liberal and every Progressive who wants to promote tax reform must understand the AMT, why it has failed, and how to fix it.

The AMT is not a new idea. Two generations ago, the federal tax code was already overloaded with various tax preferences and loopholes. With help from their friends in Washington, rich taxpayers had figured out how to dodge the 70 percent marginal rate. So reformers came up with a reasonable and popular idea, a minimum tax. The original concept was simple, but its application became very complicated and ultimately counterproductive. As they say, the devil is in the details, and that certainly applied to the AMT. The complexity-devil will continue to favor fat cats unless Democrats get their act together and push for an AMT that actually works. To do so, this basic tax reform concept now needs to be polished up for the 2020 elections as a major step to fix the worst giveaways of the Trump Tax Cuts.

Today's AMT is a soldier armed only with a slingshot and one pebble. Sensible AMT reform must target *all* income sources of the wealthiest Americans who use every loophole they can to dodge taxes. The Trump AMT is like a gold-panning sieve with the mesh so wide that the nuggets fall through. As a result, most Fat Cat investors pay lower effective tax rates than many successful professional employees, athletes, and skilled managers in our economy, because the productive taxpayers with earned professional income now pay higher tax rates than the investment class that profits from investment tax breaks and inherited wealth.

A progressive, reformed AMT needs to address income inequality and tax avoidance head on, without punishing middle class Americans. And it needs to be less complicated, not more complex, so that there are fewer ways to circumvent a reasonable and fair minimum tax rate on *all* income regardless of its source.

> The AMT is the best way to bridge the gap between taxes on labor and capital. It is also the only way to provide a common tax rate for the myriad tax preferences now baked into law.

Democrats will need to educate and persuade their members on the left wing that the AMT is America's best and fairest way to bridge the gap between taxes on labor and taxes on capital. The AMT is also the only way to apply a common tax rate to the dozen or so tax preferences that have been built into the tax code to benefit the rich far more than the middle class. AMT reform can accomplish this without completely upending the entire economy and America's place in the modern global marketplace for capital investment. Smart AMT reform will still allow the middle class to benefit from saving and investing, to build financial security for themselves and their families. Smart AMT reform fosters social mobility, for young entrepreneurs and ambitious professionals who aspire to join the One Percent club; nothing is taken away from them as they climb that ladder of aspiration and success. Progressive AMT reform turns the tables on the fat cats by preserving the major investment incentives for the 99 Percenters, while closing the tax loopholes for the rich. Prudence here -- not sloganeering and class warfare -- is essential to our long-term economic prosperity as the nation that leads the Free World and the global marketplace. Only with careful design of fiscal policies can we pay for the social benefits that most Americans want our taxes to subsidize. The GOP's reckless tax cuts have opened the field for thinking Democrats and Independents to assert financial responsibility and sustainability, which is what most Americans want to see. Smart AMT reform is central to that generational opportunity. This chapter will show how to do it.

To provide some context for those in the socialist fringe who howl in the wind to promote a 70 percent top tax rate, it must be noted that back when the first minimum tax became law, the top federal income tax rate was 70 percent. And that was long before states like California and New York had jacked up their own top income tax rates to today's levels. Nowadays, a 70 percent federal rate would essentially confiscate virtually all incremental personal income at that level, once it is combined with state income taxes, local property taxes and multi-jurisdictional sales taxes. That is what prompted conservative economist Arthur Laffer to draw his famous "Laffer curve" on a napkin and then a blackboard, to illustrate with an upside-down "U" that higher tax rates could actually produce lower GDP and lower tax revenues. The point here is that tax avoidance becomes more and more aggressive the higher the marginal tax rate on the rich, so the optimal solution was never a 70 percent tax bracket -- which was almost never paid by anybody when it was on the books.

Politically, AMT reform would be half a loaf, to the Socialist extremists. But the rest of us would say that a half a loaf is far better than none. And importantly, AMT reform can actually generate more than half of the loaf of revenues lost from "tax expenditures" that favor the wealthiest Americans, as this chapter will show. It is economic ignorance and political suicide to push the tax rates beyond the point of diminishing returns. The cost-benefit for the federal budget and for Middle American workers is just not there. National economic stagnation is a clear risk of setting the tax rates unreasonably high. AMT reform is the "middle way," as the Chinese would say.

> Sensible AMT reform must target *all* income sources of the wealthiest Americans. $125 billion annually can be raised through progressive and comprehensive AMT reform.

When combined with other reforms presented in this book, a progressive AMT will raise needed revenue without clobbering the middle class. AMT reform can target the One Percenters and *not* the salaried professionals, farmers, gig workers, independent contractors and agents, and small business owners who are still reaching to achieve the American dream. That's how to win back the White House and a sustainable majority in Congress.

First, a little bit of the history of the AMT. The first "minimum tax" was enacted in 1969. That's right, it started in the Nixon era! Back then, Treasury secretary Joseph Barr identified 155 fat cat taxpayers who paid no federal income tax. None. Nada. Zero. Under the law, even without cheating, they had taken advantage of so many deductions and tax preferences and exemptions that their federal income tax was zero. This report offended public sensibility and defied anybody in either political party to characterize the U.S. tax code as progressive and fair.

Initially, the 1969 minimum tax was enacted as an add-on tax of 10 percent of certain income. It was additive; just a tax added to other taxes. We call that a surtax, similar in ways to the 3.8 percent Medicare-NIIT surtax on investment income that took effect in 2012 as part of the "Obamacare" Affordable Care Act. The 1969 surtax was "repealed and replaced" in the tax code by the AMT in 1982.

By design, AMT is a parallel tax system: Taxpayers are essentially required to calculate their taxes the "regular way," then perform a separate AMT calculation, and then pay the higher of the two taxes. For most taxpayers, this requires specialized tax software or hiring a tax preparation firm like H&R Block to run the numbers. Most taxpayers are clueless as to how the math actually works.

The AMT sought to apply a higher tax rate to a few forms of "preference" income. But it only went halfway. It included capital gains and dividend income to determine *whether* AMT would apply, but it didn't actually *apply* the AMT tax rate directly to those sources of investment income, which still remain subject to a preferential maximum rate of 20 percent. It also reduced the amount of itemized deductions a taxpayer could claim, and then applied a moderate but higher tax rate to the resulting income number. The problem has always been that these adjustments to income and deductions didn't really solve the problem, and failed to close many of the tax loopholes used by Wall Streeters, Fat Cats, and Silver Spooners.

And here's the rub: It backfired on the well-intended tax reformers of 1982. The AMT became a Frankenstein tax that did almost nothing to reduce tax inequality and tax avoidance. Instead it creeped into middle class households that were never an under-taxed population in the first place.

The irony was that two-income professional couples, especially those who resided in (often Blue) states and localities with higher taxes approved by voters and their local representatives, were hit with an AMT tax bill. They were subjected to the AMT even though they had very little Wall Street income. Meanwhile, many of the tax-dodgers living in penthouses and mansions paid very little in AMT, and still enjoyed the lower preferential tax rates on their investments.

Another flaw of the AMT has always been that its top rate has always been relatively modest at less than 30 percent, nowhere near the top rate on ordinary earned income. Today, the top AMT rate is 28 percent whereas ordinary income is taxed at 40 percent at the upper level when the Medicare surtax is applicable. A single mother's taxable salary income over $161,000 is taxed at 32 percent. So it's typically the case that capitalists and trust fund heritors will enjoy lower tax rates under the AMT than "high paid ditchdiggers"[63] working for salaries and bonuses.

---

63 This is actually a label once used by a former Treasury official to describe highly taxed professionals. True story.

The original AMT also failed to include inflation adjustments, so that each year, more and more members of the two-income professional middle class were pushed into the AMT because it took away a good chunk of their tax deductions. Mind you, these folks weren't paying AMT on oil royalties, real estate profits, commodity speculation and hedge fund management fees. They were paying AMT because they couldn't deduct their local taxes in a bizarre parallel universe.

> A reformed AMT should never apply to middle-class salary and wage income. It should focus on One Percenters.

So it was that in 2017, Trump and the Congressional Republicans "solved" the most visible AMT problem for many taxpayers. They capped the federal deduction for state and local taxes, *aka* the SALT deduction, and shaved the tax rates on ordinary income a wee bit. Instead of subjecting middle-class taxpayers to the AMT on their SALT deductions, the GOP tax bill just took it away from us altogether! So the good news is that many folks can now avoid the AMT, along with richer taxpayers. But the bad news is that millions of Americans lost a major and important tax deduction for the upper middle class in many of the coastal Blue states. Meanwhile, the richest taxpayers got the lion's share of the Trump tax cuts. For the GOP tax sharpshooters, it was sweet revenge. "Get 'em while they are down, and punish those tax-and-spend liberals where they live."

What the GOP didn't take away was the AMT exemptions for all kinds of income that capitalists have engineered for tax preferences, and income that the wealthiest families in America routinely enjoy from passive (i.e. "do nothing") investments. These tax preferences are still taxed at rates below the ordinary income taxes that apply to salaries and wages, cash bonuses, bank and money market interest, and retirement distributions from IRAs and 401k plans. In other words, the AMT has failed to make a dent in the yawning gap between low preferential tax rates for rich investors and higher "ordinary" tax rates for anybody who receives a W-2 for earned income.

So, where do we start? We begin with tax justice and broad-brush progressivity in the tax code as the first objective. Raising revenue is secondary here, although these reforms will clearly help balance the federal budget, and sustain important social insurance programs like Medicaid. However, AMT reform will never yield enough revenue to underwrite huge new budget-busting social programs.

There are three features that a progressive AMT must include: (1) It must apply to all income over $500,000 in any year for married taxpayers, $300,000 if single (adjusted hereafter for inflation). (2) The rate should be somewhere in the range of 33-36 percent of such income over that level. (3) AMT income must include all preference distributions from trust funds and beneficiary accounts except for the grantor's surviving spouse.[64] Let's take these one at a time.

First, it is important to focus and target the AMT reform where it's needed the most, and to exclude the 99 percent of Americans who are not getting or keeping rich on tax avoidance. Liberals, Progressives and Centrists can quibble over where to draw the line, but let's remember that family dynasties in America are not built and sustained by people with household incomes below a half million dollars annually. They are affluent but they are not rich. And the lower on the income scale the AMT goes, the greater the risk that Democrats will step into the trap that Congress designed in the 1982 AMT: it will creep right back into

---

64 Or registered domestic partner, which *should* be treated as equivalent to a spouse under federal tax laws. That's a completely separate discussion in which the author advocates and intends parity and equivalence.

the middle class, and those people will vote and contribute Republican just to protect their pocketbooks.

> For those making over $500,000, their AMT must tax their capital gains, dividends, interest income, carried interest, commodity trading profits, fossil fuel subsidies, and real estate loopholes at rates of or above 33 percent. For ultra-millionaires and billionaires, a higher AMT rate (but less than 50 percent), would be more feasible than a tax on wealth.

Thus, the new definition of income subject to the AMT tax must be expanded to include almost everything over $500,000. That eliminates virtually every major tax loophole, preference and exemption now allowed under the federal tax code. The AMT must tax capital gains on all investments including real estate, dividend income, commodity trader profits, tax-sheltered real estate operating and rental income, fossil fuel extraction subsidies, private partnership income, and "carried interest" loopholes claimed and collected by investment fund managers for work they perform without themselves investing, for starters.

The only exception that makes any real sense is interest on tax-free "public purpose" municipal bonds. There is a Federalist constitutional and public policy reason for this one exception, which is called "reciprocal tax immunity." As a matter of public policy, the states do not tax U.S. treasury bond interest, and the IRS does not tax state and local government interest payments to bond investors. As long as the interest payments for municipal infrastructure are "subsidized" by lower borrowing rates resulting from the bonds' tax exemption, the result is lower costs for public facilities, and that is generally deemed a "social good."[65] However, "private activity" bonds issued to underwrite sports stadiums that benefit billionaire owners of football teams are still subject to the AMT, so this issue has been hashed out already, for the most part.

The tax forms now in use already provide an easy way to identify all of this AMT income. There is a line called "adjusted gross income" or AGI on Form 1040, which captures most but not all of the income that should be subject to the new AMT. It includes many of the preference items such as capital gains, preferential dividend income, commodity trading profits, etc. All we need to do for the AMT is to add a few items such as those mentioned above on a separate form as add-on items, to then calculate what IRS can call "AMT income." Only if that total exceeds $500,000 for married taxpayers ($300,000 single) should the proposed higher AMT tax rate apply. For those coming up with a lower number, it's business as usual under the current tax code.

There are some fine points of tax policy that are explained in a foot-note here, for those interested in technical details. They are not import-ant to the 2020 campaigns. [66]

---

65 It would actually cost the U.S. Treasury less to just send checks to states and localities every year to offset the higher costs of debt service if they instead issue taxable bonds, but civic leaders fear that eventually Congress would renege and leave them with higher interest payments and lost subsidies. If such a "taxable bond *option*" were made available perma-nently on an elective basis, however, there would be no more rationale to thereafter shelter the remaining tax-exempt bonds from AMT. See Topic 29, which also explains social goods.

66 Whether there should be ANY deductions from this AMT income is debatable The SALT deductions and mortgage interest deductions have already been capped, so essentially what we have left is charitable deductions and extraordinary medical expenses. Whether to allow or disallow those deductions from AMT taxation is a secondary consideration for this book. A fair case can be made to allow one-half of those deductions to split the baby and not quibble over it. What does need to change, however, is how the Trump Tax Cuts changed the AMT *exemptions* rules to shelter and benefit millionaires. Under the AMT, there is an exemption for the first $112,000 of income for married couples, $72,000 for singles, before applying the AMT tax rate. Before Trump, the AMT exemption was phased out for joint incomes over $160,000. The GOP raised that phase-out to $1 million of adjusted gross income which is well above the top 1 percent of household incomes. To calibrate more closely to the top 1 percent income level, the exemption needs to be dialed back to the

Second, the AMT tax rate can be left at its current (26-28 percent) levels for income under $500,000/$300,000 (married/single), using the current definitions of AMT income rather than imposing a higher rate on the prosperous middle class. But for those above that level, the top AMT rate should be somewhere in the range of 33-36 percent on all AMT-AGI income over that threshold *with no AMT exemptions.* The higher number is workable if it includes and supplants the Medicare/Obamacare "net investment income tax" for these taxpayers, and the lower number can apply if they remain separately liable for NIIT.[67]

Taxpayers with total AMT income below the threshold income levels recommended here can continue to benefit from the AMT formulas as presently written. This retains an element of progressivity for the upper middle class without applying a new and higher tax rate to them. Retirees who worked hard, saved, and invested carefully all their lives in order to enjoy a moderately affluent retirement income won't pay a nickel of net AMT taxes unless their dividends and capital gains kick now them into a stiffer bracket. Young entrepreneurs and aspiring capitalists can enjoy the lower tax rates that Congress has bestowed on risk-takers as they climb the ladder of success -- until they achieve their goal of becoming One Percenters. After that, they need to step up to a higher tax rate. That's progressive.

So, how much new tax revenue could be collected from this higher tax rate, on these various forms of tax preference items? The best place to start is the "tax expenditure" for capital gains and dividends, which enjoy lower rates. That number was estimated by the Congressional Joint Committee on Taxation to be approximately $128 billion in 2018. Clearly, that gross number is higher than what an AMT would capture,

---

$500,000 level ($300,000 single) so that the exemption still protects the middle class, but phases out quickly for the One Percenters.

67 These folks can pay a blended 27 percent on the AMT income below $500,000 if their AMT income exceeds that level, and the top marginal rate above it, just to keep the calculation straightforward for that elite group.

because the official tax expenditure calculations assume that taxpayers would pay ordinary income taxes on all their preference income, whereas the AMT rate proposed here is lower. But even so, the ballpark range would be at least two-thirds of that number, and would be even more when hedge fund and private equity managers' carried interest, and commodity trader profits are included. We also now have an official federal estimate for the new private-company passthrough tax deduction, in the range of $33 billion of lost tax revenue -- of which the lion's share goes to the One Percenters. So, all told, it is pretty clear that a reformed AMT could generate something around $100 billion of new tax revenue.

Now THAT is real money! This $100 billion can be raised annually without driving upper middle -income voters to the dark side. Nor would it drive investors to the Cayman Islands and the Isle of Man to evade U.S. taxation.

Third, and this will prove to be one of the three most novel and agitating ideas proposed in this book, an individual's AMT tax base should include ALL distributions from family trusts and similar transfers at death unless the beneficiary is the deceased grantor's surviving spouse or legal equivalent.

> A reformed AMT should also tax the trust fund distributions received by "Silver Spooners" from their parents' and grandparents' estates.

This is how a reformed AMT can begin to address wealth inequality and tax equity at the same time. What this means is that trust fund beneficiaries who were not married to the grantor must pay the AMT tax on their entire annual distribution, including both income and *principal,* if their annual income including such distributions exceeds the $500,000/$300,000 threshold adjusted for inflation.

For example, if Donald Trump hypothetically has created a family trust that passes assets to his spouse Melania and his children and grandchildren, the money each child and grandchild receives from the trust each year would be subject to the new AMT, regardless of whether it is income or principal. As his surviving spouse, Melania would receive her distributions subject only to AMT taxes on the income generated by the assets in her trust account (and not the principal in which she has a legitimate non-taxable marital interest).

Note that there is no exception for municipal bond interest in this case. That's the one exception to the exemption of muni bond interest discussed previously. Trustees can always shuffle the deck with the investment portfolio if it's in the beneficiary's best interests to invest elsewhere. In 2013, only 4 percent of the assets in taxable estates consisted of state and municipal bonds, which is trivial in the aggregate. The actual budgetary impact on states and municipalities from making this sliver of their bond interest taxable is negligible. Furthermore, that issue of Constitutional law was already decided by the Supreme Court in 1988 in *South Carolina v Baker*, which held that by law, Congress can tax muni interest if it so wishes, despite the public policy reciprocal immunity concept. And as to public policy, the idea that trust fund babies should pay no income tax whatsoever on a guaranteed investment is far more contrary to public policy than the taxation of their allocated muni bond interest.

Now, the Freedom Caucus, Heritage Foundation and the conservative think-tanks will squeal that taxing trust principal received by an heir is unfair. First, they will claim that because some of it is principal, it should not be taxed because it's not actually income, as would be interest and dividend income, rental income, etc. But to the recipient of trust distributions, it's all "found money" for which they did nothing except to get born to wealthy parents or to cozy up to a rich benefactor. Trust fund capital was never earned and saved by its recipients, so it's not double taxation. Scientists have been unable to identify a single human genome that includes include a DNA strand to which dollars are attached. Nobody in America could be more deserving of the AMT than a trust fund beneficiary.

Here's the rebuttal to the claim that it cannot logically be taxed as income. The IRS and the states regularly tax lottery winners for the income they receive from buying a winning ticket. Becoming a non-spousal trust fund beneficiary is no different than hitting the Powerball jackpot, tax-wise. Those lucky folks are the winners of the gene-pool lottery. In our random genetic universe of human evolution, they won the rich parents. And they took no risk in doing so; it's really that simple. They did no more to deserve their windfall trust fund principal than did the Megamillions winner. Both winnings should be taxed. And even with this proposed AMT reform, the biggest Powerball winners will still pay a higher tax rate than a trust fund baby, even though they actually paid cash for their ticket.

From the standpoint of mitigating wealth inequality, the AMT is actually a better vehicle than an estate tax. The best way to avoid concentrations of wealth is to diffuse it. That means, to spread it out. If a billionaire wants to create a trust with 100 beneficiaries each receiving less than $500,000 annually, instead of three children and four grandkids, to mitigate AMT taxation upon the heirs, we should cheer her on. Society has a much better chance that some of those 100 beneficiaries will put their share of the inherited capital to work productively as innovative entrepreneurs and professionals, than would a handful who collect coupon and dividend income as idle rich.

The same logic can apply to all other types of distributions received by non-spousal heritors. For example, a beneficiary designation on a brokerage or bank account[68] to a party other than the decedent's spouse would be subject to AMT taxes. Likewise, the second-to-die owner-ship of land bequeathed first to a farmer's spouse as a life estate, with the remaindermen interest to the children, would be subject to AMT taxation when the land title ultimately passes to the children.[69] Please note that this rule does not need to apply to retirement accounts like IRAs and 401(k)'s, for those below the $500,000 One Percenter level. Those assets are already subject to ordinary taxation during the life-time of the recipient through required minimum distributions based on life expectancy.

Next, the "death tax hit squad" on the right will undoubtedly complain that it's double taxation, at least for the handful of trust benefi-ciaries whose grantors' estates actually paid an estate tax. Given the size of the federal exemption from the estate tax in the Trump tax law, which is now $11+ million per person and almost $23 million for a married couple, there are not that many estates that are even subject to an estate tax anymore. It's something like 1,900 in total nationwide, and less than 1/10th of one percent of all estates. Since 2001, the number of taxable estates has declined by 96 percent, as Republicans have chiseled away at the estate tax at every turn. So we're not even talking about the One Percent here, we're talking about one-in-one-thousand of those who pass on each year. That is the richest of the rich. And most of them find ways to chisel down or evade the estate tax in other ways. The average tax rate on taxable estates was 17 percent at last count. The GOP has served its masters well.

Even so, the argument about double-taxation can be easily dismissed by assigning each federally taxable estate a subsequent deduction to

---

68 Sometimes called a Transfer on Death (TOD) registration, which is equivalent to a bene-ficiary designation for a retirement account.

69 As noted below in this chapter, special tax rules already apply to farms and can be adapted to provide for multi-year payments of taxes on the remainderman interests in a family farm. Higher dollar limits would be appropriate.

beneficiaries for the percentage of estate principal that was actually paid to IRS in estate taxes. For example, a $100 million-dollar estate that paid $20 million in estate taxes after all exemptions and deductions would have a 20 percent factor that could be deducted from the principal share distributed to each beneficiary other than the surviving spouse. If a taxable beneficiary receives $600,000 from the trust fund of which half is principal and half is investment income, then 20 percent of the principal ($60,000) could be exempted from that year's AMT tax base.[70]

With this formula, two new lines on a one-page AMT tax form will determine first whether a beneficiary's trust fund distributions are subject to the higher tax rate, and if so, how much. That is a simple and recurring calculation, not something that requires fancy math and a CPA to recalculate. These family trusts are already required to file a tax return (Form 1041), so compliance and cross-checking by IRS is readily feasible. The paperwork should be no different than any other kind of 1099 forms that taxpayers receive for interest, dividends and pensions. For other types of inter-generational transfers at the time of a donor's or spouse's death, these can be accomplished when title is changed at the financial institution or local government (usually county) offices. As one-time events, conveying a form similar to the 1099 filing regularly issued by title companies and brokers would not impose any egregious administrative burdens.

A good argument can be made also that this estate-tax credit should not apply whatsoever for grandchildren and other so-called genera-tion-skipping beneficiaries. Trusts have too conveniently been used since the early industrial Gilded Age of the late 1800s to evade estate taxes and perpetuate family dynasties. If Uncle Sam subjects the silver-spoon grandkids to a 33 percent AMT on their inherited boodle every year, it's hard to feel sorry for them that the estate also had a tax liability.

---

70 To achieve neutrality, the precisely correct tax-geek math would be somewhat different, but let's not get "too deep into the weeds" here. The concept of an offsetting compensatory credit is what is important.

Many on the far left would favor a higher rate, but the goal here is to set rules and rates that are not so punitive that they galvanize big money donors and lobbyists in opposition.

> The tax code already allows farmers to spread out their estate taxes over 10 years. Nobody needs to sell their family farm to pay their estate tax.

And then there are the farmers. Anybody who grew up on a farm can understand and respect the values of these families. Their forefathers and mothers worked, often for generations -- with the sweat of their brows, the blisters on their hands, and broken bodies by age 60 -- to build a legacy for their descendants. It was their dream, an American dream that rightfully deserves its place in our social fabric. The vast majority of farmers who are hardworking stewards of the land are entirely exempt from the estate tax. The U.S. Department of Agriculture now estimates that only 0.35 percent (1 in 300) of farm estates will ever pay any estate tax under current law. So as far as AMT taxation goes, let's not forget that here we're talking only about those who receive distributions over a half million dollars in any one year. These rare few are already One Percenters, not clodhoppers. There is already a mechanism in the tax code that enables farmers to spread out their estate taxes on real assets over ten years to avoid having to sell the family farm. This provision can easily be tweaked to avoid any conceivable need for liquidation by "family farm dynasty" operators. The timing of these tax payments is less important than the requirement that they be paid. The farmers who inherit the very largest agribusinesses will have to pay up, just like any other fat cat. Unlike their middle-class neighbors and field workers, these millionaires are modern managing operators and not yesteryear's hardscrabble pioneers -- which is how the self-interested and ideological opponents of the estate tax still cunningly portray them.

By now, some readers will wonder how much additional tax revenue this tax on trust and financial-account beneficiaries would raise, to help fund our government properly. Here's a ballpark estimate, calculated by the "bar napkin" approach to approximation: According to the latest available IRS tables on this subject, the assets in estates with more than $10 million (approximately the current exemption level) hold roughly $100 billion in assets each year. Over time, the annual distributions of principal from trusts should be roughly equal in magnitude to principal held or transferred into the trusts at the grantor's death. Eventually, the spousal distributions (except for the portions consumed) will be redistributed to other heirs, so most of that portion will remain in the proposed AMT tax base. So $100 billion is a very rough proxy for the amount of principal that transfers annually to all heirs, including spouses, relatives and others, whether in or outside of a trust.

Now, this is where it becomes particularly challenging to make accurate revenue estimates without accessing the confidential IRS tax databases: Trusts are only a part of the picture. Many assets transfer at death through beneficiary designations and other legal devices. There are several ways that family dynasties can assign and pass along their wealth, and if an AMT tax begins to hit them squarely, their tax lawyers will take measures to sidestep it somehow. One Percenter families can establish LLCs for their closely held businesses and legally make their kids partners and co-owners during the parents' midlife at bargain valuations through a "gifting" process each year. This is perfectly legal, to incrementally give them partial shares over time that will never be part of the parents' estate. Family farmers often create "life estates" for their spouses in their wills so that only the children's actuarially reduced "remainderman interest" in the family land is estate-taxable. This typically often keeps the next-generation's actuarially reduced property value below the estate tax exemption amounts.

In comparison, beneficiaries of IRA and 401k accounts will already be paying ordinary income taxes at a higher rate than the corresponding

AMT, so those assets should not be included in a tax reform revenue calculation. As readers can see, the tax-code writers will have their hands full in their efforts to apply an AMT as broadly and even-handedly as humanly possible. Every well-intended exemption becomes a future loophole, with the tax accountants and attorneys standing by on the sidelines looking for their next opportunity to sell their services to wealthy clientele.

So it's best to assume that maybe only one- third of this $100 billion annual estate number would fall into this beneficiary bucket, and of that, less than one-half would be taxable under this particular AMT rule. That gets us to something around $10 billion annually, possibly a bit less, of potential new and unprecedented AMT revenues from trust principal distributions alone. That is about two-thirds of what the entire estate tax now yields in the aftermath of the Trump Tax Cuts. And nobody can dare call this a death tax, because it would be payable entirely by the living when received.

"And just one more thing" as the TV detective *Columbo* (Peter Falk[71]) liked to say in the late 1960s: As discussed elsewhere, heritors[72] presently enjoy a special windfall in the current estate tax laws, which exempt untaxed capital gains accumulated during the deceased's lifetime.[73] Dynastic wealth loves this loophole, because profits embedded in grandpa's riches can pass from one generation to another without ever paying a capital gains tax. AMT reform needs to incorporate this untaxed appreciation in its overall structure in the deceased's final 1040 tax return. The officially estimated annual cost of this tax exemption is

---

71 Coincidentally a graduate of the Maxwell School of Citizenship and Public Affairs at Syracuse University (where the author was first schooled in public finance) before Falk switched gears and became an actor. Falk died in 2011.

72 A heritor is a person who inherits, whether by will, trust, life estate, beneficiary designation, etc.

73 See the discussion of "step up" capital gains taxation in Topic 13.

$60 billion, but only about half of that could realistically be realized if surviving spouses remain exempt[74], as they are under general tax laws. Applying an AMT rate rather than an estate tax rate could require a further adjustment, but it is probably safe to assume that the tax reform revenue yield using the progressive AMT rates outlined in this chapter would be more than $20 billion annually from this one item alone.

As they say on the farm, that's not chicken feed. But it clearly won't pay for Medicare for All. What it does accomplish is making an important step back in the direction of tax fairness, which is the progressive principle worth fighting for, along with all the other AMT reforms described previously, which are the primary revenue drivers.

In summary, AMT reforms can raise around $125 billion annually (plus or minus) from the One Percenters. AMT reforms can establish a common denominator for the tax rates that apply to all their income sources and tax preferences, no matter how hard they work to weasel out of the higher ordinary income tax rates paid by wage and salary earners. And the beauty of the AMT is that it leaves all the existing tax incentives and preferences in place for ordinary folks in the middle class who work and save to achieve a better life -- and maybe someday themselves become affluent enough to have to pay AMT thereafter. For once, Congress would be working for the benefit of middle-class Americans. In other words, it leaves alive the heart of the American dream that the capitalist class has used to justify all these tax breaks for itself. But instead it shifts them to the 99 Percenters and away from the One Percenters. Fiscally literate readers can call this "Progressive Tax Policy Jiu Jitsu."

---

74 The surviving spouse should "inherit" the deceased's partner's original tax basis with no step-up, so that ultimately, the entire capital gain will be taxed when assets are sold or re-distributed.

TOPIC 19: Financial transactions tax: The case for an FTT

Most Americans have always been skeptical about Wall Street. This has been true generally among Democrats and especially Progressives. Financial markets are where many Far Cats make most of their money, and it's the home base of U.S. capitalism. This is where rich people manufacture, sell and trade paper, not things. Wall Street is where shady people can make fortunes, some of it through scams that rob the little guy, often through trading and gambling with other people's money. Nobody there ever seems to go to jail when things blow up in their face. The Big Banks in New York lend money to Wall Street and make fortunes when times are good. But when their leveraged portfolios blow up, and stock and real estate bubbles burst, taxpayers get stuck bailing out these banks who then plead that they are "too big to fail." To many rank-and-file, mainstream Democrats and Independents, as well as the Progressives, it's "heads they win, tails we lose."

> Centrists are cautious about overdoing financial industry reforms for fear of gumming up the gears and losing our international leadership.

It's no surprise, therefore, that a declared democratic socialist like Bernie Sanders would want to tax Wall Street. Centrists, on the other hands, are cautious about overdoing financial industry reforms for fear of gumming up the gears of an otherwise effective system of allocating capital and fostering business successes. Albeit flawed, the American financial system has generated and facilitated prosperity for many of us, including small investors. Nobody can point to a superior model or better results elsewhere.[75] Centrists and Liberals share a belief that capital markets must be regulated and overseen at the legislative level, but otherwise left alone on a day to day basis. This governance model is known as "Nose In, Fingers Out" (NIFO). Only the socialist fringe would try to legislatively commandeer the companies' governance (let alone ownership) and assert themselves into the process of allocating capital.[76] As with most Americans, Centrists shudder at the idea of politicians effectively becoming executives or lead directors of companies owned fractionally through their pension funds and IRA accounts.

In between those two ends of the Democratic spectrum are voters and members who blame Wall Street when its excesses create wealthy tycoons at the expense of the little guy, and bubbles that burst. Yet many of these voters and their friends chase after the next shiny new thing like Bitcoin and brag about their brilliant successes in their IRA account when times are good or they hit a winner in the IPO lottery. In short, Democrats are a bit schizophrenic about Wall Street, but they know there is "wool to be shorn" in the financial services sector, if they could just figure out a way to trim the sheep for some revenue without mistakenly gouging into the flesh.

---

75 Marx, Lenin and Mao all failed. Xi is trying something different with a state-directed model to rival capitalism in the global economy. Time will tell, but few Americans would willingly trade into that system at this time in history.

76 California Democrats have, however, required that boards of companies domiciled there must include a female member, which is a notable step into corporate governance. The German model of worker representation on company boards is attractive to those leaning left, but seems unlikely to take hold in the U.S. until a "board of visitors" or "advisory board" model first proves successful in practice somewhere, and not just in ivory towers.

> A well-designed FTT will tax Wall Street far more than Main Street. Markets are unlikely to suffer if rates are high enough to collect $150 billion/year, but our nation's financial industry will become uncompetitive globally if Congress tries for more than that.

That is where the financial transactions tax (FTT) comes in. Some on the Left want to call it a "speculation tax" because that makes it easy to point fingers and it fits their class-conflict, us-vs-them narrative.[77] Liberals would be more inclined to look at the FTT more pragmatically and systematically as a way to first raise some significant new tax revenue without any real impact on the 99 Percenters, while helping to curb some of the parasitic trading done by high-frequency traders and market insiders that does very little to promote economic efficiency while lining their own pockets. Liberals will point to the founder of modern macroeconomic theory, John Maynard Keynes, whose new paradigm in the 1930s legitimized deficit spending during recessions. He was himself a speculator, and proposed a financial transactions tax in 1936 during the Depression to reinforce the new federal securities and exchange laws, and to curb manipulation, "churning" and market volatility using economic tools, with only a secondary interest in their revenue potential.

Financial analysis in the pages below will quantify the levels of revenue that could realistically be raised by a national FTT tax that

---

77 The "speculation" narrative over-simplifies and misdirects. Most high-frequency trading is relatively low-risk "scalping" and "front-running," which plucks profits from the gap between prices paid and received by other investors. It is generally not speculating, which requires much higher risks taken with only an informed hunch about the future of prices. There indeed are speculators in many of the markets discussed below, but they are only a fraction of the picture, and far less dominant in the institutional markets which dominate the trading volumes.

applies universally across all the major financial markets. The analysis of each market will explain why there would need to be different rates for different types of transactions, but that becomes a tertiary concern.

First, we need to know where such a tax would apply, and where it wouldn't or shouldn't. Once the "taxable universe" is better defined, we review how markets and market-makers and traders operate, and where all the transactions take place that would be taxed. Most of the politicians and candidates who advocate a transactions tax don't even know where all the trading occurs, who does it, and what are the instruments. Few of them know a whit about securities valuation and options pricing theory, nor the analytics used by swaps dealers and hedge funds. They would not know a stock-pricing algorithm if they saw one, nor whether it is a formula for speculation or investment. Failure to know the marketplaces and instruments will simply enable wily trading companies to concoct end-around strategies to evade the tax, and profit from their creation of new vehicles that don't even exist today. The Whack-a-Mole paradigm applies here, if the FTT is not comprehensive and savvy by design.

Then we have to take a look at how much such taxes would interfere with the "smart" part of capital markets, which is the efficient allocation of capital. Readers must understand who would ultimately bear the cost of a national tax on financial transactions. If it turns out that ordinary people ultimately pay most of the costs as a result, as its opponents will try to argue, this idea will likely die at the doorsteps of Congress. Just as one example, care must be taken so that the FTT does not punish or even touch farmers who pre-sell their crops directly to their local grain warehouse at a set "forward" price, in order to pay their operating expenses before their harvest. Instead, the FTT would apply only when the grain warehouse sells a futures contract on the Chicago commodity exchange in order to hedge its pricing risks, completely invisible to the farmers. Nowhere in this chain of events is there any speculation by the farmer or the warehouse.[78]

This chapter will also provide some ballpark estimates of the revenue potential the untested new tax regime could yield regularly and sustainably. Some of the potential revenue of an FTT will never be collected if it actually does have the desired effect of reducing incentives to over-trade, "front-run" the little guys, and speculate. Markets must adjust to the costs of collecting these taxes and new trading behaviors. The only certainty we have at this point is that transaction volume will go down, if such a tax is imposed. The open question is whether that is good or bad for the American economy; if done right, it can be good, and if done wrong, it will be harmful.

The analysis here begins by identifying the taxable universe for a financial transactions tax. The best way to think about this is that the tax applies to transactions involving financial instruments -- securities, not things. Now, some far-left theorists may claim that this doesn't go far enough, that we should tax credit card transactions (which pay for goods and services, not securities) and insurance premiums such as car insurance, medical insurance, and life insurance. After all, those are "financial transactions" in a sense. But they differ fundamentally from financial transactions which involve trading, and it is the trading of securities and financial instruments that is the primary focus of this section. Importantly, the ultimate cost of a tax on non-trading transactions will almost certainly be passed along to the consumer, not the insurance and credit card companies, just the way that gas and electric companies pass on their taxes to the end user. So a tax on such

---

78 On the other side of the futures trade, there could be an individual speculator or hedge fund, but it also could be a large commercial company that exports the grain, or a foreign country that buys the grain. Anybody seriously interested in this issue can easily view the "Commitment of Traders" report of the Commodity Futures Trading Commission, a federal regulatory agency, to better appreciate the role and volume of speculation. The Chicago Mercantile Exchange produces a visual, user-friendly summary of its traders' positions.

transactions becomes an offbeat consumption tax and is most likely to be regressive (hurting smaller consumers more than the rich). If we are going to have a consumption tax, it would be smarter to make it broad-based, like a value-added tax (VAT) which is discussed in Topic 20, and avoid stepping into the taxation of consumption with the FTT. Further, there is no "speculation" or "churning" or "front-running" to cure, when it comes to using one's credit card or buying life insurance.

For clarity, the FTT might best be thought of as a financial *trading* tax, if it becomes important during political debates to differentiate this concept. If Wall Street profiteering from the purchase and sale of financial instruments is the target, there is no sense in causing collateral damage to the entire population by extending the taxable universe beyond the markets described below. For the same reason, this analysis excludes purchases and sales of mutual funds and similar long-term investment vehicles. The funds themselves would pay an FTT tax when they buy and sell securities inside the fund, so double-taxation to the investor is unwarranted and contrary to the public purpose.

The most obvious markets to be subject to an FTT would be those where stocks, bonds, and other financial instruments such as futures and options and "swaps" are traded. Each of these operates a little bit differently, so the following pages provide some context in how these markets operate. Also, it turns out that "one size won't fit all" when it comes to the best tax rate. Instead, it would be smarter to levy a slightly different tax rate or formula in certain markets, depending on how typical instruments are traded and in what units (lots or sizes). Minimum transaction sizes differ markedly across these markets. The way that traders and brokers are compensated in various markets also different, and the FTT must be calibrated reasonably and realistically in the context of other trading costs in order to avoid disrupting the normal and efficient way that free markets establish prices and allocate capital.

To provide a common denominator for this calibration discussion, which will be essential if the FTT concept is to be written into law, all readers need to understand the concept of a *basis point* (BP). A basis point is 1/100th of one percent. That is 0.0001 times the principal or market value of a given trade or transaction. For a stock or bond purchase of $25,000, one basis point equals $2.50. For a million-dollar bond trade, one basis point would be $100.00. By itself, one basis point is nothing, to the average retail investor. The impact of a basis-point financial transactions tax on a long-term investor is not even a rounding error. But to a Wall Street trading house that buys and sells huge blocks of securities at lighting speed using computer-driving trading algorithms, it could add up to real money in just one day. So the first takeaway for readers should be that long-term investors like pension funds that buy and hold big baskets of stocks and bonds, and ordinary retail investors who buy and hold mutual funds in their IRA and 401(k) accounts, a basis point or two will have virtually no impact on their long-term rate of return on investment. Despite right-wing efforts to demonize the FTT, it won't hurt Main Street, granny's retirement fund, or Junior's college-savings account.

It's the short-term traders and trading houses that will bear the brunt of an FTT that is calibrated in a few basis points. But if the tax-and-spenders on the left wing get too greedy in their rhetoric and calibrating their tax bills, then the frictional costs to the markets, society and average investors will begin to pile up and gum up the gears of modern capitalist markets. That unwanted doomsday scenario will be the opening salvo of the Wall Street lobbyists and the conservative think tanks who will fight this tax tooth and nail, using every scare tactic available to their public relations and lobbying firms. So it's really important to get the math right and set realistic, small basis-point parameters when discussing the entire concept of an FTT, the tax rates themselves, and making ballpark revenue estimates.

> A financial transactions tax would apply to stocks, bonds, futures, options, swaps and currency traders. It would not apply to retail credit card and insurance transactions. An FTT is a tax on *trading*, not investing.

So let's start with the stock market. Most readers have heard of the New York Stock Exchange (NYSE), which is the grand-daddy of American stock exchanges. The NYSE is where stock traders historically met and conducted their trades in-person on the floor of the exchange, until modern technology allowed most trades to be conducted electronically. Of course, there are still floor traders and market-makers at the NYSE who provide liquidity (a buy order to match every sell order, and vice versa). Many readers also know about NASDAQ, the National Association of Securities Dealers Automated Quotations. As its full name implies, the NASDAQ was always an automated exchange where buy orders (bids) and sell orders (offers) were registered and posted virtually on a gigantic automated bulletin board where brokers and dealers could see the last trades and current bids and offers. It never had a physical trading floor like the NYSE.

Another term of importance here is the "spread" which is the difference between the highest current bid and the lowest current offer for a specific security.[79] The spread is where market-makers and professional trading houses make a lot of their money. When retail investors place a "market order" they agree to pay the bid or asked price on the opposite side of their trade and essentially forfeit the spread in order to complete the trade -- even though that may be higher or lower than the

---

79 The bid is what price a trader will pay, and the offer (or "asked") is what a buyer must pay the trader. Normally there is a small gap between the two.

latest comparable bid or offer traded. The middle-man[80] is the trader, who steps in to take the market order and capture the spread. Not every trade will prove profitable to the traders, because prices fluctuate and this moment's bid price can quickly become the next moment's asked price or worse, but over time, the skilled insiders in these markets will enjoy profits from the laws of probability. Fifty years ago, the common bid-asked spread in most stocks was 1/8 of a point ($0.125) or even a quarter in some cases, and stocks were priced in those fractions, with commission rates set by the exchanges through mutual agreement of the brokerage community and its regulators. Over time, market deregulation allowed the brokers to set their own commissions, and the prices of stocks moved to decimals. All this has been positive for investors, as bid-asked spreads have become more and more narrow. Most of the big-name and widely traded stocks now have spreads of just a few pennies,[81] and many of the large brokerage houses charge $4.95 or even less to process an on-line order for a stock trade (vs $30 or more for telephonic broker-assisted trades).

Historically, the bid-ask spread was a profit source for the floor traders and market makers on the NYSE, and the dealers who represented client buyers and sellers on the NASDAQ. These players on the Wall Street stage simply took the other side of an order from a natural person or an institutional client like a pension fund or a mutual fund.

---

80 As with other traditional linguistic references to the male, the term here is intended to include both genders, although the industry remains male dominated.

81 Stocks in companies, and securities in general, that trade less frequently can have much wider bid-ask spreads, which are necessary for the market-makers and traders to take on the risk of filling the order and holding it until they can find an offsetting or reciprocal trade to "unwind" their position. In a fast-moving market, this spread can widen significantly, especially if there is no liquidity (volume). By reducing liquidity provided by frequent traders, a financial transaction tax that is egregious in proportion to other trading costs would further widen this spread and work to the disadvantage of investors on both sides and not just the middle-men.

The brokerage houses also collected their commissions for a fixed fee. This was business as usual on Wall Street.

But in the recent decades, new technologies and strategies have emerged that have enabled hedge funds and other high-frequency traders to execute "HFT" trades at rapid-fire speed using information advantages and computer trading algorithms to capture more and more of the bid-ask spread by trading privately offline. Often, these high-frequency traders can drive prices in one direction by "piling on" to a trade or market news in ways that are actually disruptive to orderly trade processing. Some of these firms actually locate their computer systems as close to the exchanges as physically possible with high-capacity fiber-optic cable in order to receive trade information, place orders and clear trades with a nanosecond advantage. Ordinary investors and even professional money managers working for pension and mutual funds cannot compete with these HFT traders, who have engineered a systematic way to front-run the orders of natural buyers and sellers. When news reporters explain a sudden plunge in the price of a given stock or stock index, it's often attributed to HFT and "algo"[82] traders who have actually overloaded the circuits of normal market price discovery in their automated quest for instantaneous profits.

Where an FTT can play a positive role for American society is to return to the arguments presented by John Maynard Keynes all the way back in 1936, which is to curb this kind of market manipulation. A tiny transaction tax will not eliminate all the high-frequency trading, but it would change the economics favorably to discourage at least some of the excessive trading. The problem for Congressional tax-writers is that nobody on Capitol Hill can know for sure just where the tipping point will be in discouraging HFT abuses, and what impact that would have on revenue estimates. If Democrats do prevail in 2020 elections and succeed in pushing the FTT concept forward, the professional House

82 Algorithmic, or quantitatively- and formula-driven.

Ways and Means tax staff will play a key role in collecting as much expert intelligence as possible to help in the appropriate calibration. But it should be obvious to all readers that the active, self-interested players in this game have all the information advantage, so that only time will tell where the FTT rate(s) should be set. Without *a priori* rules and formulas to follow, some of this calibration may require trial-and-error. Clearly, such high-frequency tax rates cannot be set in stone, so a neutral and non-partisan regulator of FTT rates may be necessary to adjust or even waive the taxes in periods of market instability or changing economics. Any rigidity or over-reaching in the setting of an FTT tax rate on stock trades would inevitably invite a backlash favoring repeal and not just recalibration, so caution is the watchword here.

> A financial transactions tax could justifiably help reduce the federal deficit, but it is fantasy to believe it will fund Medicare for All or Universal College tuition.

With all these caveats, here is a ballpark estimate of the potential revenue yield for an FTT on stocks alone (not bonds and derivatives, which will be described later): The latest available total for the total value of transactions on the NYSE was something in the order of $25 trillion annually.[83] Similar transaction totals for NASDAQ, which actually covers more companies, are above $40 trillion. When the fringe Socialists hear numbers like that, they think they have found their gold mine. But in the context of Medicare for All, and free college education and $6000 checks to everybody earning less than six figures, the feasible

---

83 Stock transaction totals include electronically traded funds (ETFs) which are common investment instruments used by retain investors especially, to achieve low-cost diversification. They trade like stocks.

limits of an FTT on the stock market are not so grand by themselves. A 5 basis-point tax (0.05 percent or 0.0005x) on stock trades would generate annual federal tax revenue of approximately $30 billion. That estimate applies if the tax applies only to purchases: If both buyers and sellers are taxed, the number would double. But that assumes that the tax does not result in dramatic reductions of HFT trading which would reduce the volume and hence the federal revenue.

At most, the annual FTT taxes on the U.S. stock market would buy two weeks of single-payer universal health care. As readers will see, an FTT across all markets would buy five weeks of Medicare for All every year.

In the big picture, a 5 bp FTT tax on stock purchases is trivial to the long-term stock market investor who is seeking average compounded annual returns of 1000 bps, even if it applies on both purchases and sales. But Democrats must think about the "sticker shock" or "mental anchoring" that will be common with smaller investors when they get their trade confirmations.

To put 5 bps in perspective, the FTT would either directly or indirectly cost a middle-class retail investor of $10,000 more than the visible online brokerage commissions typically charged on their order confirmation. Now some of that tax burden would likely be absorbed by the brokerage community and the market-makers as a cut into their profits, but you can see where this is headed. An explicit FTT on the little guy could be a public relations disaster, so thought must be given to eliminating or reducing the rate on smaller, single trades *that are not repeated in that day.*[84] That exempts the little guy, but the HFT crowd cannot

---

84 "Odd lots" representing less than 100 shares, represent approximately five percent of all trading in the national market system, and some of that includes HFT transactions that are broken into small trades. An exemption for small retail traders would not impact federal revenue materially.

slice up their tickets into multiple millisecond trades in order to avoid or reduce the tax that should apply to their lightning-speed churning.

Next, we need to scope the bond market. Unlike stocks, most bonds are traded "over the counter" and not on an exchange.[85] Bonds are debt instruments, and are issued by the U.S. government (Treasury bonds, notes and bills), municipalities, other nations ("sovereigns") and corporations. Total trading volumes in the bond market are actually larger than the stock market, although it is mostly institutional. Small investors usually cannot buy individual bonds in small denominations at competitive prices, so they typically invest through mutual funds that combine investor dollars to manage large diversified portfolios of multi-million and billion-dollar size.

At the institutional level, bond traders profit from the bid-ask spread, similar to stocks, but there are typically not explicit commissions on the high-denomination trades. Retail brokers may charge a small transaction fee (often $1 per $1000, or 10 bps, and nowadays even zero for U.S. treasury securities) to process customers' orders to buy and sell bonds, but the professionals live in a world of basis-point spreads. Whereas a 5 bp FTT tax would be less than half of what a retail investor ultimately pays both directly and indirectly to buy an individual corporate bond, that would often exceed the entire spread on a jumbo institutional-sized trade. And most investment professionals, regardless of political affiliation, and even those on the buy side representing retail investors, would consider a 5 bp FTT on all bond trades to be egregious.

Bonds are also less prone to high frequency trading, which requires large outstanding issuance and volumes. So the FTT rationale of curbing speculation and over-trading does not apply very well in this market.

---

85 There are bonds that trade on the NYSE but most of the action is over-the-counter, dealer to dealer.

One additional fly in the ointment from a tax policy standpoint is that unlike stocks (which are perpetual), bonds mature. So long-term buyers do not sell them, they just hold them to maturity. So a question arises as to whether it is equitable to tax the investor who sells a bond and not the investor whose bonds just naturally mature. That issue can be argued either way, but it illustrates how these various financial markets are not homogenous, and why a single blanket tax rate on all transactions is not likely to work.

From an investor's perspective, bond yields are much lower than the long-term returns on riskier stocks. Presently, U.S. Treasury bills, note and bonds have annual yields of 2 to 3 percent, which is perhaps one-fourth of the expected return of stocks over a decade. A 5 bp FTT takes a much bigger slice out of the long-term bond investor's income. This is one more reason that a uniform tax rate is unfeasible.

To be realistic, an FTT on bond trades at the level of 2 bps ($20 per $100,000 or $200 per million) would probably not be crushingly distortive or disruptive to capital markets. Estimates of total trading volume in the bond market are not easily found,[86] but the revenue range is probably in the magnitude of $35 billion annually at the 2 bp FTT level, if applied only to purchases, and maybe $10-15 billion more if applied to sales of bonds before expiry but not if held to maturity. [87]

Now we have to enter the corners of the financial world that are unfamiliar to most readers: derivative securities. A derivative is a

---

86 The trade association, SIFMA, summarizes trading volumes on page 34 of its *2018 Fact Book* that total $750 billion daily.

87 A minor adjustment of the tax rate might be necessary for short-term T-bills which are sold for holding periods of less than one year. A reasonable discount on the FTT should be considered for these and other money market instruments such as commercial paper and bankers' acceptances, many of which mature in 3 months or less. For bond dealers who finance their inventories with overnight lending (often through "repurchase agreements"), an FTT exemption for these financing transactions is appropriate. Otherwise, this tax will gum the gears by interfering with market liquidity.

security whose price is derived from another security. For our purposes, this includes futures contracts, options, and swaps.

The U.S. futures industry began in Chicago as the nation' agricultural marketing hub, where the Chicago Board of Trade was founded to provide a way for farmers and their local warehouses to sell grain in advance of harvest, to pay bills they incur whilst growing their crops. A future is a contract to buy or sell a given asset at a specified price at a specified time in the future. Farmers could sell their corn to the local warehouse on a forward contract[88], and the warehouse could in turn sell a futures contract in Chicago to offset its risk that the price would decline after they agreed to buy the farmer's corn in advance. Futures trading is commonplace in the agriculture industry (wheat, corn, soybeans, orange juice, even eggs and lumber) and the metals (gold and silver) and petroleum markets (oil, gasoline, diesel and natural gas). Eventually, these exchanges began trading in financial instruments like stocks, bonds and currencies. Even today, these contracts are sometimes called "commodity futures" although physical commodities now represent only a fraction of the financial activity on these exchanges.

Futures markets have "commercial" traders whose core business is the production and storage and transport of these commodities, and "speculative" traders who place bets on future prices. Both are essential to successful futures markets. There must be a buyer for every seller, and often times it is the speculator who takes the opposite side of the trade. Just like the stock exchange, these trades were originally done in-person on the floors of the futures exchanges (called "pits" for their physical, octagonal stairsteps on which traders could stand to see each other). Contracts are all standardized: Wheat, corn and soybeans trade in 5,000 bushel lots for delivery and expiration in various future months on specified days. To exit a trade in futures, one simply reverses the

---

88 A forward contract is similar, but is a private agreement between a producer and a warehouse or commercial buyer. A future is traded on an exchange.

position and sells an offsetting contract for what they had bought, or buys contracts equivalent to what they had sold (short). [89] The magic of the exchange is that the counterparty of each buy and sell transaction can be different, and the exchange guarantees that they will live up to their obligations when the contracts expire.

To ensure that traders meet their obligations, the futures exchanges operate on *margin*. A buyer of 5,000 bushels of soybeans at $9.00/bu does not pay up $45,000 to control a contract with that nominal value. Instead, the buyer and seller each post prescribed *margin deposits* with the exchange, through their broker, of a small percentage of the nominal value of the contract. That might be as little as $3000 for "initial" margin. But if the prices go the wrong way, the owners of that contract must post additional "maintenance" margin immediately to assure the exchange that they will fulfill their obligations. As the clearinghouse, the exchange thus provides liquidity and absorbs all price risks or margin deficiency. They and the member-brokers police this aggressively throughout the day and overnight, to avoid customer defaults and the possibility of a market crash. These practices have been time tested and pose little risk to the general economy or retail investors.

Relevant to the FTT, In the 1970s, some bright financial experts designed futures contracts on financial securities, including both Treasury securities, currencies, and stock indexes. Nowadays, the volume and magnitude of futures trading in these financial instruments is far, far greater than the activity in the agricultural and physical commodities.

---

89 Short selling is common and normal in the futures trade. Only famers, producers and warehouses have physical commodities to deliver. All the other traders who sell a contract are expecting to buy it back later, at a lower price. There is an age-old adage in this marketplace that "He who sells what isn't his'n, must buy it back or go to prison." And pay a margin call to the exchange if the trade loses money.

Futures are not for Little Leaguers. Although there are thousands of odd-lot traders who dabble in this speculative corner of the markets, most of the trading is done by large financial houses. A Wall Street hedge fund can use futures to take a large market position quickly and anonymously, and usually for less cost than by trading the actual stocks or bonds. Many public pension funds use futures to manage portfolio risk and shuffle positions quickly with less frictional trading cost than owning and selling the underlying securities. Futures have proved to be the most efficient way to hedge and trade most listed currencies. Some of these trades can be hedging transactions, where the investment house is offsetting its own position by taking an opposing futures position and thereby locking in a price. Other trades are purely speculative, as a bet that prices will rise or fall the way the trader expects. In Chicago, there are "locals" who "day-trade" these contracts, always closing out their positions before the end of the day, and trying to profit from price fluctuations during the day. Like the market-makers on the stock exchange, these "scalpers" can profit from agile intra-day trend-following and capturing attractive spreads on market orders. Unlike the high-frequency traders in New York, the locals in Chicago are mostly market-makers who make pricing more efficient. Like certain intestinal microbes, they are considered to be beneficial parasites. The locals will hate a tax on trades and without doubt, an excessive FTT tax rate will interfere with market operations.

Contract sizes may vary, but for Treasury bonds the standard is $100,000 face value. For stock indexes, the S&P 500 futures are 250 times the current market index, which could easily be $700,000. So one of the natural policy questions for FTT advocates is whether the tax should apply to the contract value or be charged by the contract. Historical convention on these exchanges has been for fees to be charged per-contract, and the calculation of a tax dependent on the nominal value of each trade would introduce complications that are not worth it for the sake of this book. Tax policy writers would need to grapple with these issues. Simplistic calls to "tax the greedy speculators" will fall on their face in the real world, unless Democrats bring market expertise and savvy to the tax subcommittees' work sessions.

In addition to futures, these exchanges also trade options. Options are typically associated with retail speculators trying to gamble on price changes with less capital at risk, but there are also institutional hedgers who offset risk or capture option premiums. And the market value of each option contract can differ widely depending on the underlying stock or index price, the payoff terms when the option expires, the number of days until expiration, current market volatility,[90] and other factors. Options-trading volume is much smaller than futures, approximately one quarter of all trades, so the revenue gain from a tax on these transactions is relatively minor compared with the other categories described and quantified here[91] Therefore, for this purpose, it is simpler to calibrate an FTT tax revenue on the basis of dollars per contract rather than basis points. There are simply too many variables that can clutter the calculations without yielding any real insight or perspective to the reader.

Without getting too deeply into the weeds, the average daily trading volume at the Chicago Mercantile Exchange (CME)[92] alone is creeping close to 20 million contracts (futures and options), so annual contract volume would be an order of magnitude of 5 billion traded contracts. A $5 FTT on both sides of each traded contract would therefore generate approximately $50 billion of federal revenue.

90 University of Chicago finance professors Fischer Black and Myron Scholes are legendary for their mathematical models to price options on the basis of time and volatility.

91 Although the author recognizes that a higher percentage of "long" (buy-side) options trades expire worthless, so some trades would be only one-sided for tax purposes.

92 The venerable CBOT merged into the CME in2007, making CME the premiere and dominant exchange for futures and options in the U.S.

So that we don't rile up the farmers, it should be noted that farmers can continue to forward-price their crops with their local warehouses, without any FTT tax. A forward pricing contract is not a futures contract. Those who deliver physical goods to their local warehouse or grain merchant outside of the exchanges would not themselves be taxed. Night-time farmer hedger/speculators who play the CME futures markets "on the side" would, however, pay the FTT tax on their financial transaction, because they have then entered the world of derivatives and not forward delivery.[93] The local warehouse (which may be owned by a large grain co-operative, a private company like Cargill or NYSE-listed Archer Daniels Midland) would be more likely to trade in the futures on large scale, and they would be subject to the FTT on their hedging transactions, just like Exxon would pay a $5 tax for hedging a 1,000-barrel crude oil contract worth $50,000.

Although the FTT revenue estimate for futures and options above is based on a flat tax per contract, this need not be the only formula. It may be more equitable to set a low minimum dollar amount for the tax on each contracted traded, plus a basis point tax on total contract value. In the example of the S&P 500 futures contract at the CME, its economic value is ten times the value of most agricultural futures contracts. A mere one basis point FTT tax on a single S&P future would generate $70 in revenue. By comparison, a one basis point tax on a Eurodollar currency contract would generate $15 in tax revenue. So readers can quickly surmise that the futures and options exchanges would be a ripe source for FTT revenue, especially if the tax-administration systems can be designed and operated efficiently at these exchanges and trading houses.

This brings us to the swaps market. The swaps market is where the Big Boys and Girls play, with serious money. There is no retail

---

93 CME grain contracts are settled with certified warehouse receipts. Farmers don't pull up to the exchange and dump off a truckload of corn, and speculators don't have to worry that said corn will be dumped on their driveways.

market for swaps, this is almost entirely institutional capital. There is not an organized, formal exchange for swaps contracts. They are traded through a dealer community, [94] and are essentially private, bilateral contracts that trade one security or cash flow or any other claim on financial or real assets, for another. Often, the instruments are different in these trades: A swap could involve a trade between two principals of a certain number of Japanese yen for a different denomination of British pounds. Or it could involve a promise to exchange the interest payments on a half-billion dollars of Treasury bonds for the dividends on a basket of stocks, or the interest due on Eurodollar deposits. The length of each swap agreement is negotiated by the parties, and there is no standard maturity or tenor (time period). Each contract has financial terms that are custom-crafted, although there are common terms in many of these agreements so that parties know their legal obligations and the "rules of the game" in advance.

> Most of the financial transactions that would be subject to an FTT are institutional, not retail investors. It will hit hardest at the high-frequency and "quantitative" traders that some consider to be market parasites.

One of the largest swaps markets in the US is the credit default swaps (CDS) market, wherein one party assumes the risk that a private company or a country (like Tesla or Venezuela) will default on its bonds and other debt obligations during a specified time period. The CDS market is a vital engine on Wall Street, as it enables sophisticate players to lay off their credit risk (or take it on, for a fee) without

---

94 The International Swap Dealers Association (ISDA) is the prominent trade organization which has crafted model contracts and deal terms used more commonly in the USA.

anybody else knowing it. Credit swaps enable low-risk investors to own higher-risk paper and contractually transfer the default risk to the CDS counterparty.

The relevant size of the swaps market for purposes of taxation is hotly debated. The notional value (i.e. the principal amounts) of these deals is huge, but the actual dollars at risk can be much smaller. A swap on two similar interest rate streams, or a currency swap, can have far less capital actually involved from a risk standpoint. In 2018, a prominent industry regulator claimed that the U.S. currency swaps market, with (then) over $179 trillion of notional volumes, actually exchanges risks of $15 trillion, a mere eight percent of the face value.[95] Using similar math, the overall swaps market, with annual reported transactions over $500 trillion, would have an at-risk measure of $40 trillion.

What we do know, from professional studies, is that the economic value of swaps transactions is roughly equivalent to those on the futures market, at least for government bonds and currencies. This is helpful in ball-parking a feasible tax revenue estimate for the swaps marketplace alone. If the estimated revenue yield from a $5 FFT on each futures and option trade is roughly $50 billion or more annually, then a similar revenue yield should be feasible from the swaps market. Note that this works out to one basis point on the "lower" estimate of capital at-risk in the swaps market just cited in the previous paragraph. A one-basis-point tax on both sides of these transactions (entry and exit) would thus generate closer to $100 billion from the swaps market alone, perhaps the most potentially revenue-rich of all the financial markets.[96]

---

95 Christopher Giancarlo, Chairman of the U.S. Commodities Trading, as quoted by Reuters February 1, 2018.

96 A further nuance is that many swap contracts have a lifetime beyond one year, in which case the number of transactions in that year is less than the outstanding contracts. But offsetting those longer-term deals are a huge number of short-term swaps that have total tenure of less than three or six months. Arguably a more equitable FTT tax structure for swaps would be an "annualized" tax based on the tenor of the agreement, so that a three-month swap

What we also know, for all of these derivatives transactions (futures, options and swaps), is that the primary players are companies, not individuals. The tax incidence (who actually pays) is therefore most likely to fall on public and private companies (capitalists) that play most heavily in this marketplace. This tax will come out of their profits, with only a small sliver passed along to Joe and Mary Little on Main Street. So a thoughtful Liberal must ask whether the financial industry can reasonably be expected to bear the brunt of these sharply focused taxes on transactions that are their lifeblood. This is not a trivial question, and it becomes an important "macro" issue. Picking on Wall Street is a popular theme for Progressives. Popular sentiment against big banks, hedge funds, brokerage houses, speculators and insurance companies is clearly negative if not punitive. But a pragmatist must also ask whether the American financial industry can actually bear this much tax burden without becoming uncompetitive in the global marketplace for financial products and services.

The analysis so far has focused on how much revenue can realistically be generated from FTT taxes on various markets within the financial industry. This bottom-up approach has sought to postulate tax rates that appear to be both reasonable and feasible from the standpoints of both collection (the administrative and billing process) and economic friction (minimal market disruption). From the standpoint of a given market participant in a given trade, it will be hard for opponents of an FTT to argue that a tax of one or two basis points, or $5 per futures contract trade, would bring trading to a collapse. In the case of high-frequency trading (HFT), however, there would be a desirable effect of discouraging and shrinking undesirable market activity, as

---

would be taxed at one fourth of a basis point at entry, and a two-year swap would be taxed at two bps. Whether this over-complicates the tax regime for the sake of equity is debatable but worthy of industry input.

long as the tax is calibrated cautiously -- and possibly even re-calibrated after its market impacts are measured and audited.[97]

Adding up all the markets discussed above, we have a potential bottom-up estimated revenue yield from a family of modest and cautious FTT tax rates that collectively could total up to a ballpark range of $200 to $250 billion of annual revenue without causing undue trading friction at the per-transaction level. These numbers are consistent with estimates cited by several political candidates on the Democrats' left wing. But what works at the micro level may not work at the macro level. The question that Congressional tax committees would have to ask is whether aggregate numbers at this level are sustainable at the level of the financial industry: Can this many feathers be plucked from the golden goose without emaciating it?

For perspective on this point, a survey of industry revenues and profits across various sectors of the financial services world is required. There is not a convenient single source for that information. Revenues of money center banks are roughly $750 billion. Investment services companies (brokers and managers) collectively generate $300 billion in revenue, and insurance companies a similar amount. Of this, far less than $1 trillion is likely to be associated with trading activity. Profits, as reported for tax purposes (with all the various loopholes that are employed) are difficult to measure properly. But we do have a way to gauge the "real" expected long-term (sustainable) profitability of the financial industry, by looking at how capitalists and investors actually value their businesses. The total market capitalization (market value to investors) of the financial services sector of the S&P 500 index is roughly $7 trillion. This sector index and its market valuation excludes all the smaller companies in the financial world, and includes only the largest of the large banks and insurance companies. It does not include

---

97 The Controller General and the General Accountability Office (GAO) are well equipped to provide a post-enactment report to Congress, to clear the air on market impacts.

private companies, partnerships and hedge funds that trade in financial instruments. But it's a fair proxy for what most readers would call "Wall Street." For our purposes, we can divide this market capitalization by the industry's average Price/Earnings ratio which is approximately 15x. That gives us an "imputed" profits total of approximately $450 billion for the S&P 500 Financials. Note that if this level of profits were not expected by investors, the combined market value of the stocks could not possibly be worth what investors are paying for them.

> An FTT that collects much more than $150 billion annually would benefit London, Singapore and Hong Kong far more than the American middle class.

In this context, a fair-minded person would have to suspect that an FTT tax bill across the industry that siphons away almost one-half the industry's top-dogs' total profits is simply not realistic or healthy for the economy. This perspective is important, and essential for Democrats on the far Left to understand, as their first instinct is to tax the bankers, brokers and speculators until it hurts, and then tax them some more just for good measure. Even if the revenue feasibility analysis were to include all the other, smaller Wall Street players who also profit enormously from financial transactions, it seems unrealistic to believe that a total tax bite of more than $100 billion annually from this sector can be sustainable and globally competitive in the long run. An additional $50 billion would probably be derived from clients and principals in these transactions, including retail investors and investment funds. That makes $150 billion of annual revenue a realistic estimate of achievable and reliable tax yield.[98] Incidentally, that number is roughly *triple* the

---

98 The author acknowledges that a larger ratio for the principals' share of taxable transactions could make a higher estimate possible, but there is insufficient data to support that

total FTT revenue collected worldwide by all other countries presently. It is reasonable to suspect that higher "blood-sucking" revenue targets from an American FTT would drive financial market participants overseas. London, Hong Kong and Singapore would flourish at the expense of New York City and Chicago. In the long run, excessively high FTT tax rates would be counter-productive.[99]

TOPIC 20: The Value Added Tax (VAT): A viable funding source for universal health care?

"It is a signal advantage of taxes on consumption, that they contain in their own nature a security against excess. They prescribe their own limit, which cannot be exceeded without defeating the end proposed; that is, an extension of the revenue."

Alexander Hamilton, Federalist No. 21

So far, all the tax reforms discussed in this section could be combined to produce new federal revenue in the range of $500 billion annually.

---

conclusion given the absence or opacity of subsector industry data. At most another $25 to $50 billion might be possible, but is regarded here as unlikely.

99 Obviously, an international tax treaty to levy FTTs across the G7 "free market" nations (along with Singapore) would be mutually advantageous for all, as a mechanism to curtail industrial tax-shopping. It also begs the question of whether Chinese leaders in Beijing would impose an FTT on Hong Kong trades. Clearly, a global trade and tariff policy based on intimidation and belligerence will never result in an FTT pact that puts the US on a level playing field with our financial-markets competitors.

Those are meaningful numbers. But the federal budget deficit is now running at a rate of $1 trillion annually --in peacetime, with unemployment claims their lowest in 50 years, when social "safety net" spending is lowest at any point in the business cycle. The esteemed father of modern macroeconomics and deficit spending during depressions, John Maynard Keynes, would have declared that today is a time in the economy's business cycle when national budgets should be balanced in order that subsequent deficits can provide the automatic stabilizers in the next recession. He did not advocate large surpluses, but he did believe in "dry powder." Keynes would have been shocked to see where modern fiscal policy now finds itself, with huge debt loads that constrain the nation's fiscal flexibility. During recessions, deficits balloon as tax revenues shrink and social welfare spending expands automatically to provide benefits to unemployed workers and their families, so today's deficits will be dwarfed in the next recession and the issuance of more debt could become more treacherous than ever before.

it should be obvious by now that taxing Wall Street and Fat Cats will not alone be sufficient to underwrite all the major new universal benefits programs that Democrats are debating. Free public college tuition and fees for all 20,000 students now enrolled nationwide would wipe out a third all that new tax reform revenue, even without forgiving or subsidizing any of the massive $1.5 trillion of student loan debt already accumulated. Senator Kamala Harris's proposed $6,000 annual tax credits and checks for all Americans earning less than six figures would cost more than all the tax reforms, with nothing left over for any other social programs or deficit reduction. And Medicare for All starts with a price tag even higher, just to provide health insurance to the nearly 30 million citizens now uninsured, even without counting the under-insured, and assuming that everybody else would magically pay their current premiums without any kind of federal subsidy (that others receive). A single-payer system would require three times what tax reforms can finance.

That leaves Democrats with the unhappy choice of either abandoning their 2019 campaign rhetoric that advocated these new spending levels, or raising taxes on the general population -- and not just the One Percenters. Nobody on Capitol Hill wants to raise taxes on the middle class, but the fiscal truth is that middle America is where the revenue is, because that is where the greatest volume of income is earned and spent. Wealth may be top-heavy and concentrated with the rich, but income and tax revenue is more evenly distributed on a "rightward-tilted" bell curve.[100] And wealth can only be spent once, not annually as needed for ongoing social programs. Fifty percent of the US population is middle class, so if Congress wants to raise major new revenue, it has to start there.

Without instituting a new tax such as the FTT discussed previously, the conventional wisdom would call for a Democratic Congress to raise the personal income tax rates back to or even above the levels that prevailed under the Obama and Clinton presidencies. That requires a major tax increase on middle- and lower-income families, in order to produce the revenues required for budget-balancing and major new spending programs. The economics of a huge income-tax increase for these purposes were described previously in the section on progressive taxation, and that scenario is bleak at best. Ultimately, that may be what it will take, but it is not likely to be popular. When was the last time that somebody was elected President on a platform of raising income taxes on the middle class? It's just not a very attractive campaign strategy, even if the budget experts all tell us that eventually an income tax increase will be inevitable if only to wrestle the out-of-control federal budget deficit down to a sustainable level.

---

100 More like a "reverse Poisson distribution."

> A VAT is regressive, unless coupled with progressive tax reforms explained previously. But it makes the most sense as a funding source for universal health care solutions and college tuition and loan relief.

This brings us now to a completely different solution to the problem of raising the new revenue needed to fund universal social programs, starting with a universal health care plan for primary/basic care. As discussed in the first section of this book, the road to expanded health care access will be complicated and most likely will involve a mix of public-sector and private-sector components. But it will take literally hundreds of billions of new tax dollars to underwrite a national system of universal care, even at the most basic and essential levels. Those mega-billions of new tax revenue are needed even if a new American health care system can cut out the profits of health insurance companies, *and* capture or replace (1) all the $1 trillion now spent on private and workplace medical insurance premiums, (2) the $580 billion now spent on Medicaid by the federal and state governments, and (3) the $200 billion of tax deductions and credits now given to employees and ACA marketplaces. Putting aside all the other social-welfare proposals that candidates have proposed, there just is not enough revenue to be gleaned from taxing Wall Street and the Fat Cats. The bloating costs of interest on the swelling national debt and existing Medicare funding deficiencies will eventually exhaust all of this new tax revenue, and leave little or nothing for health care reform. Don't forget that today's Medicare revenues already fall short of revenues and premiums received by about ten percent and it only gets worse after the trust fund is depleted in 2026.

Instead, it may be necessary to find another way to "fill in the holes in the Swiss cheese" that our current health care system has evolved into. This requires an entirely new potential source of tax revenue that would provide sufficient funding to launch a basic universal medical benefit that all Americans can count on -- to provide preventative and basic care without swarming the emergency rooms of hospitals and going bankrupt in the face of six-figure hospital bills. Similar to today's Medicare coverage, such a system will still require additional premiums from those with incomes above the national average; it can likewise allow private insurance options for deductibles and co-pays similar to Medicare Advantage plans. Employer-paid medical insurance supplements could be provided under this hybrid arrangement. Anybody who wants to supplement an "HMO service level" with PPO-type coverage would pay separately for that supplemental benefit option. Non-elective major medical costs would be covered universally, with private insurance available for elective procedures. Health care savings accounts could provide a modest tax incentive for workers to save up for large out-of-pocket expenses.

This chapter will not attempt to put a specific "price tag" on a universal health care model, because there are too many variables. A cost model for Health Care for all is presented in Topic 25 below. Rather, this section is focused on how to pay for basic health care for all Americans in the most equitable way, after giving every American voter a say in the process.

That brings us now to the Value Added Tax, the VAT as it will be abbreviated in this chapter. The VAT is familiar to most Americans who have travelled outside the country, whether to Canada, Mexico, Brazil, Chile, Europe, Japan, Australia, New Zealand, Singapore, China, South Korea, Russia, or United Arab Emirates. Over 150 countries worldwide have a VAT, and the vast majority of them are major U.S. trading partners as one can see from the list above. That means that U.S. consumers are already paying a VAT on goods imported from those countries because it has been built into the product prices before they arrived on American shores.

> A VAT is essentially a consumption tax, but everybody who profits from the product or service pays part of the cost along the way.

The VAT is most commonly described as a consumption tax, which is largely true, but incomplete. At the retail level, a consumer pays the VAT, and that is where the consumption aspect is most visible. To the consumer, it looks like a sales tax. But before the product gets to the consumer, there are taxes all the way down the supply chain, which are paid by each party along the way, and credited to the next buyer. So the VAT gets built into the price of the goods and services, but not explicitly like a sales tax. For example, if a General Motors dealer were to sell a customer a car under a VAT system, the dealer would include the VAT in its price, but receive a credit for VATs paid previously that were invoiced to it as part of "dealer cost."[101] It is important to notice that any parts or assembly in Mexico or Canada would have been subject to VAT in those countries, for which today's U.S. consumer presently gets no benefit or credit at the end of the supply chain. The value added in those countries would already have been taxed there, with no credit to the consumer unless the U.S. initiates a VAT of its own.[102]

---

101 This is called the credit-invoice system. It is the most prevalent tax-collecting procedure in most VAT countries.

102 In U.S. trade negotiations, this is a sticky point. The only way for the U.S. to level the playing field on VAT taxes is to impose a reciprocal tariff because we do not have an equivalent system. And that is a crude measure, because many end-products have multiple component and assembly sources in their supply chain; automobiles are a classic example. It is worth mentioning here that a VAT could extract a higher rate for goods imported from countries with unfair trade practices. The credit-invoice system can also deny credits for foreign goods shipped to the U.S. from countries that violate free trade, which has the same impact as a tariff and actually hurts the foreign competitor, while benefiting the domestic producer competitively. The final chapter in this section, on tariffs, briefly presents this concept as a more reliable and sustainable mechanism to motivate fair trade practices globally.

Until recently, the administrative costs and hassle factor for operating a VAT in the United States were viewed as a gargantuan reason to oppose it, but new "info-tech" has overcome that objection. Blockchain technology, used for cryptocurrencies, has the powerful potential to create unbreakable forgery-proof data chains for each product and its components as it moves through the supply chain on its way to the consumer. VAT payments and credits can be embedded in the product or its packaging at each step along the way. The blockchain digitizes what was originally a paperwork mountain in the VAT countries. In fact, many states might be attracted to the idea of piggy-backing their existing sales tax onto a VAT tax system to simplify operations for retailers, if a national VAT were implemented.

Many countries have accepted VAT tax treaties with the U.S. so that American tourists in their country can receive a VAT refund on their expenses while visiting there, but that is just the tip of the revenue iceberg, and pretty much irrelevant to this analysis. It is mentioned here just to avoid confusion for readers who may think they would somehow get a VAT refund on their purchases here in the U.S. For imports, any VAT's paid overseas would be deducted from the VAT at the point of sale.

The VAT has been proposed and advocated by pundits and politicians across the political spectrum. Even Senator Ted Cruz of Texas, whose place on the political spectrum is about as far right as a Democrat can imagine, had once proposed a VAT to replace income taxes. The right-wing Heritage Foundation also would like to replace income taxes with VATs. (Suspicious Democrats will smell a rat.) But an income-tax replacement is not the concept and strategy proposed here.

Because it is primarily a consumption tax at the end of the supply chain, a VAT is regressive in the sense that lower income and middle income families spend a much larger percentage of their income on consumption (and less in savings), than to those who are more affluent and especially those who are filthy rich. A lower percentage of income is paid in tax at successively higher income levels, even when you count the yachts. So Liberals have historically shunned the VAT as an inferior substitute for a progressive income tax. The purpose of this chapter is to encourage Democrats to take a second look, to think back to the legacy of FDR (as explained below), and to look at a comprehensive financing plan that has many progressive elements, not just one piece of it.

> A VAT in the USA makes sense only if it provides new revenue for a major new program such as universal health care.

Where tax policy debates have differed, however, is where a VAT might fit into the overall tax system if it were to become a *new* revenue source, not a *replacement* for income taxes. Here, the political divide differs. Many conservatives, who instinctively never met a tax they didn't hate on its face, are reluctant to introduce an entirely new revenue source to the federal system. They figure that "Tax and Spend Liberals" will do just that: start small with a VAT, and grow it over time, and layer it on top of income taxes and local property taxes. Some conservatives in state-level offices and legislatures also fret that a VAT could eventually overlay their state sales taxes and discourage voter approval of one of their primary revenue sources – and their best alternative to state income taxes.

Like it or not, health care insurance is a regressive cost. In the context of funding a national health care program, a VAT is actually the most well-suited tax to mirror the inherently regressive nature of basic everyday household health care expenditures. The VAT actually aligns revenues with expenses across income levels better than any other achievable solution. The people who most need a helping hand for health care subsidies are those on the lower rungs of the income ladder, so the VAT's tax revenue as a percentage of personal income is actually better aligned across the full national spectrum of taxpayers' income than any other tax.

This logic is not new; it goes back to the New Deal. A VAT for universal health care is analogous to FDR's payroll tax for Social Security, which was discussed in Topic 12. Especially when one considers cost burden to hospitals and the Medicaid system, which is paid for by those in higher income brackets, the "premiums proxy" aspect of a VAT becomes much more defensible. It addresses the highly visible "free rider" problem that is so commonly attacked by many Trump supporters who resent paying taxes for health care that they see others receive for free. Even though the total taxes paid for VAT by those in the lower end of the income spectrum will never come anywhere close to the value they receive in medical benefits, it avoids the stigma of a "welfare giveaway." The "regressive" VAT comes closer to the Social Security model of payroll taxes paid by everybody as a social-insurance program, which was an essential to Franklin Roosevelt's 1935 campaign for universal Old Age and Survivors Disability Insurance legislation. The VAT is the closest feasible tax proxy for mandatory national health care in which everybody is required to buy insurance. Nobody can call it a Robin Hood tax solution to fund socialized medicine through blatant income redistribution. It's how other countries pay for health care!

On its own, however, the VAT is not the entire fiscal solution. The other tax reforms need to be part of a "package deal" in order to turn the regressive VAT tax into a progressive total tax package. Such a progressive package must also reduce the federal deficit, to relieve younger generations of the national debt monkey that their elders have put on the backs of Millennials and collegians. This way, all the progressive tax reforms outlined previously would be coupled with the VAT, in order to reduce federal budget deficits while also funding the Liberal-Progressive benefits agenda. That way, Wall Street and the One

Percenters would pay the lion's share of that half of the funding plan as a "package deal." All taxpayers would know that for every dollar of new VAT funding for health care, another tax dollar from those with higher incomes will go to eliminate the budget deficits that will otherwise hobble America's younger adults even more than today's $1.5 trillion college debt.

> A VAT could be a rational centerpiece of a comprehensive national tax reform plan to reduce deficits and fund "Basic Health Care for All" plus public college tuition relief. But are voters really willing to go that far?

To further overcome revenue-regressivity, a VAT must be combined with a *progressive* national health care *funding* system that starts with the new tax revenue, and replaces and restructures a meaningful percentage of employer- and individual-paid medical insurance premiums for *basic* care. Medicaid would be coordinated or subsumed so that those with low incomes would receive their basic benefits along with everybody else. Those in higher income brackets would pay supplemental premiums for their basic coverage, just the way more-affluent senior citizens do now already, with Medicare.[103]

In providing universal coverage for those under age 65, current retirees' Medicare benefits can be left unchanged, as would existing Medicare taxes and discounted premiums for retirees.[104]

---

103 The Medicare surcharge is called IRMAA, which stands for income-related monthly adjustment amount, which can result in a monthly Medicare premium over $500 monthly (vs $135 standard) for taxpayers with adjusted gross incomes over $440,000.(married).

104 With the possible exception of a reduction of premiums for the elderly if VAT taxes produce sufficient revenue to overcome the growing annual deficits in that program.

If a VAT were approved for this purpose, the revenues should be reserved first and foremost for basic national health care. Just as Social Security and Medicare taxes are earmarked for those sole purposes, Americans would not want to see politicians dipping into the cookie jar for other purposes. Any surplus from VAT revenues should be used to reduce premiums, shore up the Social Security and Medicare trust funds, broaden benefits or reduce the budget deficit. The VAT should never fund national defense or farm subsidies or pork-barrel infrastructure, for example. Those conditions must be part of the deal and immutable. Likewise, the revenues from progressive companion tax reforms described earlier that target affluent taxpayers, the wealthy and Wall Street should focus on deficit reduction, not new spending. A "lockbox" provision to enhance credibility is discussed later in this section.

To be clear, a VAT will never by itself provide enough new tax revenue to fund single-payer Medicare for All, or even one-half of that cost. The "package deal" outlined here must include a realistic financial model for bare-bones basic health care, income-based premiums and supplements, and other tax and deficit reforms, in order to make the numbers work.

Americans who want additional benefits could then shop for private insurance supplements, similar to Medicare Advantage for deductibles and co-pays, and higher-tier benefits such as PPO access to physicians of choice, non-essential or elective surgeries and private hospital rooms. A universal system will never be able to afford and finance "Cadillac" health care for all, but basic preventative care, maternity coverage, acute and emergency care, and major-medical insurance (with bankruptcy-free income-based deductibles) should be available and attainable with this pricing structure. This system could also allow for fair-market credits ("vouchers") to consumers and employers who elect to purchase equivalent private insurance outside of the nation's basic medical coverage. This would promote competition and allow private-sector and non-profit insurers to compete on costs vs services, while maximizing the continuation of private insurance premium revenue needed to avoid higher taxes. Consumers who opt out at fair value would have complete freedom of choice of doctors and insurers, at a dramatically lower cost to taxpayers than a single-payer system.

There is no way that this formulation of a VAT to fund basic universal medical costs, when coupled with a progressive premium structure, can be called regressive overall. A thoughtful combination of taxes, income-based premium surcharges beyond basic universal benefits can be shown to be moderately progressive in every sense known to the financial and political worlds.

What is not certain, without extensive financial modeling beyond the research capacity and resources readily available to this author, is what level of VAT taxation would be necessary to provide the basic benefits to all citizens below the current Medicare eligibility age of 65. Would housing be excluded in exchange for a higher rate? If a ten percent VAT would not cover all the costs, what rate would? Alternatively, if the VAT and other achievable savings and cost-transfers in both the public and private sectors are not sufficient, then what would be the ground-floor monthly premium for everybody regardless of income? Presently the monthly premium for Medicare participants is $135, which would generate revenues systemwide of $450 billion annually for those below age 65, but that number is too optimistic in light of low-income and indigent families with children.

As with Medicare today, income-based premiums could be collected through payroll or by CMS[105] direct billing, with IRS 1040 tax returns the ultimate collection-enforcement instrument for delinquent payers. For those financially unable to pay that premium, a backstop

---

105 CMS is the Centers for Medicare and Medicaid (billing) Services

Medicaid program with would still be needed, but its enrollment would be limited.

Matching the necessary VAT tax rate with the national costs of basic care per capita[106] is an exercise that the Congressional Budget Office (CBO) is certainly capable of performing, if policy-makers can define the scope of services and expenses to be covered. What we do know already is that a VAT of 5 percent across the board on all goods and services was estimated by the CBO last year to raise more than $300 billion annually once it is up and running. That level does not appear on its face to be sufficient, so it would appear far more likely that a VAT tax rate of 10 percent or more would be necessary. The international average for VATs is 18 percent,[107] and the average US sales tax is 5 percent, so something in the range of 10 to 13 percent for a national VAT would be consistent with overall rates overseas. Keep in mind that VAT rates in many countries exceed that level, but one must consider both the separate sales taxes and the total tax burden on citizens and not just the VAT in isolation. As a percent of GDP, total taxes paid by taxpayers in the US are lower than most OECD countries, at roughly 25 percent of income, but a 10 percent VAT on top of that level would probably put Americans above median and into the "higher taxed" family of developed countries. Of course, there would at least be a widespread social benefit gained in return for this tax increase, which would be basic universal health care coverage that is already available in almost all other developed countries. The obvious question is whether the

---

106 For perspective, in 2014 the average annual employer-sponsored medical insurance premium for those outside Medicare was $6,000 per single person and Medicaid spent $6,600 per participant. *New York Times,* September 22, 2014. These numbers now approximate $7,000 annually. Workplace family health coverage costs averaged almost $20,000 in 2018 according to Kaiser Family Foundation survey data reported in October 2018. Medicare costs over $16,000 annually per participant 2017 using CMS data for the 44 million beneficiaries.

107 Organization for Economic Cooperation and Development (OECD) data compiled by Emily Condos for the National Association of Home Builders, August 7, 2015.

American public – and the electorate – will put up with higher taxes to secure these social benefits.

Opposition to a VAT would arise from farmers and exporters who now escape tariffs on their products. A VAT across all products would raise the cost of their goods to overseas purchasers, and that will cut into their export sales and profits. For farmers, a reasonable concession is to set a lower VAT rate on foodstuffs, which is done in several countries. This has the progressive benefit of lowering the ultimate cost of food to lower-income consumers and keeping American farm products competitive overseas. The White House has also proven quite adept at providing offset subsidies to farmers caught in the vise of trade negotiations and tariffs, and a comparable system of credits or exemptions for their exports could be explored.[108]

> Politically, a VAT must be designed carefully to avoid negative impacts on farmers, retirees, homeownership, and world trade.

Another, possibly superior approach to the farm and food problem, which has never been articulated before but is well worth considering here is to exempt raw US products from the VAT entirely, until the point at which they are processed. Corn that is grown in the United States would not be taxed under the VAT until it is purchased by an ethanol plant or a breakfast cereal maker. The VAT on the processed products would only be on the difference in price between the price paid for the raw commodity and the final price paid by the consumer. Raw vegetables and fruit at the grocery would not be taxed under this kind of

---

108 Continued subsidies could run afoul of WTO international trade rules, however.

VAT exemption.[109] Milk and fresh, unprocessed domestic meat and fish would be exempt.[110] Imported foods would be subject to VAT on arrival at customs. Wheat sold to Japan in its raw form would never be subject to a VAT but the added cost of making noodles in the U.S. would. Crude oil delivered to the pipelines and refineries in Texas would not be taxed at the well-head under the VAT. After cheese is processed from milk, wine is fermented from grapes, or a refinery converts crude oil to gasoline or diesel, the cost of that process (including profit) is subject to VAT, but the underlying cost of the raw materials would never be taxed.

This "USA home grown" exemption would keep American farmers competitive in global markets, and avoids the paperwork burden that they all hate. It is also good for consumers, especially those who avoid processed foods. A foodstuff exemption would actually make a broad-based VAT more progressive with respect to lower income households. Likewise the American petroleum industry will not be taxed for value-added on the natural resources it extracts from the ground, as this VAT would apply only for their added costs and profits from processing, shipment and retail distribution. This tax differential for native raw energy production would be beneficial throughout the economy, and to be politically correct, it could be coupled with a "Green" reduction or elimination of the petroleum industry's tax-avoiding depletion allowances for fossil fuel extraction. This *quid pro quo* would give liberals in Congress a bargaining chip for taking on that special interest lobby on their lucrative home turf.

---

109 Although frozen vegetables and fish are "processed," an exemption would be easier to administer than processing credits all the way up the food chain after the farmer or fisher sells such produce at wholesale.

110 Purists could quibble that chickens are now raised in farm-factories and that milk is processed, but broad exemptions are recommended so that Democrats can show farm families that they are on the same team, and lower-income consumers spend a disproportionate share of income on basic foodstuffs so the broader exemption is technically progressive. The exemption should not reward filet mignon, king crabs and Copper River salmon at the expense of hamburger and ground chicken.

With these exemptions, it can easily be shown that the overwhelming majority of American farm families and almost all of their workers would be better off with a VAT to pay for their basic medical care. The farm community pays for its own medical insurance without any assistance from corporations. Farmers are typically self-employed and most of their field workers receive little or no medical coverage through payroll. Once their apprehension about VAT impacts on their exports are addressed, any remaining objections from rural America would be ideological -- and actually contrary to their real economic interest.

Realtors and their lobbyists can be expected to object to a VAT, which would increase housing prices and potentially make homeownership less affordable. Most nations exempt rents from the VAT, and rental income is already subject to income taxation, so that issue can be dispensed with quickly. First-time buyers should be exempted from the VAT, to support homeownership and promote lower-cost entry-level housing construction (builders will quickly figure this out). Beyond that, however, a broader tax base is defensible. In some countries, new home construction is subject to a VAT, which will push up housing prices generally, including existing home values. Existing home sales would be subject to a VAT on the owners' profits (net sale proceeds minus purchase price and the cost of improvements) not the entire price. The taxable profit should also be adjusted downward for general inflation which should be exempt from VAT on housing. An owner who sells a house for a 20 percent net profit could be subject to a one-time VAT equivalent to roughly 2 percent of the sales price, far less than the realtor's sales commission. Readers should not forget that homeowners already enjoy a large capital gains exemption for their primary residence, so the VAT on their profits from sales net of inflation is a fraction of what many would pay in capital gains taxes even at today's low rates.

Elderly voters now receiving Medicare benefits may object to a VAT that "gives them nothing in return." That is a lot of voters: 44 million Americans are now enrolled in Medicare. Sadly, 23 percent of married retirees -- and 43 percent of single retirees --now rely on Social Security alone for 90 percent of their income. A VAT would clearly make their subsistence even worse. To address these concerns, Congress would have to institute a refundable federal income tax credit for VAT taxes paid by lower-income senior citizens. This could be itemized, or standardized with a flat dollar amount, or a percentage of taxable income up to a statutory maximum. Similarly, any VAT legislation should commit the new tax revenues from that population cohort to the Medicare program, to offset the expanding deficits in that program without raising Medicare premiums and payroll taxes more than necessary. Nobody on Capitol Hill wants to tax middle- and lower-income elders for benefits they consider to be "already earned." That said, a fair argument can be made that any VAT on wealthier elders is just collecting from them their fair share for benefits that exceed the money they have themselves paid into the system.

* * *

Taxation is, in fact, the most difficult function of government and that against which their citizens are most apt to be refractory. The general aim is therefore to adopt the mode most consonant with the circumstances and sentiments of the country."

Thomas Jefferson: Introduction to Tracy's *Political Economy*, 1816.

Even if they sweep a majority in Washington DC, Democrats would need to tread carefully before they try to invoke a major new national tax like a VAT on their electorate -- even if the end result is their cherished dream of basic universal health care. The ACA-Obamacare political saga showed everybody in politics how quickly good intentions can become ensnarled by political opposition. Politicians come and go, so the very legitimacy of one transitory electoral majority can unravel in the face of organized opposition and a contrary successor.

> A national referendum on a new VAT-centered tax reform package (to pay for federal deficit reduction, basic health care for all and universal public college tuition) would require broad political support. For Millennials and collegians, it could be their best and only shot at fiscal fairness before time runs out.

To pull off the financing strategy necessary to achieve a generational change in national health care in the United States through a VAT, Democrats might be wise to "put it up for a vote" of the entire electorate. This would give all Democrats elected in 2020, as well as their colleagues on the other side of the aisle, precious political "air cover." A referendum would also "seal the deal" politically, so that repeal would require a future Republican regime to openly and conspicuously reject a voted mandate -- even though a shadow plebiscite would not be required to repeal a bill that was once submitted to voters and approved by a popular majority.[111]

Although familiar in parliamentary systems, a national plebiscite is not part of the U.S. Constitution. Our founders were wary of runaway democracy, and established the three branches of representative government with sacrosanct checks and balances. Unlike state constitutions which provide for legislatively crafted referenda in half the states, and

---

111 If this concept advances to actual bill-drafting, it could conceivably include a provision that requires a supermajority in both houses and a Presidential signature to repeal certain core provisions, if the foundational bill were to pass the referendum vote after signature by the President. It will take legal scholars and Constitutional experts to craft any such "Denver boot" provision.

petition-based initiatives in some, the federal constitution says nothing about submitting a proposal to the people for their approval. Bills passed by Congress must be approved by the President, unless a veto is over-ruled by a legislative supermajority in both houses. Indeed, there is a Constitutional timeline required for Presidential review of a bill passed by Congress when it is in session: Article 1, Section 7 sets a ten-day limit on vetoes or else it becomes law (during normal sessions). Ten days is clearly insufficient to call and conduct a national referendum. So even if the Democrats wanted to engineer such an approval process to secure voter ratification, how could they?

Constitutional scholars have mulled over this issue from time to time. One legal scholar has suggested a non-binding advisory vote that would advise and guide the President. Problematically, that seems to run up against the ten-day veto clock sitting on the President's desk. But what if the Congress instead were to pass a VAT-for-health-care bill with explicit provisions to take effect ONLY if the president signs the bill AND a simple majority of qualified voters subsequently approve (ratify) the bill in the next national general election? This kind of a federal referendum on one of the most important public policy issues of the century would generate one of the most spirited, substantive political debates in U.S. history. For those who truly believe in democracy, this scenario would be appealing. It would require the Democrats, if they were to succeed in 2020, to craft a very thoughtful and complete legislative package that can win in plebiscite.

Politically, a national referendum on health care financing through a VAT would be hard for Senate Republicans to filibuster. Simply as a matter of optics, who can argue against "letting the people make the ultimate decision?" This does not mean that the minority party would not use every legislative stall tactic and blocking maneuver in its arsenal to fight this idea, given that the voter turnout at the polls could potentially crush them in the next election. For Democrats, it could be a win-win scenario, if their political base is solid.

Needless to say, a national referendum or plebiscite on universal health care funded by a VAT would invite heated opposition. The insurance lobby would instinctively oppose it for cutting into its markets, even though a hybrid system still leaves the affected companies a wide field for individual premiums and group benefits plans. With all the powers granted them by the *Citizens United* court decision, they will spend millions if not billions to fight it. Conservatives want nothing to do with any kind of "free" medical benefits, even if premiums are funded largely by a VAT that captures revenues from those who are presently uninsured and get a "free ride" in the emergency rooms and via Medicaid. They will also instinctively oppose a new tax, especially if it pays for benefits presently funded by group insurance premiums underwritten by businesses that finance their campaigns. If the "package deal" includes other progressive tax increases focusing on One Percenters, the opposition donorship will be even stronger.

On the positive side politically, most hospitals and nurses would support this model, as a far superior alternative to the current system of indigent and emergency care, and the underpayments that they receive through Medicaid and Medicare. The current system is bleeding them with unfairly low reimbursement rates for the uninsured, and this public-private hybrid can give them the reliable revenue stream at fair value that they need to sustain their operations. Doctors are largely unaffected by this model; they can decide which networks to join, and where they prefer fee-for-service at their own billing rates. There would not be a national monopoly, monopsony, universal price controls or socialized medicine.

Doctors who elect to provide basic primary care will undoubtedly face a standardized pricing table for eligible services and procedures similar to Medicare today, and the insurance companies will continue to bargain for allowable rates, just as they do presently. But this hybrid system would provide much more pricing and fee flexibility to doctors than single-payer Medicare for All.

Some labor groups will object if their employer-paid medical insurance becomes taxable income under a package deal,[112] and their members would pay more in VAT as consumers than they now have withheld for medical insurance in their paychecks. But that ignores the immediate savings that this program gives to employers on their group insurance costs, which can be shared with the workers in the form of higher pay or supplemental insurance coverage at employer expense.

Bear in mind that the cost of basic health care would no longer be a workplace obligation, as that would transfer to the national program. If relieved of basic healthcare costs funded by a VAT, employers nationwide could readily provide supplemental policies and still pay employees enough cash to pay any additional taxes for those benefits. From a union perspective, these packages can be bargained collectively. Every union worth its salt should be able to negotiate extra wages and higher salaries to offset this new tax on group supplemental medical insurance; that is between them, the employer and their members. Given the cost-shifting that most employers have already pushed down to the worker level for payroll deductions and co-pays, and the Obamacare taxes already now required for today's high-cost group insurance plans, it will be a small minority of bargaining units that have anything to complain about, and none of them should suffer if they do their jobs at the bargaining table. The VAT is actually a better deal for most rank-and-file union members than an equivalent payroll tax or progressively higher income tax.

Employers nationwide would enjoy lower labor costs. Their group insurance bills could be cut in half or more in most cases. Premiums paid by most employees through payroll deductions would be chopped significantly, and in most cases that would offset the taxes they would then pay. No employers would be required to provide medical insurance,

---

112 To raise revenues to cover expanded costs, Congress may need to eliminate the tax exemption employees receive for employer-provided insurance. That tax expenditure exceeds $145 billion annually, which could be redeployed instead of raising taxes otherwise.

so the ACA mandates would be unnecessary. When the tax burden of a VAT is considered, it must be remembered that the labor costs of production and doing business nationwide will be reduced significantly by the transfer of basic health care costs away from the workplace. Corporate profits will actually increase commensurately, which will please investors in companies with large labor forces.

State and local governments and all their taxpayers, employees and retirees would also benefit directly. Many of these jurisdictions have promised retirement health care benefits to their employees and never bothered to put money aside to fund these promises actuarially. Their pay-as-you-go shortcut has now amassed a $1+ trillion unfunded liability.[113] For public employers of police officers, firefighters, teachers, road workers and others who typically retire before age 65, a universal national medical insurance plan would solve a huge financial problem for those jurisdictions. Tens of millions local property taxpayers and perhaps half of the nation's residents who pay state taxes would be relieved of the albatross of unfunded retiree medical liabilities for these public servants. That money can be better spent on schools, public safety, roads and bridges, or used for local tax relief. A basic universal medical plan would provide a bridge to Medicare benefits for these early retirees, and relieve states and localities of a crushing financial burden. Public pensioners, even those already now on Medicare who worry whether their pension plans will remain solvent, can breathe easier if they know that ballooning retiree medical costs will not bankrupt their employers. Needless to say, these are powerful and reliable constituencies in the Democratic party who can be mobilized to get out the vote for a VAT.

---

113 2013 data ($696) collected by the Boston College Center for Retirement Research, Paper number 48, March 2016, would support an updated estimate in the range of $1 trillion. That study estimated that local government obligations were likely to be double those of the states. The Pew Research Center study in 2018 put the number for states alone at $696 billion, and local government obligations may equal or even that number for county, municipal and school employees.

With VAT-funded Basic Health Care for All, the states could be relieved of their Medicaid costs, which would free up $200 billion in their annual budgets to sponsor tuition relieve for public colleges, universities and community colleges.[114] Collegiate tuition relief could actually be the hidden jewel in a "package deal." Voters could be presented with the opportunity to solve three problems with one tax package: health insurance for all, college tuition relief, and a solution to the federal deficit. A potential fourth component could be a multi-trillion-dollar infrastructure program, funded by other tax reform revenues, as described in Topic 29. For this to work, a "lockbox" provision could assure voters and taxpayers that the new revenue from a VAT would be spent on those purposes only, and not diverted to any other spending spree. This could be the "*New* New Deal" or the "Better Deal for America" if ratified by voters.

In a national referendum, voter turnout would be huge. Democrats can only benefit from a surge in new voters as millions of uninsured voters would have strong incentive to cast their first-time ballots. If the VAT tax rate and the core package of basic health care benefits and premium surcharges are properly designed in the bill to be submitted to the electorate, citizens will vote their interests more than their ideologies. The potential to also eliminate the financial burden of college tuition on the middle class could further tip the scales favorably. That does not guarantee voter approval, however. The idea of a VAT tax will be unknown, new and scary to many voters. The history and conventional wisdom of referendum politics is that most voters will pull the "No" lever when in doubt. It would require a brave Presidential candidate to advance this message in the general election, unless more work is done to refine the concepts outlined in this chapter. But party leaders, the platform committee, and convention delegates deliberating the

---

114 The fiscal factors supporting this opportunity are discussed more extensively in the Health Care chapter, specifically the section on universal health insurance.

platform in Milwaukee should come prepared to consider this solution to the party's Rubik's cube of universal health care.

TOPIC 21: Tariffs

· ·

"You can fool all the people some of the time and some of the people all the time, but you cannot fool all the people all the time."

Attributed to Abraham Lincoln, posthumously[115]

Tariffs are taxes on specified imports. For decades, the public finance community has universally dismissed tariffs as a major revenue source, and never as sound public policy. But we now live in a Wonderland world in which the incumbent White House leadership has declared that the tariffs it imposes on recalcitrant trade partners are a core element in its negotiating strategy. Never mind that economic history takes us back to the ill-fated Smoot Hawley tariffs of 1930, which financial scholars almost universally blame for the ensuing global depression. Tariff retaliation, trade protectionism and competitive currency devaluations back then resulted in shrinking exports for all nations and caused a downward spiral of economic activity worldwide. In the

---

115 Historians dispute the source. In 1887 a Prohibitionist named Wheeler attributed Lincoln. Whether or not Lincoln actually said this, popular culture and advertising widely cited him by the turn of the century.

words of George Santayana, "Those who fail to learn from history are doomed to repeat it."

As a political party that lost part of its base to candidate Trump in 2016, Democrat politicians are now more vocally sympathetic to the plight of American workers whose livelihoods have been jeopardized by foreign competition, especially in the manufacturing sector. For their constituents, the tariff game looks like a great way to level the playing field for U.S. producers in specific industries. Never mind that America's consumers pay the actual cost of those tariffs through higher prices, and never mind that U.S. producers lose access to foreign markets as a result of reciprocal tariffs that a trade war invokes. Only time will tell how the Democratic candidates position and pitch their trade and tariff policies, and the Milwaukee convention will have to address this issue, because the incumbent President surely will.

A tariff is ultimately paid by the consumer, in the form of a higher price for the imported goods. Although the offshore producer may shave its price fractionally to keep its products competitive with those made in the USA, the ultimate result of almost all tariffs is higher prices for the American consumer. For U.S. producers of exports to other countries, the end-game result of a tariff war is a lost market overseas, as our soybean farmers have painfully learned from the ongoing trade spat with China. To offset the predictable retaliatory tariffs on U.S. grain, the Trump administration has bestowed subsidies to farmers to buy their votes -- although the farmers themselves would tell us they prefer to keep their markets rather than collect federal welfare checks in the form of trade subsidies. Politicians come and go, but competing overseas grain growers never go away.

Economists spurn tariffs as inefficient at the global level, because the low-cost producer is usually the most efficient, and the protected producer is less efficient and could better use its resources elsewhere (in theory, which assumes that there are other options). The problem with this theory is that in the U.S. we have failed to find the alternative employment for the laborers who get laid off when factories are built overseas to operate at lower costs. For them, there is no ivory-tower world of perfect competition and other places to work. Also, there are a few "strategic" industries where a national interest can be identified (such as steelmaking, to ensure that U.S. supply chains remain intact to build battleships in the event of war). The resulting real-world problem is that many companies and workers want their interests to be protected from foreign competition, so the tariff game becomes a political football once the door is opened in Washington DC. Politicians are the winners ultimately, as they gain self-interested votes and campaign money by protecting specific industries.

In a world in which a billion humans are living with average incomes only one-tenth of those of the U.S. level, there will always be cheaper labor somewhere else. Production of labor-intensive goods that can easily be imported from high-population, low-wage countries is a losing industrial policy strategy for advanced countries.

In America's manufacturing sector, the inevitable outcome of a high standard of living in the U.S. is that our workers in plants that become cost-inefficient globally do not have shiny new jobs awaiting them elsewhere. Our failure to address this downside of capitalism lies not in the efficiencies it brings, but in the human costs that are borne by displaced workers. Losing a high-paying job that required skills and years of experience, to become a burger-flipper, is not what American workers want. So the burden of proof for Democrats is to devise national industrial policies that help smooth the transitions. Worker retraining, free vocational-technical education at community colleges, relocation allowances and tax credits to improve worker mobility, and other strategies to upgrade our workforce and our national competitive advantage are far more difficult and costly in the short run than slapping on a protective tariff, and this remains the challenge for Democrats to address in ways that voters in the nation's industrial core can trust.

> In retrospect, Congress erred when it delegated so much power to levy tariffs to the White House.

The power of taxation, which includes the power to levy tariffs, is reserved to Congress under Article 1, Section 8 of the U.S. Constitution. In retrospect, Congress was naïve and short-sighted in delegating as many powers to the office of the President as the imperious "Tariff Man" has now claimed for his grandstanding trade and border negotiations. It seems ironic and almost quizzical that the House leadership is willing to investigate many other aspects of the incumbent president's abuses of power, but leave this one hiding under a rock. Why isn't a relevant committee (such as House Commerce, or Ways and Means) calling corporate leaders to the Hill to testify on the disruption the impetuous White House tariff antics have caused to American businesses who no longer know whether they can move their supply chains from China to Mexico or just stop expansion altogether? Perhaps the party leadership and front-running candidates are waiting to first see clear, tangible evidence of the inevitable cost impact of trade wars on American businesses, consumers and families. What actually comes out of the trade wars in 2019? How will voters weigh the impacts on the general populace and the economy against the favors bestowed selectively on Trump-base manufacturing workers who benefit from trade protectionism? Time will tell.

What we know from the standpoint of fiscal policy is that tariffs are an unreliable source of federal income, especially if the White House remains mercurial in its application, and relies more on tactics and unpredictability than on strategy, global leadership and partnership in its trade negotiations. The latest White House budget touts the tariff revenues, which it projects to be $100 billion annually, as a new revenue source to pay for such costs as farm subsidies to offset the global market share lost because of its trade war.

Except in declining industries with fierce, unfair foreign competition, most Americans are supportive of a level playing field for free and fair trade. Many Americans are uncomfortable with bullying and erratic negotiating tactics. That said, this political issue is likely to fester. Specifically, a long-term change in Chinese legal structures will be necessary in order for U.S. intellectual property rights to be enforceable in a country that does not even allow its own singers to enjoy copyright protection. Those unfamiliar with Marx-Mao-Xi thoughts on private and public ownership will underestimate the years it will require to establish Western legal protections for businesses operating in China that we take for granted in capitalist democracies. It seems unlikely that photo ops and handshakes at Mar-a-Lago will make that happen quickly. China's trade delegates are playing the long game, not a stock market game or a re-election game.

> China's leaders are playing a long game, not a stock-market game or a re-election game.

What can be said for sure is that tariffs are a volatile source of federal revenue to support ongoing domestic programs and military preparedness. They are unsustainable and unstable one-off revenues in the hands of the current incumbent President. As with one-time revenues and extraordinary revenue windfalls received by state and local governments, tariff revenues should be used for deficit reduction and nothing else, to avoid dependence on them as a funding source for ongoing activities.

Rather than tariffs on selected products, a Value Added Tax could help level the global trade playing field for the U.S. and produce sustainable, reliable revenues. A VAT can also include a higher rate or surtax that applies to imports from countries such as China that engage in unfair trade practices. Likewise, the credits normally given to importers for VAT taxes paid by foreign suppliers in their country can be denied if the World Trade Organization determines that their trade practices are unfair.[116] Both of these measures would favor domestic production, which would appeal to American workers and provide a clear incentive to other countries to reform their practices. Any VAT proposal should include these elements.

TOPIC 22: Wealth Tax

Several candidates on the Progressive wing have proposed a wealth tax, aiming their sights on the accumulated capital owned by the richest Americans. A small but vocal group of sympathetic billionaires has also put themselves on record in favor of a tax on their disproportionate wealth or income. The targets are usually taxpayers with household assets above $50 million which is commonly deemed Ultra High Net Worth (UHNW) and constitutes roughly the wealthiest 1/10th of One Percenters as measured by assets. Proposed tax rates may differ, but are usually in the range of one to three percent of assets above the level deemed to be "rich," with some proposals stepping up the rate for wealth above $1 billion.

There is no doubt that such a tax could raise significant revenues, at least on paper. A recurring two percent tax on assets over $50 million could in theory generate about $100 billion annually. Some candidates will claim that the revenue yield would be higher, basing

---

116 The international system of adjudicating these disputes is slow to act, but its actions are more defensible in the long run than unilateral Presidential declarations.

their calculations on total wealth statistics and the key assumption that wealth can be measured, audited and the tax can be enforced. To avoid capital flight, one proposal includes an "exit tax" of 40 percent for Americans who renounce their citizenship to avoid the tax, which is indicative of the problem inherent in the proposal and the punitive/confiscatory mind-set of the proponent.

> A wealth tax appeals to 99 Percenters, but it would require IRS intrusion into private lives that will be called Gestapo tactics by the GOP. Who will find and assess the value of the Picassos and emeralds? Billionaires can gift assets to private foundations and claim an income tax deduction that outweighs their wealth tax. A better solution is a loophole-free AMT.

Even assuming that a bill could clear Congress despite furious and feisty GOP resistance, enforcement will be a huge undertaking, if a wealth tax is imposed. An income tax is far easier to administer than a wealth tax, because earnings and profits are much harder to disguise and under-report. Financial wealth such as stocks and bonds are far more traceable than the economic value of privately held companies and non-marketed real estate. Appraisals would be needed for every major asset that is not regularly traded in a marketplace like stocks and bonds. Who will hunt down and put a fair value on the Picassos, private jewelry and other fine art? The IRS staff would have to be expanded dramatically and equipped with investigative subpoena powers that will spawn poster-child horror stories that will make the political fights over estate taxes look like a cocktail party.

As a practical matter, many of the billionaires have and would increasingly create a charitable foundation to hold their wealth. To avoid wealth taxes, they will take an income tax deduction for the conversion to foundation ownership, which actually reduces their federal income taxes, and the foundation will thereafter be exempt from the wealth tax.

Bedrock Conservatives will argue and undoubtedly would sue, that the Constitution precludes taking of private property without compensation, and that a Wealth Tax does just that. As historians know, the "Takings Clause" was intended to accommodate government's legitimate eminent-domain actions but was written in light of the revolutionaries' bitter memories of the British Quartering Act. The 14th Amendment extended its protections to actions by the states, where property taxes have long been upheld, so it seems unlikely that a wealth tax would flunk Constitutional muster. But there is no doubt that it would be challenged in courts and ultimately end up before the Supreme Court.

A wealth tax brings us full circle to the role that property taxes played in colonial and post-Revolutionary America. Back then, the "landed gentry" were the largest and most affluent taxpayers. Property ownership was the primary indicator of wealth prior to corporate industrialization. Property taxes are now the province of local governments, so taxation of those real assets at the federal level would be duplicative. However, most of the wealth held by the richest families is not in their mansions, but more often through their ownership of profit-making companies.

Without setting up an entirely new and intrusive tax regime, an equivalent result can be achieved by taxing the income from those assets. For example, two percent of asset values is equivalent to 29 percent of income on those assets if they return seven percent annually, which is a reasonable proxy for pretax investment returns on diversified portfolios. (Public pension funds commonly assume a seven percent return for actuarial purposes and design portfolios accordingly.) If wealth is the target, an Alternative Minimum Tax rate that imposes a surtax of 29 percent on unearned income[117] over $3 million annually would have roughly the same effect as a two percent tax on the assets.

On its face, however, that add-on seems close to confiscatory, if coupled with a higher (33-35 percent) top AMT rate as described previously. This tends to support the inevitable claims of GOP opponents that the taxing tribe is going too far in their hunt for scalps in the wealth-tax forest.[118] However, a more sensible 10 or even 15 percent AMT surtax on billionaire and ultra-millionaire income might be politically defensible and achievable -- but only if Democrats successfully sweep in the 2020 election. If Republicans retain control of the Senate, or even just their ability to filibuster any major new tax to oblivion, then the Wealth Tax or any kind of AMT equivalent will be Dead on Arrival.

---

117 Unearned income includes stock, bond, real estate and business income. It could also include all income subject to the AMT.

118 It can readily be shown, with simple math, that a proposed three percent tax on wealth each year would reduce the taxpayer's net return on investments to one percent annually, after taking inflation into account.

PART III:

Health Care Finance

....

*"America's health care system is neither healthy,
caring, nor a system."*

Walter Cronkite

Will health care take center stage in the 2020 election? Convention and election dynamics are impossible to predict too far in advance, but almost everybody involved in the political process expects that health care policy will be one of the key issues that Democrats will advance in 2020. Escalating costs of medical care and health insurance are consuming more and more of household income each year, making this a mainstream bread-and-butter issue and not just a philosophical or ideological issue like abortion, LGBTQ rights, immigration policy and Supreme Court nominations.

Early in 2019, the "Medicare for All" slogan gained traction in the media, and continues to hold strong support in the party's left wing. On the other end of the political spectrum, Republicans hate the idea. After doing all they could to dismantle the Affordable Care Act (Obamacare), Republicans failed to pass a viable replacement to fulfill their "Repeal and Replace" rhetoric when they held a majority in both houses of Congress. Instead, it now appears that their election strategy will be to simply oppose whatever the Democratic party advances as its platform theme, and brand it as the forefront of socialized medicine. Ultimately, the philosophical divide between the two parties' polar wings will likely center on individual vs. collective choices, free-market insurance vs universal coverage.

> It now appears that the GOP strategy will be to simply brand whatever Democrats propose as "socialized medicine." Candidates who fail to present a workable plan will deserve that label.

What gets lost in the ideological "battle of the bases" is that the American health care system is unique in the world. Our multi-payer system has evolved over decades into a hybrid financing blend of privately paid and employer-supported health insurance for those who can afford it, and government subsidized health care coverage for retirees and the poor through Medicare and Medicaid. Sadly, for the many millions of Americans who remain uninsured, and others who are significantly underinsured, they are the 21st century equivalent of the impoverished lower class in the time of Dickens. Lacking preventative care, their ultimate access to the system too often is hospital emergency rooms and acute care facilities that essentially subsidize non-paying indigent care with funding and fees from others (often without much luck). In the U.S., the medically uninsured constitute an underclass whose size is equal to those receiving federal food stamps.

The challenge for Democrats is figuring out how to finance affordable universal access to health care. The winning strategy cannot break the bank, alienate those who do pay, and drive medical costs even higher by flooding a finite supply of medical professionals and facilities with new consumer demand that will only add to pricing pressures.

Today, medical costs are paid by multiple payers including individuals, employers, the Medicare trust fund, and federal, state and local governments. These direct payments are supplemented by a convoluted and often invisible stream of taxpayer subsidies to the various participants. Money flows through insurance companies and a medical services industry comprised of private, public and non-profit providers with for-profit suppliers. Consequently, any plan to provide for universal coverage will have winners and losers. Health care reform is truly a Rubik's cube for Democrats, as Hillary Clinton quickly discovered when tasked with that role as First Lady in 1993.

> There are many who believe that Medicare is free health care. They are unaware of Medicare's income-based premium structure.

In the face of this complexity, there are many in the social-democrat and Progressive camp who believe that the only solution is simplicity: They would eliminate all mainstream private-sector health insurance and adopt a single-payer system along the lines of Medicare. Some of those who support this view are under the naïve belief that Medicare is free health care, which is what they are mistakenly expecting from Medicare for All. They are unaware of Medicare's income-based premium structure for retirees. Putting aside for now the problems of how to pay for it and who wins and who loses, most single-payer advocates believe that the purchasing power of a national health insurance authority will drive down costs of health care enough to make it affordable. Without ever studying the financial statements of a major company in the industry, proponents of a single-payer system expect to reduce costs for everybody, by eliminating the profits and administrative costs of private insurance companies. The obvious question is whether that cost-savings opportunity is enough to really matter. Later in this Section, the industry's profits in the health insurance business will be compared with total spending for health care nationwide, to provide a financial perspective on this expectation. (Hint: they are a small percentage, less than advocates of a single-payer system would like to portray.)

Another model for health insurance reform is the so-called "Medicare option," or the "Public option." This limited-cost, incremental step to broaden coverage is more popular among Liberals and Centrists. The Public Option school-of-thought does not attempt to provide coverage for all, but rather to expand access to Medicare[1] and provide an affordable alternative to private insurance. The core idea is to leverage the purchasing power and non-profit cost structure of the Medicare system to drive down costs. What most politicians who advocate this model have failed to do so far, however, is to explain how they would price this option, and whether it should be made available to employers. Moreover, they have failed to excite the Democratic party's Liberal-Progressive base about their pragmatic vision.

For perspective, our Medicare system spends over $13,000 per participant annually. The national average for health care spending is roughly $12,000 per capita, but these costs are not uniformly distributed. For the average American below age 65, health insurance through employer plans and Medicaid costs more like $6,000 to $7,000 annually per person. Private insurance spending nationally works out to roughly $5,500 per capita, which includes high-deductible policies with limited benefits. Demographically, average annual medical costs are much lower for young singles than for married couples with or expecting

---

1 Some proponents believe Medicaid could be expanded similarly, although they rarely explain how such an option would work, That said, the Medicaid delivery system could be a vehicle for a public option, as long as state governments can administer it. More on this, below.

children, and then for older adults with increasing age-related medical expenses before they attain age 65.

For retirees and elders with significantly higher average costs, Medicare is pre-funded and subsidized through payroll taxes during workers' lifetimes. It is widely considered to be "earned" upon achieving age 65. Participants' premiums are income-adjusted, with a premium surcharge for those with higher incomes. One size for all Americans does not fit all very well in this situation.

Although Republicans failed to achieve Senate approval of their healthcare bill in 2017, with the late Senator John McCain casting a memorable opposing vote, their ballyhooed concept of healthcare block grants to the states must be held up to daylight to see if it offers a feasible strategy -- or at least a logical component that could help broaden coverage, albeit less than universal. The decentralized, neo-federalist block-grant philosophy runs counter to the instincts of most Democrats. They see a Trojan horse that ultimately leads to cutbacks when budget cuts for "discretionary social spending" become inevitable. However, there could be a block-grant stepping-stone on the political path toward broader or universal coverage, as discussed below. Objectivity requires that this discussion include consideration of any merits that could come from the other side of the political aisle. If states are truly "the laboratories of our federalist system of governance," then a quest for novel solutions should include that possibility.

> Neither party has spent any political capital addressing the supply side of the health care marketplace.

Interestingly, neither party has spent any time or political capital addressing the supply side of the health care marketplace, other than the drug industry, which has become a favored punching bag. It's easy to point to big pharma profits, but nobody wants to attack the family doctor.[2] Congress has been clueless in appropriating money for research grants for drug research that enrich venture capitalists without requiring a cut for the taxpayer. Little rhetoric or imagination has been devoted to ways that the U.S. might expand the supply of medical practitioners or the delivery systems themselves. Most politicians are reluctant to take on the medical establishment, doctors in particular. And aside from trying to rationalize a complex and fragmented medical data industry, Democrats have done little to include supply-side economics in their toolkit of remedies. Progressives and many Millennials fret about free college education, but they have no plans for how to expand the supply of licensed doctors in this country other than to import them from overseas. Feminists abound in the Democratic party, but little attention has been given to the opportunities to modernize the nurse-practitioner market and the remaining gender biases in medical practice, where progress has been notable but incomplete. Nobody has a plan to expand the capacity and output of our nation's teaching hospitals, which would require an "infrastructure" investment (for buildings, facilities, teaching clinics and instructors) that should be equal in importance to fixing potholes – and probably with more long-run impact on the national pocketbook, dollar for dollar.

As the analysis in this book drills down into the health care sector and ways to unify it, readers must appreciate that achieving a national consensus on major issues has become increasingly difficult in a Western world of fragmented and polarized electorates. Putting together a strong coalition of competing views on health care policy will present a huge challenge to the Democratic party, regardless of who heads the ticket in 2020. Has the financial strain of health care costs on

---

2 Interestingly, salaried doctors in the USA do not earn significantly more than Canadian doctors on average, about $300,000. Although specialists in private practice earn more, they take business and liability risks that should not be overlooked.

American households finally reached the tipping point where voters will put aside their differences and demand action even if it means new taxes? If the only achievable solution is to cobble together a multi-payer hybrid solution with multiple revenue sources, can Basic Health Care for All be translated honestly and convincingly into campaign sound bites?

SYNOPSIS

No lasting improvements to the affordability of health care in the U.S. can be achieved without first understanding the numbers. In this country, we collectively spend almost $4 trillion on health care annually, about $12,000 per capita. That works out to 18 percent of gross domestic product (GDP, the total of all economic activity in the USA). Of that, the federal government already spends over $1.1 trillion on our behalf, including $700 billion through Medicare. Nationwide, another $600 billion is spent through Medicaid, the federal-state program for lower-income Americans especially children, for which 62 percent is funded federally with 38 percent paid by the states collectively. $70 billion is expended annually for veterans' medical benefits. Uncle Sam also spends about $50 billion annually subsidizing state-level insurance exchanges under Obamacare; these invisible payments are often overlooked.

Government's role does not stop there, however, because $150 billion of income tax receipts are passed over each year for workers (private, public and non-profit) whose employers purchase medical insurance for their employees. Those employer-paid premiums are not only deductible as business expenses by taxable private firms, but more importantly, they are also exempt from all the employees' income taxes as "fringe benefits." States also forgo their income taxes on those premiums, costing them more than $30 billion annually. Government budgeteers call this a "tax expenditure."

Our multi-payer system has many hands that feed it. The employers themselves spent $880 billion of their money outright on group insurance benefits in 2018. Individuals paid hundreds of billions of dollars for private insurance policies including those issued through the state level insurance exchanges. To that, one can then add in the Medicare advantage insurance policies purchased by the elderly, and everybody's deductibles and co-pays. Payments out of pocket now exceed $360 billion annually, and prescription drug spending exceeds $300 million outside of Medicare Part D.

Any program that tries to replace all those various sources and uses of health care funding will displace well-established, ongoing contributions already made by employers, governments and individuals. The private insurance industry sits in the middle of all this, but only for a fraction of all the financial activity. So it is inevitable that whatever the outcome, there will be winners and losers, even before the alternative funding sources are considered. And the stakes are very high.

Polling data in 2019 indicates that the general populace is supportive of extending national health insurance to cover more people, but that support drops as soon as the question includes an income tax increase to pay for it. As with so many government programs, majorities favor the idea as long as somebody else pays for it. "Don't tax you, don't tax me, tax that guy behind the tree" is a timeworn slogan that resonates in the health care debate.

Medicare benefits could be offered at-cost as an option for all Americans and all employers without replacing the entire private sector system. Because it operates without profits and with lower overhead costs than private insurance companies, a public option through the Medicare administrative system (CMS) could deliver processing cost savings of $400 to $500 per year per participant. This can be accomplished without new tax revenues.

> It would take $1½ trillion of new annual federal tax revenue to replace all the non-governmental payment sources. That number would require massive new taxes on the middle class, not just the rich.

On the other hand, the economics of a complete take-over of the health insurance industry are quite different and far more disruptive. If social-democrats and Progressives seek to replace all the non-governmental payment sources for health care with taxpayer dollars, it would take at least $1½ trillion of new annual federal tax revenue. That number cannot be raised simply on the backs of just the wealthy on a sustainable basis. To put that number into perspective, the federal income tax collects $1.8 trillion annually from individuals, and the top tax rate is 37%. Using middle-school math, an 80 percent increase in income tax rates across the board would invoke a tax rate of 68% on the top-bracket taxpayers in order to fund nationalized health care. That ignores state and local taxes which would consume another 10-15% of those taxpayers' income in many Blue states, for a combined top rate as high as 83% -- which flunks the smell test as confiscatory. Meanwhile, budget deficits for other national spending will continue to escalate dangerously without remedy, so obviously, that math simply doesn't work. Any attempt to reconstruct the national health insurance complex will probably require some kind of hybrid solution that effectively leverages existing premium and payment sources, or an alternative, new revenue source. Although many public-policy and public-finance professionals might consider a new tax to be the best achievable strategy, it remains to be seen whether any candidate can rise to the occasion to present a palatable solution that a national majority of voters can understand and support. The narratives in this Section will address those options and the relevant fiscal considerations.

"Public Options" (expanded Medicare and Medicaid)

"What Americans want is more affordable health care"

Susan Collins. Senator (R), Maine

TOPIC 23: Medicare at Cost.

....

The least costly way to expand health insurance coverage, but with more benefit for those now insured than for those still uninsured, is to offer Medicare-administered coverage to all citizens at the actuarial cost for their demographic group. This would be a non-profit insurance system running in tandem with Medicare as we know it now, offering similar benefits, but with premiums based entirely on what the accountants calculate to be the average costs for each age group and family size. Costs and premiums could be determined regionally to reflect differing costs of living and income levels in rural Mississippi and West Virginia vs urban San Francisco and New York City. Young singles would pay less than their married cohorts, and their premiums would be lower than their parents approaching retirement age with higher average medical costs. Families would pay more than individuals, but less than per capita.

To implement such a program without swamping the medical services industry and the agency running it, implementation would best begin with those aged 50 and over, and then work down the age ladder each year to younger pricing groups until the option is available to all citizens after three or four years. Each year, the system actuaries would study actual costs nationwide for each cohort group and make premium adjustments to reflect the experience of each pricing group.

> Medicare at Cost could save each participant $400 to $500 annually. It's a great place to start. But that does not give us free health care.

Instead of private insurance, there would be no corporate profits, much lower overhead costs, and group purchasing power through Medicare's ability to dictate or at least negotiate better pricing, which most Democrats and Independents would applaud. Defenders of the status quo would point out that the share of Medicare expenses consumed by administrative costs has risen dramatically over the past 20 years, so it's not a free lunch.[3] That said, there would be some obvious administrative and overhead cost savings, and no need for marketing expenses and profit margins, to service the population that opts into Medicare at cost. For the purposes of this section, an estimate of such premium cost reductions in the range of $400 to $500 per year per participant is sufficient for discussion of the fiscal factors. (The components of this estimate are presented later in Topic 25 on universal health insurance coverage.)

If offered at-cost, as outlined above, there would be no additional federal expenses and no need for additional taxes. Program administration costs can be included in the premium structure. This is the "pure" public option, in the sense that it simply offers the Medicare benefits to all Americans on an optional non-profit basis. Undoubtedly there would be many employers who would jump at the chance to save $400 annually per (single) enrollee for themselves and their employees, if the

---

3 Source: Peterson Foundation graphic, *Composition of Medicare Spending Over Time.*

Medicare agencies are actually able to deliver such savings per capita. Employers would be able to purchase coverage either by formula based on their average workforce demographics, or they could be experience-rated just as they are now for larger employers. There could be favorable group-pricing schedules for employers who collect premiums through payroll, again with cost-based regional premium adjustments. As for who pays what share of the group premiums, that would be an employer-based decision. Collective bargaining would continue to apply where the workforce is unionized.

One advantage of this program design is that there is no social stigma attached to optional Medicare participation. Unlike Medicaid, which is viewed by the populace as "welfare" and thus a handout, Medicare is broadly seen as an earned benefit. Joining Medicare early through a program billed as "at-cost" would give participants a sense of dignity and fairness. Every consumer and employer would view their premiums as "non-profit pricing," which is presumably lower than private insurance pricing. Consumers would become much more familiar with the ins and outs of Medicare rules long before they retire, making the transition to retirement benefits smoother and arguably more natural. Workers who leave a job would no longer need a mandated employer-based COBRA benefits continuation entitlement, because Medicare-at-cost would be available to them without the risk of expiration. Having an at-cost option for older workers who may take early retirement could also relieve pressure on employers with older workers and retirees. State and local government employees who enjoy pre-65 retirement medical benefits could be reimbursed by their employers for part of their at-cost Medicare premiums, which could be lower than what some group insurers now typically charge early retirees. This portal also would provide an option to current workers when the day inevitably arrives that Medicare eligibility age (65) requirements must be raised to match those required for full Social Security benefits, (which is now age 66 and will escalate by law to 67 in 2027, with more adjustments still needed actuarially for increased longevity).[4]

If Progressives and Liberals insist that there must be a subsidy built into this kind of Medicare expansion, there are two paths to consider, and they need not be mutually exclusive if the funding sources are secured. One path is to extend Medicaid eligibility rules separately as described in the next segment. The second path is to provide a tax credit for those participants who join Medicare at-cost, calibrated on the basis of their income. For an example, Congress could start with a scaled-down version of Senator Kamala Harris' proposed $6,000 credit for every household making less than six figures as a template, focusing it instead on expanded health coverage and nothing else. A more-realistic earned-income healthcare tax credit might be feasible in the range of a few thousand dollars for citizen[5] households earning less than the national median income, who elect to pay the optional Medicare-at-cost premiums. Costs at that level could realistically be funded by one of the various tax reforms quantified previously in Part II. Whether this public option is just a transition step toward universal coverage, or the best achievable outcome, will depend on a multitude of tax and spending decisions in 2021 and beyond. The next Congress must also grapple with the already-ballooning deficit, and the competing proposals to help with other challenges facing the 50 percent of Americans who don't have enough savings today to cover even one minor hospital procedure.

---

4 A reduction factor, similar to the age 62 early retirement option for Social Security, could readily be administered in this expanded Medicare system. Just like Social Security for early retirees, individual premiums for Medicare would be higher for their lifetime for those who elect to commence subsidized retirement benefits at the lower age.

5 Note that undocumented aliens would not qualify for this subsidy, as described here, if only to forestall predictable conservative backlash. See alternative matching-grant cost-sharing concept, below.

TOPIC 24: Medicaid expansion.

....

The second strategy for a Public Option is to extend Medicaid, which is the national low-income health insurance system that provides federal and state assistance to households below and slightly above the poverty level. Most readers would be surprised to learn that 39 percent of all children are enrolled in Medicaid, and that Medicaid covers a total population of 75 million Americans. To participate in the Medicaid program under the federal rules, states must meet various matching contribution requirements. Presently, the states collectively pay about 38 percent of total Medicaid costs. Most readers are unaware of how much the states already now spend on Medicaid, which averages more than one-fourth (26%) of their budgets nationally. That works out to four times what states spend on roads, bridges and public transportation, and more than double what they spend on higher education.[6]

To expand Medicaid coverage to the currently uninsured and under-insured, one feasible method would be to expand Medicaid but with an income-based premium structure and a higher share of costs to be borne by participating states. This leaves the ultimate decision on pricing and eligible income levels to the states, which would probably help in attaining bipartisan support in Congress from GOP members who adore local determination and decentralization of power. Just as an example, Congress could approve a maximum federal contribution of 50 percent to the cost pool for new participants above current income thresholds that would then receive "extended Medicaid" in any given state. Then as long as each state contributes at least 25 percent to the costs for each additional participant, they could (in this example) each

---

6 If states were relieved of their financial obligations for Medicaid through a universal insurance system funded by a new federal taxing source, such as the VAT discussed previously, then their budgets could readily afford to underwrite free tuition for in-state students.

set the ground rules for premium structures, co-payments and other eligibility standards. If additional federal taxpayer funding for this expansion is limited, then the federal share or the income limits could be reduced, in order to fit into the national budget. With 30 million potential new eligible enrollees each requiring at least 50 percent of $6,000 of insurance coverage per capita, the price tag for this option would be $90 billion *for starters – until the crossovers start.*

> If subsidized medical benefits are to be offered to all citizens in lower income brackets, there will be cross-over from those currently insured, and costs to taxpayers could explode.

As that last clause hinted, there is problem with this model that must be acknowledged. If medical benefits are to be offered to all citizens in the lower income brackets, even with an income-based premium, there will be cross-over from currently insured participants who also want the subsidy. Certainly there will be many of today's under-insured households who would then expect cheaper, better benefits, as well as many small employers who would stop providing workplace medical benefits if their workers can then "get Medicaid at taxpayer expense." So the number of actual participants in an expanded, subsidized Medicaid program would almost certainly exceed 30 million. This crossover will drag the program costs higher, with no behavioral experience to help the actuaries make accurate estimates of the optional participation rates. Herein lies the problem of trying to re-wire the current system. Just how much crossover the actuaries would predict is beyond the scope of this book, but the problem stands there before us, and would have to be quantified by experts and research on this issue.

For the uninsured with incomes above the national average, and not covered by an employer, a Medicaid extension would have to offer them the coverage at cost with a small federal matching grant of perhaps ten or fifteen percent to states that offer an equivalent sharing of premium costs. That would make for a small and fiscally manageable subsidy that clearly chips away at the number of remaining uninsured and underinsured. It could also provide the foundation for premium-paid insurance of undocumented workers, who would have to enroll and declare their status in order to qualify.

A Medicaid expansion strategy with required premiums could offer a political solution to the Democrats' problem of coverage (at cost) for undocumented immigrants.

Another variation on the Medicaid extension option was suggested earlier, which is to use federal block grants to the states as a way to enable them to spend the money as they wish on the Medicaid extension with as few strings attached as possible. If a matching source of new revenue can be established through tax reforms, the block grant approach could be a viable bipartisan strategy to extend existing Medicaid benefits to uninsured and underinsured citizens who would pay an income-based premium determined by each state. A minimum state-paid component of this elective process would be required, with each state to determine for itself how to come up with its share of costs and whether its taxpayers should support broader coverage. The result would be lower subsidies than those now given to existing Medicaid recipients, with a lower cost to the federal taxpayer but a higher cost to state taxpayers whose elected officials would then determine the level of market penetration they can afford to underwrite. This formulation would provide am important safety net for those who opt in. It could provide a path toward more universal coverage.

Republicans would clearly prefer this option, simply as a matter of their federalist-decentralist DNA. Red states would be able to shuffle the funds as they see fit, without bureaucrats in Washington DC telling them how to spend the money. As suggested before, many Democrats will balk at this solution, for some of the very reasons that Republicans would advocate it. If today's primary federal budget deficits are not cured, it is much easier to cut and eventually unwind a block grant program in times of fiscal stress and budgetary crowding-out, whereas a formula-based "entitlement" program will be harder to choke off. Thus, the issue here ultimately boils down to pragmatic politics: if the only way to get to first base in the expansion of affordable health care access for all U.S. citizens is through a bipartisan block grant program to extend Medicaid benefits, then the Centrists and most Liberals would take half a loaf and keep working for the other half.

Neither of these strategies will establish universal health care, but they would make significant headway in the right direction. The price tag would depend on the levels of federal subsidy provided, which will also require cost-sharing with the states and the enrollees. The employer-based insurance system would remain intact and private insurance companies can still operate at a smaller but still manageable level of profitability. The federal programs would provide a public-sector yardstick and price competition for private industry that keeps everybody on their toes.[7] And the leap from there to viable national health insurance options would be much smaller in later years.

---

7 Those familiar with the Tennessee Valley Authority may know that one of its stated goals was to provide a national yardstick for understanding the pricing economics of power generation, so that rate-setting boards at the state level would have access to comparable data from a not-for-profit enterprise.

TOPIC 25: Universal health care coverage

....

This brings us to the knotty problem of how to transform today's hybrid system of public and private health insurance into universal coverage. With the federal government now paying about one-fourth of the total cost of health care in our country, how could it even be possible to underwrite a complete takeover of the nation's medical establishment? As explained previously in Part II, there simply are not enough tax sources available to the U.S. government to underwrite a single-payer system *and* rebalance the nation's existing budget deficit enough to avoid running all other "discretionary" social programs including higher education, food stamps, public housing into the ground in 15 years. To Republicans and many Independents, it looks like an impossible dream simply on the basis of cost.

As to cost, there is no question that a single-payer system could eliminate certain expenses now inherent in the multi-payer system with private insurance companies serving as intermediaries. For the sake of this discussion, it would arguably be possible to eliminate the entire 320,000 workforce employed in the private health insurance industry, and replace them with triple the headcount of workers at the federal processing agency CMS, which presently employs only 8,000. A workforce reduction of 300,000 personnel averaging $80,000 annually for employee compensation including commissions could save a single-payer system about $25 billion annually, and another $5 billion could be eliminated from office rent and redundant computer systems along with promotional and advertising expenses. That totals $30 billion, but that number is a tiny fraction of what some advocates of the single-payer concept have presumptively cited as the potential for "administrative waste" in the industry.

As for the private-sector insurance industry profits, they are not inconsequential but they also are not the dominant element in the total financial picture -- especially if the choice is between new taxes and existing payments by employers and other premium-payers in the current system. The health insurance industry collects about $1.1 trillion in private premiums annually, and the average reported profit margin In this industry sub-sector is relatively low at roughly five percent, sometimes lower. So the total savings from eliminating the profits of all health insurance companies would be about $50 billion after taxes annually, nationwide. (Recent industry data are actually lower.) Along with other obvious expense reductions, that adds up to $80 billion in potential savings for the 180 million insured consumers of private individual and group policies, which works out to $450 per person per year that Medicare-at-cost could reasonably save the average customer. That represents a savings in the order of magnitude of five to seven percent of paid premiums.

> Saving $80 billion by eliminating the entire private insurance industry will not give us free health care in a $4 trillion marketplace. That is only a 2% cost reduction.

By hypothetically eliminating the private insurance industry, a potential of $80 billion in savings sounds a big number to voters who live within budgets in thousands and not twelve-digit numbers. When compared with the $4 trillion spent each year on health care in the U.S., those potential cost savings represent a measly two percent. Health insurance company profit margins are lower on average than the margins of most Fortune 500 companies. From the federal fiscal perspective, $80 billion is just a down payment when compared with the added taxes necessary to provide universal coverage. Those numbers are 15 to 25 times larger. Using the fringe socialists' anti-profits axe to fund universal health care costs would be like cutting down a Sequoia tree with a kitchen knife.

Part of the problem with moving to a single-payer system is that the current multi-payer system has many contributors to the total cost who would be relieved of their obligations under a universal program. There is no magical nor equitable way to require them to keep paying what they do now, if Uncle Sam starts footing the bills for all those now outside the system. Even if a universal program were means-tested, the subsidies required for citizens now paying for health care and insurance themselves or through their employer would magnify the cost to general taxpayers. Because employer contributions to group medical insurance plans are not uniform, there is no equitable way to replace their premiums which total $880 million annually. Nationalized health insurance would become a windfall for those employers. This would be a clear benefit to corporate investors and some sectors of the American economy, but there is not a convenient way to transfer those dollars into the U.S. treasury. This "free substitution" problem can be solved only by retaining or recapturing as much of the current non-governmental contributions to insurance costs as possible. That requires a plan to structure premiums and service levels in a way that requires income-based contributions for basic care and additional unsubsidized premiums and payments for "extras." In other words, it cannot be free health care for all without a massive new tax regime.

One of the recurring complaints about the present health care system is that Americans over-consume medical care, spending more per capita and more as a percent of GDP than any other country, without a discernable difference in health outcomes. Undoubtedly, much of this can be blamed on Americans' hyper-consumption of potato chips and fast foods, and how much we spend on prolonging the lives of elders in their last 60 days, which are subjects beyond the scope of this book. But one avenue for systematic reform is to properly price, and stop subsidizing, premium-care service levels. A cost-controlling system cannot subsidize premium care. Presently, the tax exemption of employer subsidies for group health insurance gives workers an incentive to over-consume their insurance coverage. Even with increasingly higher deductibles and co-pays shifting a higher fraction of costs to employees, most employer-paid medical benefits plans still subsidize at least part of higher-end coverage such as PPO plans. If universal medical coverage is to be provided, it will need to incorporate ever-more-accurate pricing structures so that the true cost of premium and elective care is paid without subsidies, by the consumer directly or through taxable employer contributions.

The bottom line is that if Medicare for All means universal access to health care at current Medicare coverage levels through a single-payer system at nominal premium cost to citizens, is impossible to finance without at least $1.5 trillion of new tax dollars to pay for it. Even with a huge increase in income taxes, income-based premiums similar to Medicare today, plus all the potential tax reforms targeting the One Percenters and Wall Street that were described previously, the math simply does not work. There is no way to raise that much new revenue without bleeding all other discretionary social programs to zero in 15 years. By then, escalating federal interest costs, defense spending and the entitlement programs will chew up all available revenue. Deficits matter, the swelling cost of interest on the national debt will continue to crowd out social programs, and Medicare for All sloganeering simply ignores that problem.

For the democratic socialists and their supporters in the Progressive wing, that is a message they do not want to hear. They may remain convinced that somewhere out there they can locate and shake down a Money Tree that will cover the costs. Prior to the Milwaukee convention, all that fiscally literate Liberals and Centrists can do is to ask them to explicitly list and quantify where they will actually find the money, and hold them accountable for their Pinocchios.

> This does not mean that universal coverage is impossible to attain. What it means is that free money is impossible to attain.

This does not mean that universal coverage is impossible to attain. What it means is that free money is impossible to attain. However, a well-designed transition over time to a universal system of affordable basic care is potentially achievable, if Democrats are willing to do the hard work to make it happen. And an enduring, irreversible fast-track solution is also conceivable if the party is brave enough to put it up for a national vote in 2022.

Nobody can say right now whether the best strategy is to start with the Public Options described previously, and work step-by-step on a long-term plan to attain universal coverage for basic health care, or move more quickly to install a national plan "while the iron is hot." That depends on who wins the primaries and the nomination, and how the electorate responds to whatever vision the Democratic party formulates at its convention and presents during the 2020 campaign.

As a "stake in the ground" or a "strawman" example, what follows is a description of "Basic Health Care For All," if Democrats are willing to bite the bullet on the controversial taxation strategies it will require, which are a tall order to say the least. After describing the cost components, policy framework and rationale, the taxation requirements and options will follow.

The basic building blocks of Basic Health Care For All include:

1. Retain Medicaid as it operates presently. This requires the states to continue their contributions and cost-sharing for low-income coverage.

2. Provide all citizens a low-premium national insurance option for basic medical care including preventative care, wellness programs, and HMO-level medical services and major medical insurance, to require cost-sharing by the consumer -- with reasonable income-based bankruptcy-free stratified deductibles and co-pays. Call this Medicare Silver. (Retirees get Medicare Gold.) With non-profit administration, this should cost $400 to $500 per year per person less than what private insurance companies would charge for an identical benefits package.

3. For low-income participants who enroll in Medicare Silver, offset their premiums with an earned income tax credit that diminishes as their earnings approach the nation's average household income.[8] Their individual premium cost net of the tax credit will be higher than Medicaid. To receive a full tax credit above a basic subsistence level, the enrollee must work and earn income. The size of this tax credit will be determined and limited by the revenues available, so a revenue plan is instrumental here.

4. Medicare Silver premiums will be income adjusted. Participants with higher incomes must pay higher premiums, as they do now for today's Medicare for retirees. But to be equitable as well as realistic, Medicare Silver premiums will be higher than Medicare Gold, given that the latter have been earned by retirees over a lifetime of prior employment and contributions. There is no "prepaid" trust fund to subsidize the Silver program, even on paper.

5. Employers may pay some or all of their employees' health insurance premiums, with that decision made internally by each organization. Medicare Silver and affiliated supplemental plans

---

8 That median was $61,000 in 2017. It could be adjusted for regional cost-of-living differentials.

will no longer be tax deductible for the employee, although private companies will continue to deduct their payments as a business expense. For many, a cafeteria plan arrangement could give employees an elective after-tax allowance (that could be used otherwise for Roth 401k contributions or other nondeductible benefits). Existing collective bargaining agreements and laws would apply, although renegotiation would be expected at many workplaces. The self-employed would deduct one-half rather than all their medical insurance on their tax returns, representing the "employer" share of their premiums.

6. Alternatively, employers could continue to privately pay their employees' group insurance just as they do now. Their employees could continue to enjoy their tax exemption for the employer contributions if they elect to remain in a qualified employer-sponsored plan that provides equivalent benefits.[9] These employees would not participate in Medicare Silver or a supplemental plan, but they would remain eligible for Medicare Gold when they retire.

7. Supplemental Medicare Silver Advantage insurance can be made available to all citizens individually and employers as group policies by private insurance companies who compete for that business. Consumers can elect higher service levels, such as PPO coverage, lower deductibles and co-pays in exchange for higher premiums. No federal or state subsidies apply to this supplemental coverage which would be available only to Medicare Silver participants.

8. Consumers and employers could freely opt out of the national basic care program and take a reasonable unsubsidized

9 To eliminate subsidies for premium coverage, the current cap on high-cost "Cadillac" plans would have to be reduced by capping the tax deduction.

fair-market credit[10] (voucher) with them to buy alternative coverage through state-level exchanges, group insurance companies and non-profit competitors. This "voucher" feature would be similar in concept to the educational vouchers favored by so many Republicans -- with the key difference that it would not bleed the public system when calibrated properly to cover only essential costs and avoid subsidizing the private and for-profit alternatives. The voucher feature would show that what is good for the goose in public schools is good for the gander in private health insurance. Politically, this opt-out feature would go a long way to neutralize the traditional objections to socialized medicine, and would foster competition between public and private sectors that Conservatives consider necessary and Moderates and "establishment" Liberals would deem preferable. Public-finance economists, doctors and the "medical establishment" would find this "public choice" model meritorious as the most pragmatic way to achieve universal coverage without socializing medicine.[11]

The complexity of this multi-payer model is not easily reduced to sound bites and campaign rhetoric. If mismanaged, the messaging alone could be too complex to be successful with average voters. Whether the concept of Basic Health Care for All can be simplified conceptually to its least-common-denominator is a public relations job in itself. Fortunately, there are DNC staffers and PR firms standing by anxiously that can perform this task.

---

10 The easiest administrative method would be a tax credit on the 1040 tax return, but it is also conceivable that insurance companies could be reimbursed and interact directly with the federal government's billing agency (CMS presently).

11 No claim is made here that this system would materially reduce national health care expenditures. By providing the funds for universal coverage, the demand side of the health care economy would increase, and that can only add to total expenditures. A solution would still be needed on the supply side, which is discussed in Topic 26.

The federal cost of this prototypical national insurance model will depend on the actual per capita costs of basic health insurance, the design of the income-adjusted premium structure, and the size of tax credits given to participating Medicare Silver households below the national median income level. The single most important variable will be the level of employer contributions under the new system, and the extent that employers will retain their current group policies even when other options become available to themselves and their employees. That requires sophisticated financial modeling beyond the scope of this chapter, but ballpark estimates are feasible.

> In a well-designed multi-payer system, most employers would likely continue to contribute to workplace insurance, and their costs would be lower.

Most employers would likely continue to contribute to workplace insurance of some kind, because their employees' supplemental premium costs will generally be lower than most now pay for private insurance at the basic HMO premium level that most employers use as their base cost. For perspective, the national average for participating employers' contributions is about $5,600 for single employees, or 82% of those premiums. Many of them can be expected to continue providing employer-funded health insurance, either through their current provider or through Medicare Silver at group rates. Some employers will become new sponsors under the lower-cost Medicare Silver plan, and others will abandon group policies and simply provide taxable supplemental options, or cafeteria benefits. Each of these self-interested choices will represent a step toward economic efficiency that a monolithic single-payer model cannot ever provide.

To build a total cost model for this hybrid plan design, the following elements would apply, with the caveat that this estimation process is purely a SWAG[12] using "bar-napkin precision" to deliver crude ballpark ranges:

a. Basic Medicaid expenses remain relatively unchanged, and the net additional cost of some participants moving into Medicare Silver would be relatively modest, perhaps $1,000 annually for around 15 percent of that subpopulation, which would add a cost of $10 billion annually.

b. New subsidies for 30 million currently uninsured Americans at an average subsidy of $5,000 annually, taking into account some recovery of income-based premiums from them, which would add a new cost of $150 billion annually.

c. New subsidies for 40 million under-insured, at an average annual cost of $3,000 per enrollee, for an additional new cost of $120 billion annually.

d. Basic health care costs, net of income-based premiums, for individuals and the employees now covered by group policies who migrate into Medicare Silver, would involve a population of 180 million at an average estimated federal cost of $2,000 to $3,000, would require a net annual subsidy in the range of $300 to $500 billion.[13] However, this new cost can be reduced by as much as $75 to $150 billion by a modest per-participant business tax credit for employer-paid or individual-paid health insurance

---

12 SWAG = Strategic Wild-Assed Guess

13 This incremental cost includes the net savings from eliminating tax exemption for employer contributions if everybody were to migrate to Medicare Silver. The next sentence quantifies the probable offset, perhaps $1000 per participant as a credit on the employer's or self-employed income tax return

that induces employers and employees to retain their current private coverage and opt out of Medicare Silver.

e. Total new subsidies likely to be required from the federal taxpayers would total something in the broad range of $500 to $700 billion. As readers can now see, much depends on the per capita subsidies required to replace insurance premiums now paid by employers, employees and individuals. The closer an enrollee's income-based premium structure can come to the private insurance premium costs now borne by individuals and employers, and the more that employers retain their existing plans, the lower the net new taxation that will be required. But it is almost unimaginable to believe that anything less than a half-trillion dollars of additional annual taxes will suffice.

> Single-payer is a mathematical as well as a political impossibility.

This hybrid, multi-payer model will appear too convoluted for those on the far Left who envision a big, grand and simple solution. The problem is that their big, grand and simple single-payer dream cannot easily replace the revenues and premiums now paid by others in America's unique public-private health care insurance model. If anybody can show us where they would find the additional taxes to fund all the premiums for citizens who are now uninsured and underinsured, PLUS the $1.1 trillion now paid annually to insurance companies by employers, employees and individuals, PLUS the $280 billion now contributed annually by the states directly and indirectly, we might be able to begin an intelligent discussion. But that is simply not going to happen. It is a mathematical as well as a political impossibility.

But what about compliance? Will everybody enroll? This hybrid multi-payer Basic Health Care For All plan design gives affordable options to most Americans, but it remains unrealistic to expect that the entire population will participate without both a carrot and a stick. Where Congress has legislative leverage without imposing a penalty directly as it did with Obamacare, is its ability to deny future subsidized traditional Medicare Gold coverage to elderly citizens who have declined to join the new system during their lifetime.[14] That is a deal nobody can refuse. Except the richest of the rich and a few indigent mentally disabled (who qualify for Medicaid by definition) no rational consumer would disclaim their subsidized retirement Medicare benefits, so this future-exclusion penalty provision becomes the ultimate hammer to motivate participation. In a way, this is not entirely a new idea: A similar club applies now to Medicare Part D coverage, where a failure to join at age 65 (and pay the price for income-based premiums) results in draconian fees for later enrollments, so there is an effective precedent available to assure compliance without precipitating a losing Supreme Court case that brings down the entire law.

In theory, the costs to operate a hybrid model along the outline provided above could be funded by a combination of tax increases and tax reforms presented in the previous section with that heading. Ignoring for a moment the unresolved problem of today's $1 trillion annual budget deficit (which would not be cured by the new revenues required to fund "just" Basic Health Care For All), it would take a combination of:

- A substantial increase in income tax rates for One Percenters and the entire upper middle class to levels possibly even higher than they were under Obama and Clinton

---

14 To pass judicial review, such citizens would probably need to be offered Medicare Gold *at cost* to make the "election" non-compulsory and free of duress. Note that this case is actually stronger after the Medicare trust funds are depleted.

- An increase in the corporate income tax from 21 to 25percent and a new surtax on corporate stock buy-backs

- A new financial transactions tax

- A new, stiffer and comprehensive Alternative Minimum Tax, AND

- Elimination of all various tax preferences and loopholes described in the preceding section on tax reform, including the estate tax, capital gains step-up, fossil fuel tax preferences, carried interest taxation, and private business pass-through tax deductions.

For perspective, let's start with some big round numbers here, what we call "one significant digit" data points. Without repeating the granular annual revenue estimates that are provided in Part 2 of this book, the relevant order of magnitude of each one of the preceding five bullets is $100 to $150 billion, for a total of $600 billion if all of them were enacted simultaneously. Any politician or single-payer advocate who claims that universal health care can be funded properly with just one or two of those tax revenues is either delusional, incompetent or contending for a Pinocchio award. Any one of these five revenue sources could, however, fund the two Public Options as described previously, including Medicare at Cost and a modestly subsidized Medicaid extension – which would itself be a major step forward toward affordable coverage for tens of millions of uninsured households.

Putting heath care reform aside for a moment, readers should note that a combination of *all* the tax reforms listed above will still not themselves balance the federal budget at current spending levels. That will require an even-larger additional revenue source, significantly more than just tax reforms that focus mostly on the One Percenters and Wall Street.

> The only solution that covers both the national debt problem *and* the affordable health care problem is a new tax such as the VAT, in addition to all the tax reforms in Part II. Otherwise we get health care and a sick economy with inflation and economic malaise.

The only solution that covers both the national debt problem *and* the affordable health care problem is the Valued Added Tax (VAT) funding strategy explained in the Tax Policy chapter. Even a VAT would have to be supplemented with the tax reforms listed above in order to both fund Basic Health Care for All and close the budgetary gap enough to avoid financial Armageddon in 15 to 20 years. A "lockbox" provision would be necessary to guarantee that new VAT and associated tax reform revenues are earmarked exclusively for the specified purposes and not any other new Congressional Christmas-tree spending. Notably, there is a silver lining to that approach: As mentioned earlier, a VAT-funded comprehensive health care program that relieves state governments of their Medicaid cost burdens would free up ample cash for most states to underwrite free resident tuition at public colleges and universities. It becomes a "Two-Fer" or a "BOGO"[15] package, which dramatically increases its popular political appeal for the Democratic base, and most Millennials and collegians. But not without a huge cost in additional taxes across the entire population and not just the One Percenters.

> Rational Millennials and collegians who become fiscally literate will come to realize that a "package deal" would be in their best long-term interests.

---

15 "Buy One, Get One" free, a common grocery and retail promotional slogan.

To awaken Americans to the financial requirements and implications, a six-month task force appointed in early 2021 could deliver a plan for "Universal Health Care and College Funding with a Balanced Budget," which might be the right political approach to unify a majoritarian funding plan for Congress to consider. The subtitle could be "A Better Deal for America" or the "*New* New Deal" or "America 2030." This report could accompany an incremental first step of enacting the two Public Options outlined previously in 2021, with sufficient concurrent tax reforms to pay for the associated additional costs. The problem with most blue-ribbon commissions is that their reports typically die on the shelf. The new Democratic leadership and advocates of universal benefits would have to step up and prevent that outcome. Voters and the media will need accurate, honest, actionable information, a plan of action to finally put America's fiscal house in order, and a Congress and White House willing to carry it out -- despite the public unpopularity of new taxes and intense opposition from the perennial anti-tax establishment.

Readers are left to ponder here whether this vision of a multi-payer Basic Health Care for All strategy is a pipedream or politically attainable. The objective of this section is to outline what it will take from a fiscal standpoint first, and to pencil out just a few of the most obvious basic political and administrative issues, corollaries and hurdles. The words of Alexander Hamilton, the founding forefather of "big government finances" may be worthy of reflection as Democrats assemble their tax proposals:

> "*If taxes are too high, they lessen the consumption; the collection is eluded, and the product to the treasury is not so great as when they are confined within proper and moderate bounds.*"

Federalist No. 21, 1787

TOPIC 26: Medical cost reductions

Democrats continue to favor brick-and-mortar infrastructure spending, with much of their support based on job-creation. Infrastructure discussions rarely include any thinking about health care economics. Meanwhile, the focus on universal health insurance and affordable health care typically focuses on the demand side of the health care industry, mostly on who pays and how much. The only supply side issue that has received much rhetorical attention has been the profits of insurance companies and pharmaceutical companies, which are convenient scapegoats but only part of the problem.

Where the discussion of affordable health care must now delve is into the supply side of medical services. This section offers two strategies to contribute to that discussion, with the caveat that neither of them will single-handedly make American health care cheaper than other countries'. As a nation, we spend more on health care "because we can." Ours is an affluent country populated with some unhealthy lifestyles, popular expectations that state-of-the-art biomedical technologies and chemistry will cure our afflictions, and a modern tradition of spending considerable sums on third-party long-term care for elderly patients. [16] Without belittling or dismissing the need to fix those problems outside of the fiscal arena, the macro demand issues cannot be solved readily by re-engineering the supply side.

---

16 Research indicates that long-term care costs, more than end-of-life hospital expenses, is what amplifies our national average healthcare expenditures. As a society, we Americans have outsourced long-term care, which is still traditionally provided by families, or simply not prevalent elsewhere. In America more than elsewhere, Grandma lives in a nursing home, not with her children and grandkids, during her feeble years.

> To bend the cost curve, our country needs to expand the supply and productivity of doctors, nurses and medical personnel. Tweaking the insurance system is only a partial solution.

To "bend the cost curve" in a meaningful way, this country needs to expand the supply and the productivity of doctors, nurses, and medical personnel. Although the highly efficient, innovative medical device industry does reliably produce many new ways to improve medical productivity, the U.S. has fallen short on the personnel side of the industry. We just don't produce enough doctors to meet the needs of our entire population, and to eliminate the scarcity pricing that doctors have always enjoyed.[17] Even deeper into the service delivery ecosystem, prevailing medical practices fail to optimize the use of non-MD practitioners and nurses who are capable of performing many procedures, including preventative care.

This book and its readers are not in a position to change the sociology of the medical industry. Undoubtedly there are gender limitations on workforce productivity that need to be removed, and the occupational distribution of compensation in the entire industry probably needs an overhaul. Putting those issues aside, the one place where federal spending could bear real fruit is in containing the $2 trillion of expenses we now pay for hospital, clinic, and physician/practitioner services. Imagine the savings, arguably in the magnitude of $100 billion annually, that could be derived from expanding the professional workforce in this field by more than ten percent in order to reduce scarcity pricing and promote both access and competition on the supply side of the professionals in this field. Stated simply, the country needs more

---

17 To be fair, the costs borne by medical students must be recaptured in doctors' career income, or else we need to subsidize their professional training far more than presently.

doctors. The goal here is not to punish doctors by flooding the market with more competing practitioners, but to help more medical students get the training without mortgaging their futures and taking on obscene debt themselves, and to better train and deploy those whose do not aspire and qualify to become an MD but still have plenty of heart and skills to offer in this field.

Most teaching hospitals are capacity constrained. Often this begins with their physical facilities, which were built for the instructional load several decades ago. The supply-side shortfalls do not include just conventional classrooms and labs and training clinics, but also the new technology-based opportunities to expand instructional capacity. Distance-learning labs and augmented/virtual reality training clinics can leverage trainees' and instructors' time. Capacity expansion also requires more teaching doctors, who must forgo private practice in order to teach, and that personal sacrifice may require tax incentives or other perquisites to induce a larger professional faculty. Likewise, the nursing schools and other training sites for supporting medical personnel can be expanded, and their skill sets elevated to enable these health care workers to perform routine, trainable and high-value tasks.

While we spend countless hours debating how to spend and fund hundreds of billions of dollars annually to tinker with health insurance to provide broader, affordable coverage, the lowest hanging fruit on the cost-cutting tree may be in the med-school classrooms. As part of health care reforms, Uncle Sam could well afford to spend $2 or $3 billion annually (a fraction of one percent of the current fees paid nationwide for services) to help public universities expand their throughput of trained professionals including both doctors and nurses. The long-run benefits to society overall from improved and localized access that reduces employees' lost working hours,[18] while yielding direct

18 The Integrated Benefits Institute estimates that lost work time and worker productivity cost employers $500 billion annually.

cost savings to taxpayers and consumers, would dwarf the national expenditure. Private philanthropists are beginning to step up and help with medical tuition costs, and this would be a natural opportunity for federal matching grants to encourage free or affordable med school tuition. In return, those lower-debt graduates should accept Medicare and Medicaid patients, or practice in under-served rural and urban communities for a multi-year "tour of duty" as a professional obligation. A few billion dollars of new annual soft spending on med-school tuition relief and additional faculty could probably increase the number of new doctors who graduate annually by 50%, if accompanied by the necessary capital expenditures for teaching and training facilities.

Economics 101 teaches us that additional supply of scarce talent will result in lower fees. Unlike so many debates in which education expenses are rhetorically postured as "investments" even though the supply-demand payoff is never quantified, the medical field is one where the results would be manifold, tangible, and financial.

The second realm in which Democrats can advance and underwrite a cost-reduction and cost-containment strategy in the health care field, lies right at the feet of both parties' favorite scapegoat: pharmaceutical pricing. Here, there is plenty of national anger over high priced drugs, especially those that have already recovered the original investors' research spending many times over. There is also rightful resentment that Uncle Sam helps fund research for drug therapies that later make headlines for their outrageous prices because "that is what the free market will bear."

> A strategic approach to reducing prescription drug prices is feasible but it will require legislation as well as hard bargaining.

This brings us to two approaches to cost-abatement in the drug industry: marketplace controls and reform of governmental research funding rules. The first solution includes an array of strategies that seek to leverage the federal government's regulatory and bargaining power in the Medicare Part D prescription drug marketplace and the international pharmaceutical trade. Ironically, there are many drugs that sell at lower prices in other countries because those nations have exercised their monopoly purchasing power to compel the manufacturers and distributors to sell American drugs at lower prices than they are offered on the shelf here in the USA. Meanwhile, it is the U.S that enforces the patents of these drug companies that protect their products from price competition. The patent premium is most obvious when generic manufacturers start production and sales once the patents run off. Something is simply wrong with that picture, and a concerted effort to formulate a winning strategy on behalf of American consumers will be a victory for whichever party is successful in solving that puzzle. Right now, the Trump administration is trying to use its bully pulpit to gain credit for that outcome. Time will tell whether it requires federal legislation to authorize a strong executive branch intervention in these markets to achieve better pricing.

But there is also another stage in the supply chain that has been overlooked by both political parties: the research and development (R&D) funding stage. Most American bio-pharmaceutical chemicals are developed by private companies. Very often, these firms are startups headed by a team of expert research specialists and a business executive who sometimes spend almost as much time and energy on raising the capital for their venture as they do on the science. Although big pharma companies also have their own labs to develop new drugs, the prevailing model in the industry is for them to avoid the very early-stage research which is typically a "moonshot" or "lottery ticket" exercise, and wait until the drug development teams have cleared the Stage 2 and Stage 3 clinical trials that are required by the FDA before a drug can even be considered for release to the general public. During that time period, these startup companies burn a large amount of cash, much of which is supplied by "angel investors" in the very early stages and then by venture capitalists and private equity funds as the successful projects progress through the larger and more-expensive trials. The early investors are gambling (they often call it a lottery ticket) that their little company will hit the jackpot and be acquired by Big Pharma for an investment return of 100 to 1 -- or sometimes even more if the market for the drug is large enough. These "angels" typically invest in ten or more start-ups, to spread out their portfolios' single-company risk, expecting that eventually they will make enough profit on one big winner to pay for 9 other losers and still come out way ahead of the mutual funds that invest in stock indexes.

Throughout this early stage capital investment process, many companies seek and often obtain federal and philanthropic foundation grants. In the fields of cancer and Alzheimer's research, it is not uncommon for multi-million-dollar grants to be awarded to teams exploring promising therapies. The competition for this funding is intense, and requires scientific appraisal of the biochemistry and other technical factors. Winning a grant is a big deal in the industry, and helps the research teams gain professional recognition and prestige. Sometimes the grants total up to as much as the private investors have gambled on the new drug (or molecule, as it is often known).

Some of the private foundations that give out research grants have become sophisticated enough to require an equity (stock) investment share in the startup company. Our federal government, with its sought-after research grants, typically does not demand such a piece of the pie. Investors love this arrangement, because it provides what they call "non-dilutive capital" which funds the research without demanding a share of the profits from the drug and the eventual speculative profit from selling the company or taking it public in an IPO on the stock market. This is where Democrats can lead some thoughtful reform of how our nation funds its pharmaceutical R&D. It doesn't take a genius to realize that most startup companies would be happy to give up a sliver of equity, or a royalty on the future drug sales, in exchange for the money they get from federal grantors, in addition to the credibility and prestige that goes with a grant award.

Without dwelling on the mechanics of how this can be accomplished, this chapter simply concludes with the observation that this is low-hanging fruit: Just make a royalty, or an equity stake[19] a condition of the R&D grant application and approval process. A royalty agreement could provide for a stiff "penalty rate" if the drug price exceeds an affordable level, which deters future rip-off pricing by the company that controls the patent. If the research teams, their CEOs and their investors don't want the money, they will find it elsewhere.[20] But most will be happy to oblige, especially when stock markets are in the dumps. Alternatively, the company making application for federal funding could contract to pay royalties indefinitely or until patents expire, or provide a percentage of its product to lower-income users at a discount, which would burden the later investors, but not dilute the shares of original investors directly. Either way, there are fair-share venture-underwriting profits to be captured for taxpayers' benefit. The proceeds from these investments by Uncle Sam could be used to subsidize lower prescription drug prices under Medicare and Medicaid, or to create a revolving fund for future research. All of these strategies would help

---

19 A common instrument in these situations is a cashless warrant, which enables the holder to buy shares later at a given price without putting up its own money, simply taking a profit from the change in value of the stock. For private investors, this would be a taxable transaction, but in the case of government agencies, there would obviously be no tax issues. The other investors are diluted fractionally by this instrument, but only if the science works out.

20 Alternatively, the initial private investors in startup drug research companies could be given favorable tax treatment (i.e. capital gains tax exemption) if the company were to agree up-front that its ultimate products would be subject to federal cost-containment. This could attract risk capital in specific sectors such as Alzheimer's and cancer research, although the crafting of appropriate tax code sections would leave a door open to future abuses.

reduce drug prices fractionally, but it would be an over-reach to claim that they alone would solve the overpricing problem.

The federal government has also failed to require drug researchers that receive their grant funding to agree contractually, in advance, to a "most favored nations" (MFN) pricing clause. An MFN obligation would be legally binding on their future pricing until patents expire (including acquirers), so that American consumers will no longer pay prices higher than residents in other countries for drugs funded by federal grants to American companies. Pricing in the U.S. then could never be higher than abroad, and other countries will no longer enjoy marginal-cost "product dumping" or "production piggyback" price subsidies at our expense. No other single policy change discussed here could impact the pharma industry as powerfully and U.S. consumers as beneficially. This policy would finally put Americans on a level playing field in the global pharma industry, and it may well be the single most potent policy recommendation in this section. Eventually, Congress could extend the concept to drug patent applications as well, which would really revolutionize U.S. drug pricing. More aggressively, Congress could extend MFN pricing requirements logically to all U.S. patent approvals, or levy a punitive ten percent corporate income surtax on all companies that sell U.S. patented medical products at lower prices overseas.

This section concludes with humble recognition that two examples of supply-side economics in the health care industry will not reduce overall costs dramatically. But hopefully this section will stimulate thinking by readers and their colleagues, who can adapt from these examples and use them as templates for other solutions that collectively will put a meaningful dent in the medical cost curve.

PART IV:

Infrastructure

....

"Infrastructure is much more important than architecture."

Rem Koolhaas, renowned Dutch architect, 2012

Most Americans understand and agree that much of the nation's physical infrastructure needs repair and in many cases replacement. As with health care, the numbers are huge. The American Society of Civil Engineers estimates that nationwide, the U.S. needs to spend $4.5 trillion on infrastructure upgrades by 2025. We have all seen the media coverage of old, failing bridges that pose a safety hazard to drivers. Many of our airports and transit systems are outdated and shabby. Many dams and levees on our waterways need reinforcement and rising sea levels pose new risks that require sea walls and other solutions. Stormwater systems are inadequate in flood-prone regions. The list goes on and on.

As a nation, capital investment in core infrastructure is easily defensible, if Congress can come up with a way to pay for it. Unlike annual spending for social programs and income re-distribution, capital spending can legitimately be financed with long-term bond issues to spread out the costs across generations over the projects' lives. There is an asset to match the liability, as long as taxes can cover the debt service.

Politically, infrastructure spending is popular in Congress because it produces tangible projects for politicians to showcase for the folks back home. Unfortunately, infrastructure bills also have their seedy side. "Bridges to nowhere" and pork barrel projects often have members of Congress who will vote for them despite their unworthiness. Historically, "log-rolling" of spending bills with "earmarked" capital spending projects in enough Congressional districts has often been necessary to secure a majority vote.[1] Capital projects that would never be approved by local voters, if they had to fund it themselves with their own tax money by a referendum vote, are amazingly popular if the dollars come from that special corner of heaven called Washington DC. Voters and their elected representatives, both Democratic and Republican, all love to spend somebody else's money in their hometowns.

> Capital projects that would never be approved by local voters are amazingly popular if the dollars come from Washington.

Although leaders in Washington DC have given lip service to infrastructure as an area for bipartisan agreement, Congressional action seems highly unlikely as the calendar approaches the 2020 elections. Democrats and the prevailing faction in the White House have vastly different views of how, and where to spend federal dollars on infrastructure. The first-order problem is a clear partisan disagreement over what kind of infrastructure to fund, and how to pay for it. A secondary issue is when to build it. Not only is the economy running

---

1 Log-rolling is the legislative practice of trading votes in favor of another chamber member in a *quid pro quo*. Earmarking is the designation of specific named projects or locations with specific amounts, in a general appropriation or authorization bill.

at low unemployment, but Democrats are now loathe to give the Trump re-election campaign a legislative accomplishment going into November 2020.

Democratic support for infrastructure spending is typically couched in terms of jobs creation. The party's political base includes construction unions that always want more work for their members. Federal projects typically have union-friendly contract requirements attached by law such as prevailing wage rules that implicitly require union pay scales. Although political support for infrastructure spending is invariably strongest among Democrats when the economy is shrinking and constituents are unemployed, there is almost never a bad time for building, in their minds.

In addition to roads and bridges, federal buildings and transit projects, Democratic leaders also sense grassroots agitation from the teachers' unions for federal spending on schools -- which are typically a local government responsibility -- because that frees up local tax dollars for teacher pay, and funds more classrooms to fill which in turn means hiring more teachers. But is federal funding of local school buildings just another brand of pork, in today's era of untamed federal budget deficits?

Congressional Republican support for infrastructure has been more situational. In recessions, GOP leaders have often agreed to fiscal measures that help stimulate the economy, and like any other politician, their members in Congress are equally eager to "bring home the bacon" with projects in their constituent communities. Historically, Republicans are also receptive to constituency demands for public infrastructure that supports local commerce and regional transportation advantages, like seaports, transit facilities, riverways and airports. But their limited or conditional support for "make work" employment typically fades when the economy is expanding on its own (especially when rising private-sector construction labor costs are cutting into company profits).

Where the politics of today's White House has driven a wedge between the two parties is the Ross-Navarro[2] thesis that infrastructure spending should focus on privatized projects using tax incentives rather than federal direct spending, combined with skimpy fractional federal grants to state and local government projects that lack user-paid revenue streams. True to form, this White House has never seen a private sector tax incentive it doesn't like, and that now applies specifically to infrastructure. If a project cannot produce revenue from user fees such as tolls, airport concessions, or other cost-recovery mechanisms that would reward private investors, then it is not worth building (or it goes to the back of the line). This is a game-changing political philosophy and strategy that readers must understand for its rationale, contradictions and limitations.

As to who pays for governmental infrastructure projects, the American system of federal government is unlike that of most other countries. Our national government "owns" federal buildings and major waterway infrastructure, but roads and bridges are typically built and maintained by states and their political subdivisions Highway funding comes from statewide fuel and motor vehicle taxes along with federal taxes on gas and diesel. Airports and transit facilities are typically built and operated by local or regional special-purpose districts.[3] School

---

2 At the time of this writing, Peter Navarro is a White House trade advisor and Wilbur Ross is secretary of Commerce (although speculation abounds that Ross may step down). They co-authored a controversial Trump campaign white paper on infrastructure that favored privatization strategies and major new tax incentives for private capital investment in infrastructure. They later authored a separate paper that emphasized matching grants to states and localities with very modest Federal matching shares that gained little traction politically ("Big hat, no cattle," as they say in Texas).

3 Special districts are either created or authorized by state law, and have municipal powers for a specific purpose such as airports, regional water or sewerage systems, convention-center or stadium authorities, and tollway authorities. Most have access to tax-exempt

buildings are typically the responsibilities of local school districts with funding from local property taxes and state-shared revenues from income or sales taxes. Our fiscal federalism is unique: very few other countries levy and allocate local taxes to pay for so much of their major infrastructure.

Outside of government, we have public-private partnerships and entirely private infrastructure. Although toll highways and toll bridges are most commonly constructed by public agencies because of the need to invoke eminent domain to acquire land, their ability to generate revenues by charging the users makes it possible to convey ownership or operational control to privately funded businesses or public-private partnerships (so-called P3). Finally, in the private sector, pipelines for oil and gas transmission, and electric power grids (transmission lines), are typically funded and operated by private companies that enjoy natural monopolies whose prices and franchises are regulated by the states.

> The time lags between Congressional authorization and the hiring of construction workers is notoriously long. A more agile process is needed.

Fiscal literacy requires readers to understand how these various forms of ownership and operation of infrastructure interplay with the politics of infrastructure funding. Fiscally literate readers also must appreciate that infrastructure construction costs are cyclical, and the "best bang for the buck" is usually achieved when projects are put out for bids *during* recessions when labor is plentiful and contract prices are lowest. But the time lags between Congressional authorization,

---

municipal borrowing privileges to fund capital projects, sometimes also including local or regional taxing authority.

contract awards and the hiring of workers is notoriously long and often inefficient. As a result, many job-creating infrastructure initiatives that were promoted as counter-cyclical actually become macroeconomically pro-cyclical during the construction phase. This book is the first in its field to address this challenge and offer policy prescriptions. (Hint: Engineering and land/rights acquisition can precede the contracting, in order for projects to be "ready for bids" when the time comes to goose the economy.)

SYNOPSIS

America's ability to finance new infrastructure spending is now constrained by the federal deficit juggernaut, coupled with a host of constraints on state and local government funding sources. Increasingly, the financing of public facilities must be accomplished through user fees because general tax revenues are simply not available to support unconstrained borrowing to fund capital projects.

At the federal level, the primary sources of funding for major infrastructure initiatives are general revenues (mostly income taxes), highway trust fund revenues from motor fuel taxes, and deficit spending. Because the U.S. government is perennially running budget deficits, as explained in Part I of this book, the two latter sources are effectively the only ones that matter now. With the exception of highway trust fund projects, all other federally financed infrastructure is essentially funded by new national debt.

Many infrastructure projects involve federal, state and local government funding, in what public-finance academicians call a "marble cake" of federalism (as distinguished from a "layer cake" in which each level of government performs distinctive functions). The responsibilities and authorities of federal, state and local governments for constructing and financing infrastructure projects are not uniform. The decision-making and approval processes at the state and local government level can result in long delays in breaking ground and employing workers. This decision-making complexity, with inherent process delays, results in economic inefficiencies and higher costs.

When federal grants for infrastructure projects are awarded to state and local governments, they often substitute federal dollars for local funds that would eventually have been spent anyway. In fact, projects that would never have been built at local expense are arguably inferior to those that local voters would have taxed themselves to complete. The funding rationale in those cases is weak to begin with. In other cases, one must question the "substitution effect" of simply injecting federal dollars funded by Treasury bonds to replace state and local dollars funded by local income, sales and property taxes. Funding substitution can fail to produce any long-term employment benefits, and may not result in sustained long-term improvements of infrastructure nationally. Better management of substitution effects is a missing element in traditional Congressional infrastructure authorizations. This is especially true if the policy and implementation lags for "marble-cake" projects delay the actual construction activity until months or even sometimes years after the national and local economies have recovered.

Many states and local governments have sophisticated, professional capital planning and project approval processes. To optimize the effectiveness of federal borrowing to fund infrastructure, a combination of long-term planning and timing triggers is needed. Topic 29 will present strategies to accomplish both long-term modernization of the nation's infrastructure and the effective use of construction projects to provide economic stimulus and needed jobs when the economy enters recessions.

In addition to direct expenditures funded by federal borrowing, the U.S. has several "debt management" tools to reduce state and local infrastructure costs. The carrot of lower interest costs can incentivize state and local government capital expenditures where important strategically, and also as part of a shorter-term, counter-cyclical strategy for which proper advance planning and legislative authorizations must be enacted before the next economic recession. Foresighted infrastructure financing is both possible and practical, and the results would be a markedly more-efficient use of taxpayer dollars in the long run.

Local governments have often failed to properly finance and price their local monopoly utilities for water, sewer and electrical service. A classic example is that the controversial Flint, Michigan water crisis that arguably could have been avoided if the local water utility had been operated properly with full-cost pricing per unit consumed to include a depreciation charge for timely replacement of obsolete water lines. Flint is hardly alone in this predicament, whose roots go all the way to allowing federal income tax deductions for property taxes but not for utility user charges. The problem and its solution are therefore not unique to Flint, and it must become part of a national policy to require proper depreciation accounting and user fees for utility services where full-cost pricing is feasible.

Under a full-cost pricing structure, user fees must be accumulated systematically to replace aging facilities. This "tough love" approach presents a double-whammy to low-income communities that were historically mismanaged: They will now need to pay debt service in the future for new bonds needed to upgrade their archaic systems at the same time they will pay depreciation charges for the inevitable future renovations and replacements of the new system. This does not mean that America should turn its back on Flint, Newark and others in this trap. Democrats can show their hearts and their brains by providing one-time matching funding for environmental upgrades in lower-income communities – but with the contractual proviso that proper utility pricing must be established.

> Democrats can show their hearts and their brains with matching funding for environmental upgrades in lower-income communities, by requiring proper utility pricing thereafter.

To overcome these policy-making inefficiencies, an effective long-term fiscal federalist plan for infrastructure finance must include: (1) a long-term commitment to funding infrastructure projects that modernize the American economy with jobs-creation a secondary priority, (2) modest federal matching-fund incentives for states and localities to complete land acquisition and rights, and develop "RFP-ready"[4] engineering and project plans that can be quickly implemented in the event of a recession, (3) federal financing incentives that either (a) reduce the cost of state and local government bond issuance during periods of economic recession or stagnation, or (b) promote economic efficiency and improve commerce, regardless of the business cycle, and (4) rigorous conditional funding requirements that ensure timely replacement through user fees wherever possible, because general taxation and federal deficit financing has become increasingly less feasible. For a major long-term infrastructure program to achieve Congressional approval, a bipartisan program must be designed that includes all these elements in order to satisfy competing views of the role of infrastructure and how best to pay for it.

To properly fund a one-time $1 trillion federal infrastructure spending initiative, Congress would need to raise taxes by roughly $50 billion annually and refrain from tax rollbacks for 30 years in order to pay off

---

4 An RFP is a Request for Proposal, and is the method by which states and localities award construction contracts through competitive bidding. The best time to issue an RFP is when there is slack in the economy, labor is abundant, and contractors are hungry for work, thus willing to bid lower prices than they would during periods of full employment.

the debt. Any number of tax reforms can accomplish a program of this magnitude. For example, an industrial carbon emissions (flaring and smokestack) tax could be earmarked for as much as $2 trillion of federal funding for infrastructure construction, although the revenue stream from such a tax would likely erode in a progressively Green future. To address all the structural deficiencies cited by the ASCE engineering society, a far more comprehensive tax plan would be required, consistent with the outline discussed in Topics 20 and 25.

New technologies will disrupt the traditional model for financing highways and bridges, as electric vehicles become more prevalent, making traditional motor fuels taxes insufficient to fund timely renovation of bridges and congested roads. As vehicular automation and 5G telecommunications technology advances in the coming decade, cars and trucks must pay through micro-payment systems that automatically capture the revenue needed to replace the facilities they use, regardless of who if anybody is driving and what method of propulsion is used. Rural highways, local roads and residential streets must continue to be financed through state and local taxes, because user fees will be insufficient. But wherever possible, the benefits of transportation facilities will increasingly and eventually have to be funded by those who use them, when they use them.

White House policy advisors have advocated a program of fractional incentives to private investors, states and localities. The motivations and rationales in each area are somewhat different. For the private sector, tax credits are proposed by the White House to stimulate more private investment in profit-making infrastructure. This could encourage investors to buy the "family jewels" from cash-strapped cities and counties, using federal tax credits to enhance the profitability of projects they would undertake anyway. In the energy space, it is questionable whether additional federal dollars should be devoted to expanding fossil fuel pipelines, especially when there is abundant private capital available to fund those projects at a fair interest rate that reflects the risk of existential competition coming eventually from renewable energy sources. Tax credits awarded to private investors who invest in infrastructure are beneficial to the investors, but seldom add value to the federal taxpayer who pays the subsidy. (See Topic 11 on tax loopholes.) The one conceivable exception to this could be public-private partnerships for transmission of renewable energy, such as interstate power lines for wind turbines in the central U.S.[5]

As for the small (e.g. 15 percent) intergovernmental matching grant formulas suggested by some of the President's advisors, such tiny slivers of federal aid will not induce states and political subdivisions to construct projects that otherwise would remain unfunded, unless they are revenue-producing;[6] the subsidy is simply too small to change behaviors. All that a slim factional federal share accomplishes is White House bragging rights to claim credit for megabillion dollar construction projects attributable to the incumbent's "brilliant" leadership, and that is a political trap that Democrats have learned to sidestep. A better use of federal capital at that level of cost-sharing would be countercyclical "accelerator" funding to pay the first three or four years of debt service for scheduled later-year state and local projects that can be advanced quickly to be completed during a recession.

> What the nation needs most is a long-term plan to fund and incentivize the right kinds of infrastructure projects, financed in the right way at the right time.

---

5 An illuminating story of political blockades to interstate renewable electricity transmission can be found in the history of Clean Line Energy Partners, as told in a forthcoming book entitled *Superpower* by Russell Gold.

6 See the description and discussion of public vs private goods in Topic 28.

What the nation needs most is a long-term plan to fund and incentivize the right kinds of infrastructure projects, financed in the right way at the right time. This is not a trivial ambition. With the possible exception of the interstate highway system and the federal highway trust funds, no act of Congress has looked much beyond the immediately obvious when funding infrastructure. None of those initiatives were ever described as well-planned, cost-effective and frugal in their use of resources. Topic 29 lays out a framework for just such a long-term plan, using all the available tools in the public finance toolkit that make sense in an era of fiscally literate federalism.

TOPIC 27: "Marble-cake" fiscal federalism and infrastructure policy

. . . .

"The powers not delegated to the United States by the Constitution, nor prohibited by it to the States, are reserved to the States respectively, or to the people."

Tenth Amendment, 1791

The American federalist system is unique in many ways, especially in how we finance and maintain public infrastructure. Fiscally literate readers must understand "who does what and how." Responsibility and authority for financing, building and maintaining public facilities is "federal" in the sense that the national government (the United States) has certain authorities and fiscal responsibilities, and the states and their political subdivisions have others. Private contractors are engaged to perform much of the actual construction activity, and in some cases, private companies also operate public and quasi-public facilities. This section describes the topography and anatomy of public infrastructure finance, construction, operations and maintenance.

Certain powers are assigned to the United States as the national government, by the Constitution through the Congress. Other powers are reserved to the states. In the case of infrastructure, the national defense, national parks, federal prisons, federal office buildings, interstate waterways and interstate commerce are generally the domain of the national government. States ultimately have responsibility or control over other structures and improvements in their territories, including highways and public transportation facilities, educational facilities, and state and municipal buildings. The states in turn have created or authorized political subdivisions such as counties and cities, school districts and other special districts, with various levels of authority to impose taxes and fees and construct local facilities that they operate. Although there are many similarities in how certain governmental functions are performed in each state, there is notable variation in the levels and forms of government and the specific agencies that perform them.

When we think about the most massive infrastructure projects undertaken by the federal government in the past century, the most familiar examples are the various public works built during the New Deal era of Franklin Roosevelt, and the interstate highway system promoted by Dwight Eisenhower. During the Depression, FDR's Works Progress Administration (WPA) built hundreds of public facilities in communities across the country, including not just dams on major rivers, but also schools, bridges, roads and civic buildings. The WPA was funded almost entirely by federal deficit finance (borrowed money) and cut across all levels of government in its scope. States and local governments were in cut-back mode during the Depression, as their tax revenues plunged because the economy shrank sharply. They had no money of their own for building construction. The employment that WPA provided to out-of-work citizens was widely understood to be one of its policy objectives. Under Eisenhower, the interstate highway system was a predominantly federal-state initiative with 90 percent funding provided by the U.S. in part for purposes of "national defense" and the remainder funded by the states. Creating new employment was deemed beneficial but less urgent, as that program spanned several decades.

The funding for federal infrastructure projects is derived from three primary sources; general revenues such as the income tax, federal motor fuels taxes for transportation purposes (via the Highway Trust Fund), and deficit spending which is funded by issuance of Treasury bonds. Except for projects funded by the motor fuels taxes, the distinction between general revenues and debt finance is now more theoretical than real in today's federal fiscal situation: Deficit finance is effectively the only current funding source for all domestic discretionary spending which includes infrastructure projects. Unlike states and local governments, the federal government does not issue bonds to fund specific projects or project categories, and voter approval is not required. The amount, timing and geography of federally funded infrastructure projects is determined by acts of Congress. Various federal departments then administer the expenditures, sometimes directly as federal agencies and more often by contracting with states and local governments.

> States and local governments operate under completely different rule-sets. Their incentive is to replace local taxpayer dollars with federal dollars. Congress needs a smarter strategy in the future.

In contrast to the Congressional authority, state and local governments operate under three completely different rule-sets. First, they lack the power to print money through the nation's central bank, the Federal Reserve system. Consequently, they cannot fund projects "out of thin air." Second, most states and political subdivisions must obtain voter approval to issue bonds of indebtedness, at least for general purposes, without a dedicated revenue source to pay for them. Only some local governments, school districts and special districts can raise taxes to pay for infrastructure debt service without voter approval. In some jurisdictions, such as California, a voter supermajority is required for bonds to be funded by a tax increase. Third, most states and almost all local governments are prohibited by law from running an operating budget deficit by borrowing money through general obligation bonds.[7] These fiscal limitations have important ramifications for any major federal infrastructure initiative that requires state and local funding or matching funds.

Unlike the Congress, most states and many of the larger local governments have professionally prepared multi-year capital improvement plans that identify needed infrastructure projects, the funding they require and possible sources, and a timetable for approvals and construction. A multi-year capital plan is considered a "best practice" by financial professionals.[8] State and local engineering and executive staffs know very well what structures within their jurisdiction need repair and replacement, and where new facilities are needed. Often, they have done enough rough-pencil cost estimation to have a working idea of how much funding is required. Where matching funding or potential grants are available from federal or state highway funds or community development block grants, they often establish a tentative schedule of potential project applications. At the local level, these multi-year plans are frequently presented to the local governing body for prioritization and approval, with the understanding that without formal funding

---

7 General obligation (GO) bonds are secured by unlimited pledges of future taxes to repay the debt. Revenue bonds, on the other hand, pledge revenues from various sources, often tolls and user fees, to repay the debt, although some revenue bonds also carry a secondary tax pledge, which makes them "double-barreled" bonds. As Puerto Rico's debt default has shown, such double-barreled bonds are not always as secure as they appear at time of issuance, and may become less credit-worthy than GO bonds.

8 Government Finance Officers of the U.S. and Canada, 2016 Recommended Practice.

approvals, nothing gets built. If a bond-issue referendum is necessary in order to secure voter approval, the financial and executive staffs typically develop strategies for grassroots ballot campaigns.

Instead of a federalist "layer cake" in which each level of government has distinct responsibilities, infrastructure is one of those realms that academic economists call a "marble cake." Federal money often flows down to the states for various projects, where it is matched with state funding, and from there the project may be managed by a local government or special district, most often with local financial contributions. These funding processes are often complex and depend on the type of project, the manner in which Congress makes appropriations, and the specifics of state laws with respect to both the authority to perform construction and the powers to finance it. What may be one state's project performed by a state agency could well be performed by a local government in another, each with its own unique mix of revenue sources, and approval processes. In one state, future voter approvals may be required, but in others the voters may have already approved a funding source. Yet in others, the legislature or local governing body under "home rule" may be able to green-light the project straightaway.

Obviously, the more that voter approvals and bond-financing authorizations are required at each level of government to move an infrastructure project forward, the longer the inherent delays in breaking ground, employing workers, and completing the project. This lengthy process of project and funding approvals is called "policy lag" and "Implementation lag." When infrastructure spending is approved by Congress in the middle of a national economic recession (such as the crisis of 2008-9) or a period of economic malaise (such as the mid-1970s or early 1980s, when Congress approved counter-cyclical jobs programs), the employment benefits came after the economy was already on the mend. This is not to say that the projects were unworthy, or that they failed to induce new hiring in the construction trades, but their benefits were "a day late and half-a-dollar short" of what they could have been if the legislative and approval and contracting processes were more agile. In this regard, the U.S. infrastructure policy-approvals and -execution processes are much more like an aircraft carrier than a speedboat.

Local governments will happily take a federal construction grant as a gift, but it is rare that they become incentivized to build a structure that they would not have funded on their own unless it is predominantly federally funded. Unless the U.S. pays a hefty portion of the total cost, federal matching funds in smaller ratios can accelerate a project, but they rarely induce one to occur out of thin air. Even then, the local share comes at the expense of another project that becomes displaced by the one that is funded

One of the problems with the marble-cake model of infrastructure finance is that state and local government officials are sometimes encouraged by past experience to rely on federal funding, and to replace local tax dollars with federal dollars for projects they would have undertaken anyway. Economists call this a form of "rational expectations" which in turn become part of the gamesmanship in intergovernmental finance (sometimes called "grantsmanship"). This shuffling of projects enables them to re-deploy revenues and capital on other projects that lack appeal to federal decision-makers. This is called a "substitution effect." In this way, money that would have been spent on Project A can now be spent on Project B, which would otherwise not have been built, and may never have been approved by federal decision-makers. In other cases, however, the result of federal funding is that projects that would have been funded from a voter-approved categorical bond issue (such as a statewide water resources or transportation bond program) can instead be used for additional projects, in which case the federal funding is likely to be additive. Thus, substitution effects are important to understand and manage effectively in order to best leverage federal funding. Congress has never applied this test explicitly in its legislative requirements.

The final element of fiscal federalism that deserves mention in this section is the tax exemption of state and municipal bonds (hereafter, "muni bonds"). A powerful financing tool for states and local governments is their ability to sell debt securities whose interest is exempt from federal income taxes. This power was originally perceived to be a Constitutional entitlement of the states, under the premise that "reciprocal immunity" from federal taxation was a Tenth Amendment right. But in 1988, the Supreme Court held otherwise in the famed *South Carolina v Baker* case. There, court held that the tax exemption was granted by Congress through the political process under Article One, rather than by the Bill of Rights. Thus, what Congress giveth, it can take away. Today, the tax exemption remains alive for general obligation and revenue bonds issued by the states and their political subdivisions, but interest on certain so-called private activity bonds (such as industrial development bonds issued to finance private company facilities and certain sports stadia) is subject to the federal alternative minimum income tax (AMT).

The tax exemption is a huge subsidy, because (wealthy, high-bracket) taxable investors are willing to buy muni bonds with much-lower interest rates than they would otherwise demand if the muni bonds were taxable. So the tax exemption represents an indirect subsidy of the vast majority of infrastructure projects funded by states and most localities. For top-bracket investors, the tax exemption would make a 2 percent tax exempt bond superior to an otherwise-identical 3 percent taxable bond. In practice, however, it is not the top marginal tax rate that determines prevailing yield spreads between muni and Treasury bonds (T-bonds). The muni bonds, even if insured by a third party, are considered less secure than T-bonds and they are less tradable and liquid in the after-market, so the interest-rate differentials are typically narrower. For corporations that are now subject to a 21 percent top bracket and not 35 percent, the tax exemption has lost some of its punch. In today's marketplace, a top-rated municipal bond maturing in 10 or more years usually trades at a *higher* yield than the comparable T-bond, even with the indirect subsidy of tax-exemption.[9] That is why some economists consider the tax exemption to be an inefficient subsidy.

> Congress should leverage the financial tools it can give to states and localities, to promote timely infrastructure at lower cost to taxpayers.

The authority to issue tax-exempt bonds is not deal-specific. Congress does not pick and choose which infrastructure projects funded by muni bonds are able to enjoy tax exemption.[10] That would be a nightmare administratively, even putting the policy implications aside. But Congress has previously voted to offer a temporary incentive to the states and localities in order to stimulate infrastructure spending: the taxable bond option (TBO). The most recent episode of this selective financing strategy was the temporary Build America Bonds (BABs) authority granted by Congress during the Obama administration in 2009, in an effort to stimulate more state and local government infrastructure spending during the Great Recession.

In a TBO bond issue, the state or municipality issues bonds whose interest payments are instead deemed taxable for federal income tax purposes. Instead of receiving the indirect federal subsidy, the bond issuer instead is entitled to receive a direct reimbursement for a percentage of its interest costs from the U.S. Treasury.[11] As it turns out, this

---

9 In this regard, municipalities would be better off borrowing through the U.S. Treasury, a subject to be discussed in the final section.

10 Congress has, however, made certain "private-activity" bonds that benefit private parties subject to the Alternative Minimum Tax (AMT).

11 In the case of Build America Bonds, the reimbursement rate was 35 percent in most cases, payable to the muni bond issuer that elected to sell under the statutory TBO protocol. At the

direct subsidy of the debt service costs can prove to be worth more to the issuer than the lower rate it would have received from issuing tax-exempt. And it costs the U.S. Treasury less than it would have given away to the high-bracket investors in municipal bonds if they were tax-exempt.

So why don't states and local governments simply lobby Congress to make this the universal arrangement, if it's so good for both them and Uncle Sam? There are two reasons: (1) Their policy associations believe that once they forego their tax exemption, it will be lost forever in the federal sea of red ink, and (2) a direct reimbursement of interest payments is much easier to remove or renege in a future decade than is a tax exemption that has a legal opinion behind it for the investor and a flock of investor-voters at risk. In other words, they don't trust Congress to continue its subsidies indefinitely, especially if the U.S. heads over a fiscal cliff as described in Part I. Tax exemption is at least a mandatory expenditure if not an "entitlement." As bond issuers and counterparties, they obviously prefer that the investors assume the political risk, not them.

With this as background, it is far more likely that state and local officials' support for a TBO arrangement for counter-cyclical infrastructure spending will be "situationally dependent" rather than universal. That is not to say that the authorization of a TBO option must await a recession, but it would suggest that any standing legislation to authorize TBO issues generally should require a recession-trigger to avoid making it the prevailing practice. It also stands to reason that muni bond issuers will want contractual protections on any TBO deals in the future, given the precarious environment of growing federal deficits. The final segment of this section on Infrastructure will return to this idea.

---

time, the top personal income tax rate was also 35 percent and the top corporate rate was slightly bur irregularly higher.

There is one more potential form of federal assistance to states and municipalities in funding their infrastructure: conduit financing for state infrastructure packages. What if the states (for themselves and on behalf of their subdivisions) could borrow directly from the federal government at the same low rates that the U.S. Treasury enjoys in the marketplace? As explained previously, interest rates on highest quality municipal bonds are now higher than those on comparable maturity T-bonds, because of risk and liquidity factors. This is especially true of longer-term muni bonds, which is how long-lived infrastructure must be financed anyway. So what if Congress instead gave the states access to the Federal Financing Bank (FFB), which acts as a go-between for designated borrowers? What if Uncle Sam played the role of Rich Uncle and figuratively "co-signed the loans" by borrowing in the capital markets on behalf of the states, passing on the proceeds and the repayment terms at advantageous rates? Even though these would be taxable obligations, the interest rates for the states and participating localities would often be lower than their tax-exempt bonds

For the FFB conduit to work, there will be three essential prerequisites. First, the borrower should be a state and not a municipality. Although there are some political subdivisions with high credit ratings and large issuance volumes, the credit and taxing authority of states should be required as part of any such market access that the federal government would ever extend to them. Constitutionally, the states are responsible for supervising the credits and financial practices of their subdivisions. States have much larger tax bases, less risk of widespread credit impairment from natural disasters, and far more legal authority to tax, than their subdivisions. Second, all deals through this conduit facility must carry a third-party credit guarantee (bond insurance) from a high-quality guarantor that is approved by the Treasury Secretary. The lower the state's bond rating, the higher the guarantor's must be. This makes the state's taxpayers and the private insurance company both liable for any failures to pay. Third, the Financial Golden Rule[12]: the U.S. Treasury must be obligated to withhold federal assistance disbursements indefinitely from any state that fails to meet its passthrough credit obligations (for example, highway funds, Medicaid matching funds, federal disaster relief, etc). In other words, "Don't mess with Uncle Sam." The Treasury Secretary could also attach various other strings as general conditions for gaining access to the FFB window, including a risk surcharge if appropriate.[13] The final section on strategies (Topic 29) will explain more about how this new facility could work.

Finally, on this technical topic, a cost-benefit analysis: The muni bond market has $3.8 trillion of outstanding bonds. If the entire market were to enjoy these benefits, the total annual savings for states and localities on interest costs after 10 or 20 years would never exceed $20 billion, and the initial annual savings would be $2 billion at most. To them, a 20 percent reduction in interest payments would be serious money, but at the federal level, it is peanuts compared with the increases in infrastructure it could incentivize. So there is important leverage to be gained through these tools, but they cannot be over-sold. That is why their strategic deployment during recessions is likely to be the most cost-advantageous strategy. Notably, none of this would actually cost the federal treasury a penny, given the current cost of tax exemptions. In fact, the FFB portal would actually reduce federal tax expenditures. And in recessions, it is unquestionable that the two incentives combined could stimulate significant new construction. If there is any place in the infrastructure marble cake where new leverage can be added to the mix, this will be it. The TBO is a federal budgetary wash and could actually

---

12 In finance, the Golden Rule holds that the party with the gold, rules.

13 Whether this facility can prudently be extended to Puerto Rico and other U.S. territories is debatable, in light of their unique hurricane risks and PR's recent bankruptcy proceedings. A credit conduit may be less expensive to federal taxpayers than a cash bail-out, but a third-party guarantor would have to demonstrate very deep pockets to calm inevitable critics and skeptics.

reduce federal taxpayer costs if properly calibrated. So both policies are win-win and improve marketplace efficiency. If the U.S. were a business, the CEO and CFO would implement these tools immediately.

TOPIC 28: Infrastructure economics in the digital and green era

Think back to when bottled water first appeared on grocery store shelves. Most consumers wondered "Who on earth would pay good money for something we can get almost for free?" It turned out to be an entire nation, and almost an entire world, because clean water is not "almost free," and polluted tap water has a huge cost to consumers and their entire community. Think now about what happened to the misfortunate citizens of Flint, Michigan, whose "almost free" tap water proved to be the most expensive product they ever consumed. Flint's story of dysfunctional municipal water-utility pricing, fiscal mismanagement and mistaken tax policy incentives at all levels of government is a case study in public finance and infrastructure economics gone wrong.

> The distinction between public goods and private goods is evolving. Enlightened public finance provides context in the digital and green world.

For five decades, the professional public-finance community has operated under a paradigm established by the late Richard and Peggy Musgrave in their classic textbook *Public Finance in Theory and Practice,* which was republished many times. Many of the concepts discussed elsewhere in this book are "children" of the Musgrave school of thought, including the rationale for progressive taxation and federal fiscal assistance. The Musgraves categorized public goods, private goods, social goods, common goods and merit goods[14] in ways that have influenced the financing of infrastructure. In a nutshell, here are the key distinctions and differences:

Private goods are exclusive in the sense that one person's consumption or use cannot be enjoyed by another unless they pay. Private goods are generally divisible, and the owner's rights are enforceable in court. As a result, private goods can be priced. Purely private goods can be packaged or metered. Water consumption and corn flakes are private goods. Copyrighted music is a private good, as is a patented technology. Airspace over a building is a private good, under land use law. Even if produced by a municipal monopoly like a water or electric utility, a private good's costs are recovered through the pricing mechanism as long as its fixed costs (which includes depreciation of the capital facility) are included in the price. Economists like to say that markets are efficient when the cost of production equals its marginal utility of consumption, and the proper pricing mechanisms achieve this.

Public goods, on the other hand, are non-exclusive and generally are difficult if not impossible to price individually. The air we breathe is a public good (whether clean or polluted). National defense is a public good. Expired patents, and music or literature that has outlived its copyright, are all public goods.[15] Unless abundant in nature or provided by law, public goods must be financed collectively, usually through taxation. Except for token admission and parking fees, the Grand

---

14 In all cases for these definitions, a "good" can include a product, a physical good, a service, an intangible right or power, or a facility.

15 What American trade negotiators refuse to acknowledge is that in the neo-Marxist ideology of China (aka Xi Jinping Thought), intellectual property is commonly treated there by law as a public good.

Canyon, Yellowstone, Mount Rushmore, Yosemite and Appalachian Trail national parks are public goods. Interstate freeways and rural roads are public goods, whereas local toll roads and toll bridges are private goods because exclusion and pricing are feasible and enforceable. No person has a superior right to a public good.

Social goods are the broad class of public goods that are created by a society for the benefit of all its members. Local public schools are social goods for their residents, although they may exclude non-residents. National defense and the court systems are social goods: we pay for it whether we like it or not, unlike the air we breathe which is a public good. Eisenhower's interstate highway system was funded on the premise that it was a social good, providing not only for modern transportation to benefit all, but also a military roadway for the national defense if ever the need be. In the field of infrastructure, the ability to exercise the power of eminent domain is a clear indicator that society deems a facility to be a social good by converting private property to public use. [16]

Common goods are public goods where users share a common resource, such as a commercial fishing habitat, which may be accessible to all or only to those paying for a permit. One or more parties' overconsumption can spoil the common good, as is the case when over-fishing jeopardizes the benefits for all. A polluted regional airshed would be a negative common good (a common bad): what is bad for one is bad for everybody. A freeway is a common good, but congestion becomes a common bad when the roads become overcrowded, which then imposes negative externalities and costs on all affected users. The "tragedy of the commons" is when individuals acting in their own self-interest destroy or impair a common good.

---

16 Re-privatization of such social goods is where public officials have sometimes failed to protect the social benefits originally secured. This is where public-private partnership (P3) discussions should always commence and conclude.

Merit goods are facilities and services that are deemed to be beneficial to the community overall when they are consumed. Some economists also define merit goods as "good for you" as determined by public decisions. Although users may pay a price individually, part of their cost is paid or subsidized by the community. A public high school, a vocational-technical community college, or a public college with subsidized tuition are considered merit goods because an educated and trained local workforce is beneficial to the entire community, the businesses operating there and overall economic development. A regional seaport could be deemed a merit good, even if it can finance commercial operations with user fees; local residents benefit from the employment and economic activity the facilities attract. Home residential solar panels may be a merit good if the result is reduction of air pollution from the regional power utility system. Some Democrats would say that Medicaid-funded preventative and basic health care has merit-good qualities, to the extent it reduces the demand for emergency medical care that taxpayers must otherwise bear if an indigent population relies on high-cost acute care at public expense.

As readers can discern, these definitions are not always mutually exclusive. There are many examples of public facilities and services that blur the lines that differentiate purely private from purely public or social goods. As a general rule, the closer a public service or facility comes to being a public good or a social good, the more likely that general taxes (income and sales taxes, most commonly) must be used to finance their provision because no other option is feasible. Merit goods often include a public subsidy for private consumption, but there may also be nominal fees for usage, to defray some costs. Private goods and services provided by governmental agencies, such as water, sewerage and electric utilities, are more likely to be funded by user fees. Most economists and financial professionals would argue that these private goods ought best be priced at full cost including the interest on debt issued to finance them, as well as the annual depreciation charges to put money away for future replacements. Private goods can almost universally be a candidate for privatization or at least a public-private partnership that can sometimes run the facility more efficiently (or maximize its market value better) than a governmental agency.

With these definitions and concepts in mind, we can now proceed to the modern application of public finance theory to several problems in national infrastructure policy. These include: (1) municipal utility pricing as a private good and infrastructure remediation as a social good, (2) the funding of high-volume highways, bridges and other private-passenger transportation infrastructure in the coming digital era, and (3) public-private partnerships (P3).

Municipal utility infrastructure funding policy. A political problem for Democrats with regard to municipal infrastructure is that they often are predisposed to lobby for federal funding to local governments on the basis of social equity, most notably center cities with lower-income demographic profiles. The flip side of this policy issue is that many local governments are not pricing their utility services for water, sewerage and electricity at full cost. As a result, they have failed to accumulate the requisite financial reserves through depreciation charges that would ensure they have money in reserve to pay for replacement of water and sewer lines and new treatment plants. Consequently, they have not systematically upgraded their archaic, often rotted and rusted underground pipes because that would now require them to sell bonds and raise fees for usage to cover the debt service in order to secure the funding at the same time they raise fees to cover depreciation of the new assets. In some municipalities, the water laterals and collectors are either wooden or leaden pipes that must be replaced as soon as possible, only getting more hazardous and costly to replace each year. Like ostriches, their leaders have put their heads in the sand, paralyzed and praying for the day that benevolent Uncle Sam might magically drop them some cash from a helicopter to pay for the inevitable replacement of their obsolete and unhealthy systems. Voters living elsewhere in the general vicinity can become resentful of assistance for those who benefit from what they see as "a problem of their own making."

> Obsolete and unhealthy municipal water systems reflect a failure in public finance.

In many cases, the failure to properly finance their utility operations is similar to the "kick the can" behavior of our Congress over past decades. Raising user fees is never popular, so the path of least resistance is to underprice the product (clean water and sanitary sewerage) and leave the problem to the succeeding politicians. In some cases, the local politicians' instinct to postpone the inevitable was exacerbated by a big fat excuse that Congress gave them: the property tax deduction. In the past, some municipal governing bodies chose to fund their municipal utility operations with property taxes rather than user charges, on the premise that it would be less costly to their taxpayer if the expenses were buried in the property tax bill, which was deductible on federal income taxes, rather than paid for through user fees which are not tax-deductible. That theory worked as long as the municipality had sufficient taxing authority and a strong enough property tax base, and as long as Congress allowed the property tax deduction. But fiscally literate readers know that the so-called SALT deduction[17] has now been capped, and the standard deduction has been raised, so that only ten percent of American income taxpayers now itemize deductions, and probably even fewer do so in center cities. Of those who do itemize, many will be capped by the SALT limits. Hence the rationale for taxpayer savings from reliance on the property tax to pay for utility system infrastructure is now an obsolete concept. Also, as more and more municipalities have

---

17 State and Local Tax deduction on the federal income tax, commonly called the "SALT" deduction.

now crashed into their property tax ceilings, whether by law or taxpayer opposition, it has become increasingly difficult to raise property taxes to pay for new utility systems.

The only good news in this predicament is that it is a one-time problem. A "social and merit goods" case can be made for federal funding to help upgrade and replace local utility systems that are environmentally unsound, and for which there is a clear economic inability to bear the full costs replacement AND depreciation. Where system upgrades have a clear public health benefit, federal funds could match state appropriations and bond issues to fund the system upgrades, and leave to local citizen-consumers the annual depreciation charges needed to properly fund future replacements of the utility system's infrastructure. This should not be construed as a "free lunch" ticket, however. Ideally, the cost sharing formula should probably be in the ballpark of three equal shares of one-third each at the federal, state and local levels, a true "marble cake" federalist solution. As to the timing of these programs, that issue will re-appear in Topic 29 as an example of "Enlightened Infrastructure Funding."

For municipal utility systems that have not converted to full-cost pricing, the two federal financing incentives introduced previously, the TBO and FFB, can be made available, as also explained in Topic 29.

Funding tollways, highways and bridges amid the Digital and Green technology revolutions. Our nation's historic reliance on motor fuel taxes to fund the lion's share of highway and transportation infrastructure is unlikely to prevail for more than another decade. The handwriting is already on the wall at state transportation departments, where the conversion to electric vehicles is already cutting into the number of gallons of gasoline and diesel consumed annually. With motor fuel taxes based on gallonage rather than price, the state transportation departments are already squeezed financially. They can raise taxes, with all the problems that produces at border towns where tax-shopping is already problematic, or they can raise the motor vehicle fees and excise taxes. But even with separate surtaxes for electric vehicles that try to equate the cost-per-mile of usage, there is no immediate and equitable substitute for the fuel taxes, which at least provided a rough proxy for the number of highway miles driven by a given vehicle, and its size.

Meanwhile, the auto companies and the automation technologists are moving far more quickly than the road and bridge builders, to install autonomous technologies that will revolutionize how we use and pay for cars and trucks. Ride-hailing services like Uber and Lyft may not survive with their current business models, but it is almost certain that within most of our lifetimes, most Americans will have the option to be driven on demand without a human behind the wheel, either as a rental or in a driverless taxi. Automobiles as a service, rather than a personal property, will likely be here by 2030, along with the payment mechanisms to make that possible. A decade may pass before electric vehicles (EVs) predominate on the roads, but the migration away from gasoline and diesel power is already underway.

So, where does this leave us, in the realm of personal-transportation infrastructure? It is obvious that motor fuel taxes will decline in volume and revenue capacity. This does not mean that farmers and rural Americans will all go the route of EVs any time soon, but it does mean that the federal highway trust fund cannot remain the nation's primary piggybank for Congressional infrastructure spending.

On the user side, we also know that three technologies are rapidly converging: (a) 5G telecommunications, (b) vehicular automation and electrification and (c) micropayment processing. In the telecommunications world, 5G and its successor technologies will be far more capable of externally identifying vehicles on the road at every point during their travels. Yes, Big Brother is here. Cars and trucks will not be able to cross a mile marker anywhere in metropolitan roadways without the 5G system knowing their location. To complement cell towers, the telecommunications companies are reportedly installing some 250,000 cell sites nationwide for starters, and that number will probably grow. Even without "sighting" a vehicle, these 5G devices will be able to triangulate location with high precision. Meanwhile, the newer vehicles themselves will be embedded with digital technologies that also know their locations and have computing power, data storage devices, and the ability to upload information to networks for a host of applications both voluntary and involuntary. And they will run on electricity, thereby paying a big fat zero into the motor fuels tax coffers.

> Motor fuel taxes will fail to cover highway costs as electric vehicles proliferate. Transportation agencies will soon be able to calculate and charge a user fee for every stretch of highway and every bridge crossed.

These digital forces are inevitable, and they are now unavoidable. This means that the routes that each vehicle takes will be knowable, measurable, recordable, and "price-able." Just as automated tollway systems today know what toll to charge each user's account on the basis of what entry and exit point a vehicle came into and left the system, the transportation agencies will soon be able to calculate a user fee for every specific stretch of highway driven, and every bridge crossed. All they need is a micro-payment processor to record small usage charges in sub-dollar units that are not practical and commercially feasible today, but will easily be so in a few years. Without even using one of the existing tollways in my vicinity, my car might run up a bill of 76 cents for its trip to the office five miles from home, and 43 cents each way for crossing that local trestle bridge over the town's river that was almost falling apart last year until they repaired it, and $2.75 for the highway to pick up Mom at the airport. Total of fees for me that Tuesday would be $4.37 which goes onto my account with the state DMV [18] or the metropolitan transportation commission where my digital wallet or prepaid credit card is charged every month.

Remember all those dilapidated and nearly collapsing bridges we keep hearing about? It won't be motor fuel taxes that pay for their replacement after 2030. By then, micro-tolls should be able to fund depreciation accounts to assure that thereafter, the users will begin to put away the money needed to properly repair and replace most major roads and bridges in the U.S.

Where we still have a funding problem is the financing of today's failing infrastructure before all this fancy new technology enables the U.S. to institute usage fees across the country on a widespread basis. Until then, it may be necessary to charge an annual motor vehicle infrastructure fee equal to what the average vehicle pays in motor fuel taxes each year, which is roughly $200 per auto (ranging from $140 to $300 annually on average in various states). However, that alone will not raise more than $50 billion annually at the federal level, which is hardly enough to fund a multi-trillion-dollar transportation infrastructure initiative. Other strategies and federal programs will be necessary in order to kick-start the inevitable movement toward full-cost pricing of roads and bridges as private goods, and the replacement of outworn facilities. Topic 29 addresses presents several options.

Public-private partnerships (P3). In recent decades, a number of public agencies have sold their infrastructure assets to private owners, or entered into long-term leasing or operating contracts with private entities. More recently, a few P3 consortia have organized to build and operate facilities that may require the powers of eminent domain to acquire land rights, the lower-cost financing of a municipal agency with access to tax exemptions, and the operational efficiency of private

---

18 Department of Motor Vehicles.

operators whose motives are clearly profits not a social good. In some cases, the P3 partnership involves facilities that have attributes of public goods as well as private goods, so the pricing mechanisms do not work entirely as they would for a purely privatized operation.

Some cities and counties have been compelled to sell a "crown jewel" in order to fund other obligations. For example, a city might sell its sewer treatment operation or a parking structure to a private firm in order to raise capital to shore up its dangerously underfunded pension plan. Whether the taxpayers ultimately benefit from these transactions may depend in part on the terms of the deal and how wisely the money is used, the business skills of the operator, and the quality of controls placed on the counterparty through contracts. Public agencies have often been ill-equipped to secure deals that benefit taxpayers.[19]

One thing is clear, however. P3 partnerships are likely to proliferate in an era in which public agencies migrate increasingly to user-fee pricing. More sales of crown jewels are likely if the funding problems of cities and counties with overhanging pension and retiree medical benefits obligations continue to overwhelm their annual budgets. In light of what has been written above about optimal pricing and financing of municipal utilities, and the inevitable transition of highway and bridge financing, it is likely that these public facilities are moving toward private-good pricing. Whether the facilities are thereafter operated by a government, a P3 consortium or a private company, then becomes an issue that sometimes may be driven by economic efficiency, and other times by expedience, politics or fiscal exigency. Having outspent America's ability to fund these previously "social goods" facilities

---

19 There are professional third-part advisers with requisite expertise in P3 negotiations, but many public agencies have been penny-wise and pound foolish, relying instead on naïve, undertrained and inexperienced internal staff, or worse yet, the judgements of local elected officials who may be influenced by cronies or financial contributors. Disclosure: The author was employed professionally as a senior strategist in 2008-12 by the nation's largest municipal financial advisory firm, although not engaged in its P3 advisory work.

through general taxation, as other expenditures have crowded out the subsidies previously given to "priceable" facilities, the trend will be to rely on user fees rather than general revenues hereafter.

TOPIC 29: Enlightened infrastructure funding: timing, incentives and strategies

An enlightened federal policy structure for funding the nation's infrastructure must accomplish the following:

- A long-term planning process must be established at all three levels of government: federal, state and local. State and local governments' eligibility for federal financial assistance should require formal processes for capital improvement planning and local financing strategies, and prioritization. Federal agencies can provide limited matching grants for the design and readiness of "out-year" (deferred) infrastructure projects that can be accelerated in recessions but otherwise built on schedule at local expense with an approved strategy for local funding.

- During periods of full employment, intra-state infrastructure spending is best accomplished through normal funding processes of states and their political subdivisions, at local expense.

- The long-term planning process must therefore include a counter-cyclical component that automatically triggers federal infrastructure matching funds with optimal timing.

- During economic recessions, the federal government's strategic role is to accelerate projects that are already planned and "RFP ready" in order to stimulate employment and capture the best possible contract pricing during a slack period in the construction industry.[20]

- In some cases, the federal government can accelerate state and local government projects by agreeing to pay the first three- or four-years' debt service, which would stimulate employment immediately but avoid long-term substitution effects.

- A comprehensive federal strategy must convert the financing of higher-volume highway and bridge replacement to user fees collected through micropayment technology.

- Congress should authorize matching grants for state transportation agencies to complete the design of high-priority critical bridge replacements on the basis of structural deficiency and highest-use public-safety hazards. The same legislation should authorize matching construction funds for these projects to be triggered formulaically at successive levels by a national economic recession or escalating local unemployment even if deficit finance is required. All replacement bridges should include automated toll mechanisms using the best technology then available.

- Federal matching funds for obsolete and unhealthy municipal water and sewerage utilities should require comprehensive full-cost pricing to assure future financial reserves for replacements and upgrades.

---

20 Professor Michael Pagano at the University of Illinois, Chicago, has suggested that lower-profile repair and maintenance work can also be performed during recessions to achieve counter-cyclical employment goals. (*Governing*, January 16, 2019) Substitution issues would need to be addressed by this strategy as well.

- Federal financing vehicles to reduce the costs of infrastructure debt service should include a Taxable Bond Option (TBO) and access to the Federal Financing Bank (FFB) for states and their political subdivisions. Standing authority should provide widespread access to these instruments during recessions. Access during periods of economic growth should be limited to revenue bond issuers converting to full-cost user fees, and projects that provably promote cost-efficient commerce or economic expansion.

- Except where a P3 project will modernize a project to install full-cost user fees as outlined here, incentives for private investment in infrastructure can wait until a recession. Democrats need political leverage to win Republican votes for additional job-creation projects that could be authorized at that time. Federal funds and tax credits should not underwrite buy-outs that merely transfer ownership to a private for-profit purchaser.

Multi-year infrastructure planning and federal funding authorizations. A systematic federal infrastructure plan must begin with a formal Congressional authorization that obligates funding for an extended period such as ten years. For some of the measures recommended here, the authority must be ongoing and long-term so that planners and politicians at all levels of government can set their expectations and plan the timing of their construction activity. Instead of waiting for a recession and the lengthy Congressional sausage-making legislative process, certain types of infrastructure spending and financial incentives should be triggered by the economic statistics -- whether it be two consecutive quarters of declining GDP (a standard indicator of recession) or unemployment above an acceptable level (say seven percent of a state or metropolitan region's workforce). Access to the FFB and TBO financing vehicles described below can be made ongoing for certain types of infrastructure, and conditional on economic conditions that trigger counter-cyclical authorizations.

> Instead of waiting for a recession, a ten-year plan can leverage state and local government infrastructure work on a just-in-time basis to get more bang for the buck.

Having a ten-year plan which can be renewed in the future will enable state and local decision-makers to make the most rational possible decisions for setting their priorities, allocating their own scarce resources, and timing their projects. Where projects are warranted because of environmental and health benefits, obvious tax-producing economic development benefits, or conversion to more-efficient user-fee financing, the funding authorization need not need to depend on the business cycle. Where counter-cyclical job-creation justifies the acceleration of already scheduled or insufficiently funded projects that meet qualification standards, the rules of that game can be specified well in advance so that competition for federal funding is both fair, efficient and swift.

Therefore, the universal requirement for any form of federal assistance, whether it be matching funds or financing incentives, is that the state or subdivision's governing body for that entity must approve a long-term capital improvement plan. Many municipalities already manage their infrastructure spending through a formal plan, which is deemed a best practice in the professional finance community. A formal capital financing plan identifies the construction work that must be undertaken, it schedules them chronologically and sequentially over five to seven years, and it explains the funding sources that will be needed to complete them. To be eligible for federal matching funds, the plan must be more than a wish list; it must have an authentic strategy for local financing without federal matching funds in the construction phase. Some of these plans can be funded in part by federal grants to defray part of the engineering design and even the land acquisition for "RFP ready" projects that can be accelerated in the event of a national recession, but the governing body must issue a public document that clearly announces, explains and defends its plan to go-it-alone if counter-cyclical funding never becomes available.

As a core part of this multi-year planning process, Congress can authorize a modest federal grant program to provide 50-50 matching funds to states (and through them, qualifying localities) to acquire land rights and draft all the engineering and procurement documents that will be needed to accelerate a limited number of projects in the event of a recession during the capital improvement plan's funding horizon (e.g. five years). This will ensure that a substantial number of "RFP-ready" projects can be activated quickly and cost-effectively when the economy hits the rocks and contractors are hungry for business at the lowest possible cost. Some of this federal assistance can be administered on a block grant basis, leaving a certain amount of discretion to the states in good faith, but the remainder should be allocated on the basis of merit using criteria specified by law to minimize "substitution strategies" that simply replace local funding at the expense of federal taxpayers and the national debt.

In order to qualify for access to the lower-cost federal bond market financing options, states and localities must likewise approve a multi-year capital improvement plan, along with other criteria that would be established for those two programs. The policy point here is that federal assistance is offered only to those who plan ahead and manage their resources prudently.

* * *

"We will provide useful work for the needy unemployed; we prefer useful work to the pauperism of a dole"

Franklin D. Roosevelt, 1936

Counter-cyclical infrastructure project acceleration. By having a "bullpen" of qualified, eligible and pre-approved infrastructure projects ready to enter into procurement and contracting when the economy enters a recession, the "policy and implementation lag" normally associated with federal counter-cyclical legislation can be minimized. The specific process for making formulaic grants will require more detailed legislative and administrative policy provisions than this book can offer, but the key concepts here would include:

- State matching funds are required, and for local government projects, each level should pay one-third of the cost. For facilities that can be funded with local user fees, the federal share of funding should not exceed 25 percent, in addition to access to the lower-cost federal financing vehicles described below. This basic requirement of "skin in the game" will minimize frivolous bridges to nowhere.

- Federal funding can be "first dollar in" so that the responsible government can proceed quickly while raising the necessary capital in the debt markets. However, if voter approval is required to issue bonds or raise taxes, the project cannot be federally funded beyond the plan design stage, until properly authorized.

- Another variation of "first dollar in" strategies would be for the federal government to pay the first several years of annually amortized debt service on projects in the local improvement plan that are accelerated during periods of economic recession. For example, a project originally scheduled to begin in 2027 that is accelerated during a recession in 2024 could obtain federal reimbursement for its annual debt service in the first three or four years. Federal payments could continue even longer if high local unemployment persists. Local taxpayers would gain the benefit of the new facility earlier than planned, and timely countercyclical employment is provided at a time when contractors and workers are hungriest for jobs.

- The capital improvement plan must specify exactly how that government would raise its share of funding, and also how the receipt of federal assistance will enable the jurisdiction to undertake additional projects with the money it would have otherwise provided locally. Projects with capital plans that clearly identify a multiplicative benefit from federal spending should receive higher priority, because of the leverage they provide to federal taxpayer dollars.

- Projects that improve public health, environmental conditions and regional economic development should take priority over general-purpose governmental building projects.

- There is a fiscal rationale for federal cost-sharing to prepare "RFP ready" construction plans as contingency projects. Full employment is a national objective (just as it is for the Federal Reserve, our nation's central bank). Therefore, the national interest is served by having cost-effective "quick start" projects that can be deployed semi-automatically on short notice. Economists would call these "semi-automatic stabilizers."[21] Paying a fair share of the fractional cost of an overall project, in order to be prepared and timely, is the smartest money Uncle Sam can ever spend. As with the Boy and Girl Scouts' motto: Congress should "Be Prepared" for the next recession, instead of reacting to it belatedly and ineffectually.

Conversion to full-cost user-fee financing. As explained in Topic 28, a technology revolution is inevitably changing the landscape for

---

21 "Automatic stabilizers" are federal fiscal actions that instantly increase when GDP declines and unemployment increases, such as spending on unemployment insurance, and federal deficit borrowing to cover income-tax shortfalls.

vehicular transportation infrastructure, moving the entire nation in the direction of automated micro-payments for the use of higher-volume roadways and bridges. Likewise, municipal utilities cannot perpetually underprice their products through general taxation and negligent, under-funded infrastructure replacement programs. Today's problem is how to convert these examples of "private goods" to more-efficient full-cost user-fee financing, which requires the issuance of new debt to finance the overdue renovations and the collection of depreciation charges in the fee structure to start saving money for the next round of capital renovations and replacements.

This is where federal financing can be justified, as a one-time expense to set the nation on a sustainable path toward economically efficient pricing systems. A multi-year matching grant program can be authorized that mandates federal matching funds for state and local authorities and utilities that undertake the necessary conversion to full-fee pricing as part of their capital expenditure and bond financing program. During normal economic times, the matching ratio might be 30 percent federal funding, and this ratio could be enlarged automatically during defined periods of economic recession, which would accelerate such projects as counter-cyclical at those times. For transportation infrastructure, the federal share must be sufficiently high to provide incentives to the states.

Federal financing vehicles as infrastructure incentives. Congress can authorize the Treasury Department to offer two powerful tools to states and localities that can reduce their cost of paying for infrastructure, the Taxable Bond Option (TBO) and the Federal Financing Bank (FFB). In both cases, they should be offered as incentives, rather than a permanent feature of the federalist system, except in special cases described below.

The Taxable Bond Option has been offered before, under the name of "Build America Bonds" (BABs) that were authorized for a brief period under the Obama-era's American Recovery and Reinvestment Act of 2009. Under that program, which expired in 2010, states and municipalities were given the broad option to issue taxable bonds instead of their traditional tax-exempt debt. In return, Congress authorized the Treasury department to reimburse them for 35 percent of their interest costs. There were several eligibility requirements, but the program was generally open to most forms of state and local infrastructure construction.

> The Taxable Bond Option (TBO) and Federal Financing Bank (FFB) are powerful tools to drive timely state and municipal infrastructure projects.

Since 2009, the Trump Tax Cuts have reduced tax rates for high-income investors and especially for corporations, so the value of muni-bond tax exemption is now less than it was in 2009. As a result, the indirect subsidy to muni bond issuer is lower than before, so any new TBO would not need to offer the 35 percent reimbursement rate that the BAB program offered back then. Even a reimbursement as low as 24 percent of taxable interest costs would be a cheaper way to finance for most muni bond issuers, and the Treasury department would actually spend less than it does on tax exemptions for Fat Cat investors. Where the state and local government community has indigestion is when TBO advocates suggest that this subsidy be made universal, in exchange for eliminating the muni bond interest tax exemption. They can live with the option but their opinion leaders worry that someday, Congress will renege on its promise to pay the explicit subsidies. So, any new version of a TBO must include a provision for contractual protections to the muni bond issuers that the federal TBO subsidy for any new issue is irrevocable and enforceable in court. Importantly, the states and municipalities wish to preserve their right to issue their bonds tax-exempt at any time.

With that as background, the obvious question is what should be the ground-rules for a new TBO authorization. First, the authority must be multi-year, preferably a ten-year window for new issues (which can be shortened by a future Congress, but not retroactively) so that states and localities can plan their infrastructure programs with reliance on this option. Second, the option can be made available continuously for various qualified bond issues, including those that fund projects that will establish full-cost user charges for revenue bonds issued by municipal utilities, and transportation bonds issued to fund road and bridge replacements and improvements that will hereafter be funded through tolls. Projects that fund economic development could qualify for the continuous TBO option, although the devil will be in the details as to qualification criteria. Infrastructure that meets public health or environmental improvement guidelines would also be a logical candidate for continuous TBO eligibility. Third, the TBO window should be open to all during any national economic recession. At that point, school districts can finance new or expanded buildings, cities and counties can fund new municipal buildings, and any number of other general-purpose projects financed through general taxation can be funded with a TBO subsidy. To avoid a paperwork nightmare for the Treasury department, smaller projects would have to be bundled by state bond banks acting as a conduit, so that only a select few of larger municipal deals are administered directly at the federal level.

As an alternative to the TBO, there is also an even more cost-effective and innovative way for Uncle Sam to help states and localities reduce their debt service costs, without spending a nickel of federal taxpayer money. This is the Federal Financing Bank (FFB). This subsidiary of the U.S. Treasury department was created by Congress to provide a conduit-financing vehicle for various federal agencies by purchasing their debt and funding it through issuance of lower-cost Treasury bonds. As suggested previously, the best model for expanding the FFB mission would be to authorize states to issue (or package) debt obligations to the FFB which in turn would sell Treasury bonds of similar maturity. In today's marketplace, that could potentially reduce interest costs on 20- and 30-year muni bonds by one-half of one percent (50 basis points) of principal outstanding, which represents an annual savings of 20 percent for AAA-rated issuers and potentially even more for those with lower credit ratings.

To be eligible for FFB financing, a state (or its conduit agency, if it packages subdivision debt) would have to pledge its full faith and credit or a first call on an eligible future tax stream, and secure the debt with a third-party guarantee from a qualifying highly rated private bond insurer or guarantor. Also, Congress can require that failure to repay the FFB disqualifies the state and its localities from receiving federal funds for any other purpose. Other "strings" can be attached to reduce the risk of non-payment. Even with the mandatory costs to obtain third-party credit guarantees, many jurisdictions would find this vehicle offers a lower cost of capital, and the Treasury would avoid giving away tax exemptions to wealthy investors who would otherwise buy these muni bonds.[22] The reduction in issuance volume in the tax-exempt marketplace would actually lower the interest costs and the indirect federal subsidies for everybody in the muni bond market, making the FFB window a winning strategy across the intergovernmental spectrum.

Eligible project qualifications for FFB financing could be similar to the conditions under which muni bond issuers are allowed to sell TBO bonds, or they could follow different rules. Some states already operate state "bond banks" that issue debt on behalf of their political subdivisions, and this kind of conduit financing would be a logical extension

---

22 During recessions, the Federal Reserve would be buyer of last resort for Treasury and FFB bonds, which essentially provides their financing "out of thin air." It would be the one time during each business cycle when Keynesian economics and Modern Monetary Theory both apply without the danger of inflation in the short run.

of those programs, as long as prudent credit guarantees effectively eliminate the default risks for Uncle Sam. If Democratic party leaders feel compelled to throw a bone to the teacher's unions, the best path would be state bond bank financing of public-school facilities through the FFB, with a required standby credit guarantee from the state that can be secured by recurring state aid.

The fiscal limits on federal largess. By now, there will be some readers asking, "But what about us?" School and municipal building construction is nowhere to be found in the matching-grant priorities outlined above. Unlike the heyday of FDR's Works Progress Administration, there is not a plan here for federal funding of every local government's capital improvement plan, although a case can be made for authorizing the TBO and FFB debt-service incentives to be offered to all projects that are accelerated during recessions, or funded prudently through the FFB in accordance with the preceding paragraph.

Alas, there cannot be free money for everybody. The matching-funds authorizations already presented above will require massive federal expenditures over the coming decade, financed entirely by the issuance of Treasury bonds for which there are no identified revenue sources. The construction projects that can be financed under the programs outlined above will employ thousands of workers, so the burden of proof then rests on competing interests to show that their pet projects are objectively the most deserving of federal matching funds. Given the current levels of federal deficits already accumulated, it would require magical thinking to believe that even more debt should be thrown on the backs of U.S. taxpayers when local funding sources can finance worthwhile projects. If local voters are unwilling to part with their own money to build new schools or city halls, why is it that taxpayers outside of that community should?

> Until such time as federal deficits have been properly financed, public infrastructure spending at the federal level must now be limited to three primary functions.

Until such time as federal deficits have been properly financed, the rationale for systematic public infrastructure spending at the federal level must now be limited to three primary functions: (1) economic development through improvements in transportation and transit facilities such as airports and seaports, (2) countercyclical federal spending to accelerate worthwhile and planned projects during recessions and periods of high unemployment, (3) helping states and localities finance their infrastructure debt at the lowest feasible cost without impairing federal borrowing capacity.

This does not mean that other federal, state and local government infrastructure would not be funded by a future Congress in the darkest hour of the next economic downturn, because politics and opportunism will undoubtedly give voice to such legislation. An "emergency" bill to fund pothole repairs and street resurfacing could probably pass Congress in a recession, and avoid implementation lags. But this book is about fiscal literacy and systematic public finance. The policy recommendations in this section are intended to provide a rational approach to infrastructure financing in the current political milieu. As a ten-year infrastructure plan for the nation, the priorities and strategies provided here will produce the most long-term benefit at the least cost for taxpayers. The further one goes down the slippery slope of opportunistic pork-barrel legislation, the more inefficient the overall system becomes, and the more cynical voters and taxpayers become.

A substantial new taxing authorization along the lines described in Topic 20 would be required in order to finance a more aggressive program to upgrade the nation's infrastructure on the order of magnitude suggested by the ASCE engineering society and numerous state and local government policy associations. Such a tax package would have to include many if not all the multiple tax reforms described in Part II, increases in existing tax rates, or an entirely new tax revenue source such as a Value Added Tax (VAT). That would leave nothing for other spending initiatives discussed previously, beyond Medicare at Cost. To accomplish all these objectives, a combination of "all of the above" would be necessary. No other fiscal policy solution can work if the next Congress seeks to (a) seriously address the current national debt problem, (b) dramatically expand health care and public college affordability AND (c) replace and upgrade deficient infrastructure to meet modern standards. That is a very tall order, but a "big-picture, big-tent" approach might actually succeed in cobbling together the national coalition that would be necessary to invoke such a fiscally literate tax-and-spend policy package. Readers can judge for themselves whether such a vision would ever be feasible without a "wave election." Las Vegas oddsmakers would call that a very long shot (or a sucker's bet) unless the Millennial and collegiate generations mobilize sufficiently to demand long-term fundamental change rather than incrementalism.

APPENDIX

"Pinocchio" Fact-Checking and Smell-Testing Scorecard

Ballpark magnitude of key fiscal drivers

Expense or Revenue Driver	Annual order of magnitude	Topic #
Cost drivers and accumulated liabilities		
U.S. budget	$4 trillion	Part I:
Current budget deficit	$1 trillion: $8,500 per household/year	Intro section
National debt	$22 trillion total U.S. debt outstanding	
Annual interest payments on U.S. debt	$400 billion; double or triple in 10 years	6
Increase in annual Baby Boomer benefits by 2030	$1 trillion annually of new spending for Social Security and Medicare benefits	Intro & 2,3,4
Single-payer health care tax requirements	$1.5 trillion annually	25

Expense or Revenue Driver	Annual order of magnitude	Topic #
Multiple-payer hybrid expanded health care	$90+ billion to $500-700 billion annually	23,25
Free public college tuition nationwide	$150 billion annually	20,24
Outstanding student debt	$1.5 trillion total debt outstanding	20
Infrastructure spending needed 2021-25	$4.5 trillion minimum; >$200 billion annually to properly service debt	27
$6000 tax credit to 90 mm households <$100K	More than $500 billion annually	9,20
Depletion of Social Security and Medicare trusts funds; currently running $300 billion deficits	Medicare depletion date is 2026 Social Security fund depleted in 2034	2,3,4

Expense or Revenue Driver	Annual order of magnitude	Topic #
Tax reforms		
Restore higher progressive tax rates to Obama-era levels	Less than $100 billion annually	10
Reduce and eliminate various tax loopholes*	Perhaps $100 billion annually that is not counted elsewhere below	11
Reform and increase the estate tax	$10-$15 billion annually plus possible $20 billion of capital gains step-up*	13
Raise payroll taxes to levels needed to properly fund Social Security and Medicare	$150 billion annually for each 1% of payroll in new taxes; $35 billion if wage base limit is eliminated for employers	12
Restore corporate income tax rates to levels that are still competitive globally	$100 billion annually, plus possible revenues from carbon emissions tax	14
Tax capital gains and dividends as ordinary income*	$125 billion annually*	15
Tax carried interest as ordinary income*	Included in AMT total below	16

Expense or Revenue Driver	Annual order of magnitude	Topic #
Tax reforms		
Limit the passthrough business income deduction	$30 billion annually	17
*Comprehensively reform and increase the Alternative Minimum Tax (AMT) including capital gains, carried interest, other loopholes	$150 billion; however, this replaces savings from the asterisked* duplicative items so some parts cannot be additive	18
Establish a new financial transactions tax (FTT)	$150 billion annually	19
Establish a new Value Added Tax (VAT)	$300 billion annually for each 5% of sales	20
Establish a wealth tax on ultra-millionaires	Perhaps $100 billion; highly debatable	22,18

Sources: Author's estimates based on reliable independent foundational data sources

GLOSSARY OF ACRONYMS

AGI: Adjusted Gross Income. An individual's total income before deductions.

AMT: Alternative Minimum Tax. A parallel income tax that applies a minimum tax rate to certain income that would otherwise be exempted or taxed at a lower rate.

CMS: Centers for Medicare and Medicaid Services. The federal agency (within HHS) that collects and processes insurance premiums for Medicare and Medicaid.

FICA: Federal Insurance Contributions Act. The law that requires employees and employers to make contributions for Social Security and Medicare. The current FICA tax rate is 6.4% of workers' income up to $132,900 (2019), paid by both employees and employers.

FTT: Financial Transactions Tax. A tax on the purchase and sale of stocks, bonds, and other investment-related financial instruments.

HHS: Department of Health and Human Services. The cabinet-level department responsible for administering Social Security and Medicare as well as various federal educational and social welfare programs.

HUD: Department of Housing and Urban Development. A cabinet-level federal agency responsible for various public housing programs, as well as mortgage finance.

IRMAA: Income Related Monthly Adjustment Amount. Medicare premiums are increased by formula for participants with incomes at various higher levels, so that more-affluent retirees pay more for Medicare benefits than those at lower income levels.

IRS: Internal Revenue Service. The federal agency within the Treasury department that collects and administers taxes.

NIIT: Net Investment Income Tax. The 3.8% Obamacare-ACA Medicare surtax on investment income for taxpayers with (modified) AGI over $250,000.

OASDI: Old Age Survivors and Disability Insurance. The formal name for Social Security insurance. OASDI provides benefits for retirees, as well as surviving dependents, and workers who become disabled.

QBID: Qualified Business Income Deduction. A recently enacted tax deduction for self-employed individuals and private business partners that reduces their taxable business income by 20%

TCJA: Tax Cuts and Jobs Act of 2017. Sometimes known as the Trump Tax Cuts. This law reduced personal income tax rates until 2025, eliminated various tax deductions, capped the deduction for state and local income taxes, and permanently reduced corporate income tax rates.

VAT: Value Added Tax. A consumption tax on goods and services that credits the seller for the taxes on the profits earned at each point along the supply chain.

POSTSCRIPT: RECESSION RE-SETS?

Just as this book went to press, the Trump trade fiasco had plunged global financial markets into a tailspin and raised the specter of a new worldwide recession. Nobody can write a book of this depth on the basis of weekly wiggles in the stock markets, gyrating overseas economic data, or the whimsical and erratic madness of today's White House. But Democrats on the campaign trail will be tempted to attack any signs of economic weakness, and the fringe left wing in particular will reflexively use this development to support their populist rationale for unsustainable fiscal policies and MMT monetary easing. Fiscally illiterate populists will claim that federal spending for all causes is a free lunch once we enter a recession. (Note to readers: there is no such thing as a free lunch in the history of economics.)

Nothing in the main body of this book is written for transitory economic fluctuations or "market wiggles." The long-term outlook for 2030 and beyond does not change just because a recession occurs sooner rather than later, or later than sooner. Compound interest ignores economic cycles, and in fact, recessions make national debt much worse, and never better. As Part I explained, a recession in the next Presidential term is almost inevitable because of the imbalances of the Trump Administration's fiscal and trade policies. The more important question is how should the Congress address the next recession?

On that score, the recommendations of Part IV on Infrastructure must take center stage. All the tools recommended there for counter-cyclical economic and fiscal policy management should be implemented immediately in the next Congressional session. A Keynesian economic policy analysis would suggest that any scheduled tax increases on the middle class should be deferred until the economy recovers, and caution should prevail in the adoption of tax reforms that hit the rich and corporate America too hard, too fast, too soon. But directionally, nothing changes in the long run.

Relief for student debt can logically and prudently be provided in a recession scenario by opening a federal facility to refinance student loans at three percent annual interest plus a fair processing fee, with a 20-year repayment schedule and no prepayment penalties. The government's cost of capital in the T-bond market will be lower, and borrower defaults can be recaptured through the income tax system with a first lien on borrower's incomes. Sallie Mae, SoFi and others in the student loan industry can be engaged to process the paperwork through a fast-track competitive procurement or licensing contract. An option to pledge a fixed annual percentage of future income in lieu of the debt payments could be provided to veterans, doctors, teachers and other public servants, provided that it is actuarially calibrated and does not surreptitiously become "loan forgiveness" for self-interested "progressive" voters.

Obviously, deficit reduction takes a back seat to other priorities during recessions. The concept of matching each dollar of new spending for social benefits (funded by new taxes or tax reforms) with an equal dollar of deficit reduction must wait its turn in the business cycle. Deficit hawks are not fools, and Democrats cannot die on the cross of fiscal responsibility if the populace is suffering from the Trump regime's egotistical miscalculations and reckless global economic brinksmanship.

One technical recommendation in Part I should be advanced immediately, which is for the Treasury department to sell large volumes of long-term bonds at very low rates. There has already been market talk of a 50- or 100-year T-bond issue, and that is not an unreasonable strategy if long rates fall as low as some are predicting. If nothing else, an expansion of 20- and 30-year bond issues is now fully justifiable and will help reduce the intergenerational risks of compound interest on federal debt, if Treasury can now find enough buyers willing to accept such unprecedented low yields.[23] Debt extension is not magical, but it will be timely and helpful.

Temperance and fiscal responsibility must be the watchword of 2020, not recklessness: It would be pure madness for Democrats to advocate a plunge into endless deficit finance to pay for consumption of health care benefits and college debt relief on a permanent basis. Fiscal literacy and responsibility require that the revenue side of our nation's budget policies must ultimately include a multi-year plan to restore sanity when the economy is expanding. This is not a task to be delegated to a President who emotionally tweets new federal policies on the basis of each day's news cycle. It has become the adult responsibility of the Democratic party and the Independents, Centrists, Millennials and Collegians who have learned through this book that arithmetic actually matters when deciding the fiscal burdens, opportunities and fate of younger generations.

---

23 One gimmick that Congress used decades ago to promote "long and low" bonds is to allow such low-coupon bonds to be redeemable at par for payment of estate taxes. This provides protection to the investor that future inflation will not decimate their investment. They were known back then as "flower bonds" (as in funeral bouquets). Consider it a crumb for the One Percenters and a better answer than MMT. For pension funds, a similar concept could make the low-coupon bonds they (and only they) hold be redeemable at par after a ten-year holding period from the eligible fund's date of purchase. This could help minimize capital losses in pension funds whenever inflation eventually returns.